Race Dialogues

Race Dialogues

A Facilitator's Guide to
Tackling the Elephant in the Classroom

DONNA RICH KAPLOWITZ

SHAYLA REESE GRIFFIN

SHERI SEYKA

Foreword by Patricia Gurin

TEACHERS COLLEGE PRESS

TEACHERS COLLEGE | COLUMBIA UNIVERSITY

NEW YORK AND LONDON

Published by Teachers College Press, 1234 Amsterdam Avenue, New York, NY 10027

Cover design by Therese and Henry Brimmer, Brimmer Family Design, East Lansing, Michigan. Cover photo by Patryk Kosmider / Shutterstock.

Library of Congress Cataloging-in-Publication Data

Names: Kaplowitz, Donna Rich, 1962– author. | Griffin, Shayla Reese, author.
  | Seyka, Sheri, author.
Title: Race dialogues : a facilitator's guide to tackling the elephant in the
  classroom / Donna Rich Kaplowitz, Shayla Reese Griffin, Sheri Seyka.
Description: New York : Teachers College Press, [2019] | Includes
  bibliographical references and index. |
Identifiers: LCCN 2018060734 (print) | LCCN 2019011025 (ebook) | ISBN
  9780807777701 (ebook) | ISBN 9780807761304 (pbk.)
Subjects: LCSH: Multicultural education—United States. | Race
  awareness—Study and teaching—United States. | Racism in
  education—United States. | Communication in education—United States.
Classification: LCC LC1099.3 (ebook) | LCC LC1099.3 .K36 2019 (print) | DDC
  370.1170973—dc23
LC record available at https://lccn.loc.gov/2018060734

ISBN 978-0-8077-6130-4 (paper)
ISBN 978-0-8077-6175-5 (casebound)
ISBN 978-0-8077-7770-1 (ebook)

26 25 24 23 22 21 20 19   8 7 6 5 4 3 2 1

Contents

Foreword

Race Dialogues: A Facilitator's Guide to Tackling the Elephant in the Classroom is a scholarly, timely, and urgently needed book. While there is other literature on facilitation of intergroup dialogues, none is so deeply and effectively focused on race—the elephant in the room. Political scientist Katherine Walsh (2007), while studying community discussions that were part of the national organization Everyday Democracy, commented how rare it was in these discussions that people of different racial backgrounds talked about race across race, and when they did, they interpreted life in the same city differently. Yet talking about race across race has never been more important. The United States is undergoing rapid racial/ethnic diversification of its population—what demographer William Frey (2016) calls a diversity explosion—brought about by immigration, differential birth rates among groups, and the aging of the White population. What troubles the most is that diversification has occurred with persistent racial/ethnic residential and school segregation, greater for some groups and in some places than others, and ever since the 1970s with continuing large income differences between Whites and African Americans and also between Whites and Latinos (Sugrue, 2016). Racial/ethnic differences are particularly pronounced with respect to wealth in assets that include bank accounts, stocks, bonds, securities, retirement plans, and real estate (Sugrue, 2016). The fundamental challenge facing the United States is how to de-couple the rapid demographic diversification that is occurring from both segregation and inequality so as to ensure future economic competitiveness and sufficient cohesion to sustain democracy.

Addressing this challenge, the authors in *Our Compelling Interests* (Lewis & Cantor, 2016) stress the crucial role of education in bridging demographic cleavages to ensure a more connected, democratic society. Educational institutions from prekindergarten through college will have to create ways to educate students about how to talk with each other, understand different perspectives and experiences of inequality, work together for common purpose, and build the bridging ties so needed for a connected society (Allen, 2016).

But how will educational (and other) institutions do this? *Race Dialogues* provides a powerful approach for educators to use in many settings (such as schools, colleges, corporations, and community groups) with many types of groups (preservice teachers, current teachers, university professors, youth advisors, school administrators, corporate and nonprofit leaders) to ensure nonsuperficial talk across race. In this volume, anyone interested in creating and facilitating intergroup dialogue will find how to set up a dialogue space, select participants, structure an interaction that will result in dialogue rather than debate, frame expectations including the likelihood and importance of conflict and discomfort, and set group norms that preserve confidentiality and promote equitable participation across race. The authors offer a five-stage model that constantly ties personal and interpersonal experiences to each other, and both to broader structural forces that result in racial inequality, segregation, and sometimes violence. They suggest specific strategies to be used in difficult dialogue moments, such as when some participants disengage, sometimes out of fear of exhibiting ignorance or misinformation, or resist examining how structures and institutions shape racial relations in everyday life, or display anger, pain, or sadness. They stress the multiple demands facing facilitators "to listen actively and globally . . . to mentally organize participants' comments in order to make connections between what people are saying . . . to connect comments to larger structural or institutional issues . . . to summarize specific points, and . . . to respond to painful or traumatic comments appropriately" (p. 84).

It's a tall order. But Donna Rich Kaplowitz, Shayla Reese Griffin, and Sheri Seyka not only offer rich examples of specific facilitation strategies that have proven useful in effective intergroup dialogue. They also include a detailed curriculum, grounded in research-based evidence of effectiveness, that can be adapted for use with various age groups, fit with goals in the National English Common Core, and modified for semester-long courses, one day workshops, or multiple-day dialogues. The plan for each session includes relevant concepts, specific activities, processes for making sense of the activities and what potential learning they provide, prompts for debriefing activities, and facilitator behaviors that will maximize interaction and learning. A great strength of this book lies in its many levels of knowledge—theory, research evidence, a practice-based model of dialogue about race, practice examples, and a richly developed yet modifiable curriculum. It should be required reading for anyone developing race dialogue courses or workshops.

The authors thoughtfully address how dialogue can address the fundamental challenge of ensuring connections across racial/ethnic communities and groups as the United States becomes a majority non-White country. The key, in the model of race dialogues presented in this book, is the importance the model places on educating about both prejudice and systemic racism, and both personal and social change. Participants should leave race dialogues that are guided by this model with a greater understanding of how race has shaped their own personal lives and also a commitment to work for changes in both legislation and organizational and institutional policies and practices. Dialogue is talk but not only talk: It is also collaboration across differences to sustain deliberative democracy.

REFERENCES

Allen, D. (2016). Toward a connected society. In E. Lewis & N. Cantor (Eds.), *Our compelling interests: The value of diversity for democracy and a prosperous society* (pp. 71–105). Princeton, NJ: Princeton University Press.

Frey, W. H. (2016). The "diversity explosion" is America's twenty-first-century baby boom. In E. Lewis & N. Cantor (Eds.), *Our compelling interests: The value of diversity for democracy and a prosperous society* (pp. 16–38). Princeton, NJ: Princeton University Press.

Lewis, E., & Cantor, N. (Eds.). (2016). *Our compelling interests: The value of diversity for democracy and a prosperous society.* Princeton, NJ: Princeton University Press.

Sugrue, T. J. (2016). Less separate, still unequal: Diversity and equality in "post-civil rights" America. In E. Lewis & N. Cantor (Eds.), *Our compelling interests: The value of diversity for democracy and a prosperous society* (pp. 39–70). Princeton, NJ: Princeton University Press.

Walsh, K. C. (2007). *Talking about race: Community dialogues and the politics of difference.* Chicago, IL: University of Chicago Press.

Acknowledgments

As anyone who has written a book can attest (and to shamelessly borrow from an old proverb), it takes a village to write a book. This book is no exception. When you have three different authors, at three different stages of life, with three different "villages" coming together, our gratitude flows in many directions. These pages were not written in a vacuum but were labored over while we simultaneously balanced our rich work lives with nurturing our respective families: nursing a baby, marrying off a daughter, helping one of our oldest with college applications, navigating being first-time public school parents, sending our last baby off to college, attending to ailing relatives, changing jobs, and welcoming new family members into our fold. While we have often had to pay a professional price for being working mothers, we believe that our lives as full human beings have enriched these pages immeasurably.

We are indebted to a wide array of folks who have paved the way for the birth of this book. First, we want to thank our thousands of students, dialogue participants, colleagues, and facilitators who have been our greatest teachers. We have learned something unique and important from each person who has helped us refine our craft. This also includes those who have been resistant to our mission of cultivating civil discourse about race in a variety of spaces. There are some giants in the field of intergroup dialogue who continue to be our teachers, mentors, and supporting cast including, but not limited to, the great folks at the University of Michigan Program on Intergroup Relations. Patricia Gurin, Roger Fisher, Monita Thompson, Kelly Maxwell, Charles Behling, Mark Chesler and the late Adrienne Dessel have been pioneers in this work. Many of them have been on "speed dial" for us as we ventured into the world of dialogue.

Each of us has a special team that deserves recognition here. Donna and Sheri are indebted to the support from East Lansing Public Schools. It was the courage and vision of a variety of folks to do this work despite obstacles that contributed immeasurably to elements in this book. We specifically want to recognize all the teachers who have participated in this project over the years: Emily Holmes, Cody Harrell, Jennifer LaPointe, Katy Topp, Nicole Hegglund, Adam Woolsey, Jacqueline Carroll, Jeff Lampi, Robyn Stevens, and Pat Murray. We also want to thank Superintendent Dori Leyko, former Superintendent Robyn Thompson, Principals Andy Wells and Coby Fletcher, Curriculum Director Glen Mitcham, and members of the East Lansing School Board for believing in the work and promoting it, especially when the going got a little tough.

Donna appreciates her former department chair at Michigan State University, Margaret Crocco. It was Margaret who initially said, "I think this would be an important book and you should write it!" She is grateful to Paulette Granberry Russell, special advisor to the President for Diversity, who gave Donna the space to create a vibrant dialogue program at Michigan State when others were reluctant. She is also grateful to all the MSU student facilitators who have worked with her to create the dialogue program. Donna could not have done this work without her "junta"—they know who they are—who gather around her table monthly and have kept her sane and laughing through some trying times.

She is deeply grateful to her mom, Paula Rich, and her late father, Arthur Rich, who were antiracist activists before there was a word for it. They instilled in her from the time she was a little girl the idea that you do what is right and not what is easy. And to the greater Shwam family, who as a whole share antiracist sentiments dating back all the generations we have known. Thank you for making our Thanksgivings conflict-free.

Donna is indebted to her daughter, Ariel Kaplowitz Hahn, who was first in the family to venture into intergroup dialogue work as an undergraduate at the University of Michigan and whose passion for the work inspired Donna to build the program at Michigan State University. In fact, dialogue has become a family affair for the Rich Kaplowitzes, and each of her children, Ariel, Andrew, Eliana, and Danny, has participated in or facilitated dialogues in the last 6 years.

Donna dedicates this work to her husband, Michael Kaplowitz, a facilitator in his own right, who listened patiently through years of trial and error and believed in Donna's work often at times when she was ready to move to a deserted island. Thank you, dear one.

Shayla was first introduced to intergroup dialogue by Michael S. Spencer at the University of Michigan. It was in his course during the early years of her MSW program that she felt she had finally found an answer to her lifelong frustration of seeing racial inequality but lacking the opportunity or skill to talk about it productively across race. She is forever grateful for the mentorship, support, and collaboration of naomi warren, Mikel Brown, Melanie Morrison, Lois McCullen Parr, Autumn Campbell, Dionardo Pizaña, Karen Pace, Shaenu Micou, Relando Thompkins-Jones, Kelsey Cavanagh-Strong, and Sharonda Simmons, all of whom she's had the honor of working with over the years as partners in co-facilitation and learning.

Shayla is especially grateful to the current and former leaders of the Washtenaw Intermediate School District, Scott Menzel, Sarena Shivers, and Naomi Norman, who made an institutional commitment to equity, inclusion, and social justice and have given Shayla the opportunity to help P–12 educators across the county become more socially just people and practitioners.

The educators she has gotten the opportunity to work with have not only greatly shaped Shayla's commitment to social justice, they are the teachers she has been searching for since she was a young child frustrated by the racism she witnessed in her schools and the failure of educators to help students navigate it. She remains in complete awe and admiration of the transformational work they are continually doing to change their classrooms, their schools, their districts, and themselves. Though they are too numerous to name, she could write an entire book about the hope they have instilled in her for the future of our country.

Finally, Shayla is humbled by the support of her loving family and amazing community of friends (you know you who are!). She would especially like to thank her teacher-mother, Pamela Sallee Griffin, who first modeled socially just education for her, provided much needed childcare and, as always, read through early drafts of this book; her father, Thomas, and siblings, Maiessha, Trevor, Marggy, Tori (who helped with our graphics), Victoria, and Cory, who always keep her on her toes and force her to think deeply about race; her in-laws, Maureen and Brian Dobbie; Ebony Mixon, and Jamilia McLeod, who helped watch her very attached young children; and her husband, David Dobbie, who remains her best friend, tireless editor, and "biggest" supporter in life and work. She would like to dedicate this book to her children, Asa, Mandela, and Rosario, who deserve a much better world than the one they were born into. She hopes that this book plays a small part in creating one for them.

Sheri is deeply appreciative of the continued support and understanding of her husband, Mark, and children, Kaylee and Aidan. Living, working, and attending the public schools in the same community creates overlap for each of us that has repercussions on all of us. Their support, open mindedness, and understanding that doing what is right is not always the easy route has allowed her to remain dedicated to this work. Educators, administrators, and past and present students have also molded Sheri's professional beliefs, and for that she is eternally grateful. She would not be the student advocate she is today without the students driving her to continue to fight the good fight, and support from administrators has allowed her the freedom to challenge educational norms to provide an all-inclusive learning environment.

The final group of individuals Sheri would like to thank are the parents and community members of the many, many talented and curious students she has had the privilege of educating. While many different views and opinions have been encountered throughout her career, the overwhelming level of support from many of those families was exactly what she needed to continue the fight for marginalized students striving to become tomorrow's leaders.

Introduction

One of us is a race researcher and an educator at a Tier 1 public research university; one of us is a veteran public school English teacher; and one of us is a consultant who works with districts, schools, and educators on issues of equity, inclusion, and social justice. We have worked at the forefront of public education for a combined total of 50 years and we have experienced firsthand the crucial need for accessible, immediate tools in order to facilitate difficult but critically important dialogues about race. We came together because each of us needed a text that provided detailed instructions on how to facilitate dialogues about race, and after finding nothing to meet our needs, we decided to write one.

Race is one of the most taboo subjects in the United States. Though many people talk about race when in segregated racial groups, *intergroup* race dialogue is still avoided in much of our country, including in our public schools and universities.

One of the reasons we have such serious racial divides in the United States is that most of us do not have meaningful relationships across race. We live in a country that is not only racially segregated by neighborhood and school, but also one in which "integrated" spaces often fail to produce meaningful relationships across differences. It is often easier to dislike, fear, feel threatened by, disagree with, and struggle to see the humanity in folks whom we do not know and with whom we have little connection. Though school is one place where it is possible to build relationships and understanding across difference, most teachers do not believe they have the skills or knowledge to facilitate such dialogues.

Eighty-two percent of U.S. public school teachers are White. In contrast, nearly 50% of students in the United States are of color (U.S. Department of Education, Office of Civil Rights, 2016). Unfortunately, most educators are not trained to bridge this divide because almost no colleges of education teach how to lead dialogues about race within the classroom. As a result, educators often lack the necessary tools to prevent and address racial tensions in school settings and to provide students with necessary life skills to develop deep understanding and concrete tools to live, work, and thrive in a racially diverse democracy.

Silence is deepening the racial divide (Griffin, 2015; Pollock, 2004), and the consequences are dangerous. Race-based hate crimes in the United States are rising (Martin, 2017); racial health disparities are widening (Wildeman & Wang, 2018); the United States has a greater percentage of People of Color[1] behind bars than that of apartheid South Africa (Kristof, 2014); and our schools are more segregated now than they were in the 1960s (Richmond, 2012). As the race discourse in our country has devolved into shouting matches, silence, and violence, we have seen these attitudes mirrored in our own classrooms. Though these statistics seem insurmountable, intergroup dialogue across racial difference offers us a way out. We know from more than 30 years of research on intergroup dialogue, and through our own dialogue programs, that facilitators and participants in intergroup dialogue develop concrete skills to dismantle systems of oppression in the short and long terms. This book was born out of our own critical need for a text to use in high schools, university classrooms, and teacher professional development sessions to help individuals develop key skills in dialogue facilitation (Griffin, 2015; Kaplowitz, Lee, & Seyka, 2018).

SCOPE AND CONTENT

This book is designed to provide concrete materials for teachers, professors, and a variety of facilitators to use in classrooms and beyond. Our goal is to offer readers specific skills and materials to facilitate effective race dialogues.

The first chapter examines why there is a need for race dialogues. We share data showing that race-based school segregation and race-based inequality is growing in the United States. Chapter 2 looks at what we mean when we talk about intergroup dialogue including where dialogue came from, how it is used, and what the research tells us about its results. We explore why talking about race in intimate cross-racial dialogue settings is key to dismantling systems of racial division, and we review our own research data. In Chapter 3, we provide a detailed analysis of all the elements involved in creating an inclusive dialogue space and explore a range of strategies for implementing dialogues from using peer, near-peer, teacher, or consultant-based facilitating frameworks. In Chapter 4, we provide a primer on the foundations of facilitation with very specific suggestions to facilitate dialogues about race for preservice teachers, current teachers, university professors, youth advisors, school administrators, corporate and nonprofit leaders, and anyone with an interest in promoting dialogue across race. Chapter 5 is a deep dive into the power of sharing stories, one of the core principles in dialogue. We look at the importance of asking critical questions and responding to participant comments in Chapter 6.

We advocate that when possible, it is best to use co-facilitators in dialogue, so in Chapter 7 we examine what constitutes skilled co-facilitation techniques. Because one of the goals of dialogue is to surface differences of opinion and areas of conflict, in Chapter 8 we examine why conflict emerges and how to preplan for inevitable pushback. In Chapter 9, we give very specific advice about how to handle conflict once it erupts. Chapter 10 addresses how to manage resistance among a variety of nonparticipant stakeholders, and we share our own case study with details about mistakes we have made, and lessons learned. In Chapter 11, we provide a specific curriculum for race dialogues that can be used in a variety of settings, from college courses to high school classes, and from community settings to extracurricular and professional development series. Our curriculum uses a well-researched, evidence-based practice that leads participants in thoughtfully facilitated and sustainably sequenced dialogues about race. We have facilitated this curriculum in dozens of settings with thousands of participants from high school and college classrooms to faculty and community dialogue series over the last 5 years. Throughout each chapter, we offer anecdotes and vignettes based upon our own experiences to share our hard-earned lessons. Ultimately, we present a road map for school, university, and community leaders to navigate the implementation of race dialogues in a variety of settings.

DIALOGUE: A TOOL FOR CREATING A PARTICIPATORY DEMOCRACY

We firmly believe that intergroup dialogue provides one way to address the growing racial divide in the United States. The principles and facilitation techniques shared in the following chapters are applicable to nearly any type of conflict and can be used from the Thanksgiving table to high-level political diplomacy. Though this book is focused on race, there are many social identities that impact our lives. For example, Black women have different experiences than Black men or Asian women. Those who are wealthy have a different set of life experiences than those who are poor. Members of the LGBTQ+ community experience discrimination that those who are straight or cis do not. Our hope is that our readers will be able to apply similar facilitation techniques to a variety of other identities and circumstances.

In intergroup dialogue, facilitators and participants alike learn core skills useful for participating in a functional democracy: how to listen generously, question previously held beliefs, think openly, share personal experiences, acquire new information, understand other's perspectives, and act to create social change (Schoem & Hurtado, 2001). Ultimately, dialogue is about adding to the common pool of knowledge. Participating in dialogue contributes to a larger vision of the core democratic principles upon which U.S. democracy is founded. We know from research (Gurin, Nagda, & Zúñiga, 2013) that dialogue participants are more likely to be civically engaged than their nondialogue peers. While it may seem lofty, we believe that dialogue facilitation and participation provide the basic building blocks for dismantling systems of oppression and the skills and vision to co-create a new, equitable, democratic social structure.

NOTE

1. We capitalize *People of Color* in this text as an ideological and epistemological stance toward humanizing communities that have been marginalized historically and traditionally, and to use our written voice to empower marginalized groups.

CHAPTER 1

Why Is There a Need for Race Dialogues?

A Brief Primer on Race in the United States

> Until we have dismantled the system of White Supremacy and racial oppression, we will always need to talk about it. (Oluo, 2018)

In 1999, Gary Howard published a book for White teachers who want to become more culturally relevant educators, now in its third edition, titled *We Can't Teach What We Don't Know*. This insightful refrain is one we use often when working with educators around issues of social justice. There are many reasons why it can feel impossible to talk about race and racism in schools and classrooms, from narrow curriculum mandates to the fear of angering parents if it goes poorly; but one of the biggest challenges is that when it comes to race, many of us just do not know all that much.

Although we live in a country in which race shapes every aspect of our lives, most U.S. citizens, including the majority of educators, did not learn anything of depth in our P–12 schools about the concept of race or the history and present reality of racism. The majority of U.S. citizens live in highly segregated communities in which we are surrounded by people who are similar to us, racially, economically, religiously, and politically. Most of us, especially those who are White, are taught the best thing to be when it comes to race is "colorblind"—to just pretend we do not see it (hint: unless we are actually colorblind, we *do* see race, and ignoring it is not the answer). As a result, few of us even have a good idea of what the racial demographics of our country are.[1]

As Shayla writes in *Those Kids, Our Schools: Race and Reform in an American High School* (2015), when educators attempt to tackle race in the classroom, we are often doing something in our work that the majority of us have failed to do in our lives. How can we build relationships with students from very different backgrounds than our own, when all of our friends look like us? How can we have dialogues with diverse groups of students when we have not practiced talking about race in "mixed" company? How can we confidently facilitate conversations about race with young people who

5

have been taught to see us as experts, when we know so very little about it? How can we respond to students' questions when we ourselves have so many unanswered ones? How can we teach what we do not know?

The first step in developing the ability to engage students in dialogues about race (or any social identity) is growing our own knowledge. While one book can never make up for a lifetime of missing and misinformation, our hope is that this chapter will be a starting place to help you better understand our complicated racial history and identify where you might go next in your own learning so that you can more successfully engage students in dialogues about race.

WHAT IS RACE? IT'S COMPLICATED

In the United States, the terms "race," "racism," and "racist" are thrown around with little care in social interactions and popular media. Despite the prevalence of this language, the overwhelming majority of people do not have a solid understanding of what these terms mean. In part, this is because race is a relatively new concept in human history, invented as a way to justify European domination.

Skin Color

Many people believe that race is about "skin color" and even use the word "color" as a synonym for "race." Similarly, some people believe there are significant biological differences in the very DNA of people from different racial backgrounds. While these beliefs are common, neither is true. If you take a closer look around you, you might notice that individuals from various racial backgrounds come in a range of "skin colors." For example, someone who identifies as Black may be relatively light-skinned, like the singer Beyoncé, or dark-skinned like the actress Lupita Nyong'o. Similarly, a person who identifies as Asian or Latinx may be darker skinned or lighter skinned. White people also come in a range of skin tones, from very pale to what we often call "olive" or tan. Although it is true that Black Americans are, on average, darker skinned than White Americans, the most current scientific research has concluded that there is actually no biological difference between people of different "races" (Yudell, Roberts, DeSalle, & Tishkoff, 2016). The accepted science today concludes that there is as much genetic variation within racial groups as between them. In other words, two people who are Black are likely to be just as genetically different as a Black person and a White person (Public Broadcasting Service, 2003).

You may be wondering, if race is not biological, why is it so easy to spot? When we "see" race, we are likely attending to a number of factors related to presentation, performance, and culture that we are not conscious of. Skin color may be one factor, but so is hair texture and style, way of dressing, pattern of speech, and even geographic location. The truth is, there is no single feature—skin color, hair texture, nose shape, eye shape, lip thickness, weight, and so forth—that is found only within one racial group. Instead, most of our features are inherited independently of one another (Rosenberg et al., 2002). Although there are those of us who appear to be very obviously Black, White, or Native American, people make inaccurate racial assumptions all the time.

Shayla is a Black person whose skin color and hair texture match the assumptions most Americans hold about how Black people look. However, her much lighter-skinned brother, who is also Black American, is often as- sumed to be Latino when he is in New York or Florida, and Black when he is in their home state of Indiana. Her biracial son was once assumed to be the child of her Asian friend. That same Asian friend was once admonished in a store in a Latinx neighborhood because she did not speak Spanish. Donna's daughter with an olive complexion has often been mistaken for being Latina or Native American, though both of her parents are White. We bet some of the White educators reading this book who teach in majority Black schools have been assumed by at least a few students to be "light- skinned" Black Americans.

It is because race is about so much more than skin color that since the time of enslavement some Black people have been able to "pass" as White. Ideas about skin color also contribute to the oft-asked question "What are you?" (a common microaggression experienced by People of Color) and the characterization of many people as "ethnically ambiguous."

While race and color do not align in quite the ways we assume, color is *still* a significant feature around which people experience discrimination. You can find "colorism" on virtually every continent in the world. Nearly every human society has or has had systems in place based on "colorism" that benefit lighter-skinned members over those who are darker skinned, such as the caste system in India. Like racism, colorism is rooted in White supremacy and the privileging of those seen as closer to White.

Social Construction

If race is not about biology, then what is it? Social scientists often talk about race as a *social construction*. Racial categories were created (constructed) by people (social) in power to further their own privilege and prosperity. When the concept of modern race was first invented in 1775 by Johan Fried- rich Blumenbach, racial categories were geographic: "Negroids" came from Africa; "Mongoloids" came from parts of Asia; "American Indians" were indigenous to North, Central, and South America; "Malayans" came from South Asia and the Pacific Islands; and "Caucasoids" came from parts of Europe and were so named because the scientist doing the naming believed the people of the Caucasus mountains were the most beautiful in the world.[2] By the mid-19th century, early race scientists had started engaging in faulty experiments rife with bias and stereotypes in order to rank racial groups. Despite the fact that nothing about these experiments and findings would pass the tests of modern science, their conclusions have served to justify the mistreatment and oppression of People of Color for centuries (Painter, 2010).

The U.S. government also constructed racial groups in ways that served to justify inequitable treatment. Since the early days of chattel slavery, Black Americans were subject to what is commonly referred to as the *one drop rule* in which having even "one drop" of traceable African ancestry made one "Black" by law. This rule was a way of keeping as many people enslaved as possible by denying rights to the huge numbers of children White men fathered with enslaved Black women through rape (Livesey, 2017; Morrison, 2010). In contrast, the United States' treatment of Native Americans was completely different but similarly dehumanizing. Unlike Black Americans, Native Americans who had more than a drop of anything *other than* Indigenous "blood" were denied rights. Even today, in order to have tribal membership, a person must prove that they have a certain percentage of Native American ancestry, known as blood quantum (Jarvis, 2017). Having European or African ancestry is treated as a "watering down" of Indigenous identity. This decision was also rooted in profit and capitalism. If a person must retain a certain percentage of Indigenous "blood" in order to receive rights and lands promised to Native Americans, limiting who qualifies is a way of denying them access into perpetuity.

It is clearly unsatisfactory to use geography or "blood" as the only ways of thinking about race. As we are learning from DNA testing, huge numbers of "Black" people in the United States who would not consider themselves multiracial also have ancestors who came from Europe, the Americas, and Asia because of colonization, enslavement, and intermarriage. This pattern of eclectic ancestry is true for all racial groups in the United States. White people frequently have African or Native American heritage, and Latinx people are likely to have a mix of Indigenous, African, and European heritage. Moreover, as rates of interracial relationships increase, growing numbers of people are identifying as biracial, multiracial, or mixed. As a society, we have always struggled to place ourselves within clear racial categories. If you were to look at the racial groups tracked by the U.S. Census starting in 1790 through today, you would likely notice how often they have been changed in our efforts to do so. In short, when it comes to defining race, as Shayla often says: "It's complicated."

Race vs. Ethnicity

The difference between *race* and *ethnicity* is another place of confusion for many people. The social construction of race divides humans into broad racial groups: Black, White, Asian, Indigenous American, Pacific Island-er, and now, perhaps, we would also add Arab/MENA (Middle Eastern or North African)[3] and Latinx.[4] In contrast, ethnic identities are more specifically related to culture and heritage. For example, people who are racially "Black" now live on every continent on earth. You can be Black in the United States, in Ghana, in Jamaica, in Brazil, and in Scotland. While we would not think of the African descended people from these various countries as racially different, we would likely think of them as ethnically different.

Similarly, a Jewish American student, an Italian American student, and an Irish American student may have unique traditions, foods, holidays, lan-guages, and worldviews that are connected to their specific ethnic identi-ties. But racially, they are all considered White in the context of the United States. This was not always true. In fact, when waves of new Jewish, Italian, and Irish immigrants came to the country in the 20th century, they were of-ten treated as "racial" minorities by the European Americans already here. However, what makes these European immigrants unique is that they were ultimately able to assimilate into "Whiteness" and receive all of the benefits, privileges, and protections that identity entailed in ways that Black, Indige-nous, Latinx, Asian, and Pacific Islanders have not. The idea of the "melting pot" in which people from all over the world have come together in the United States to become one American group "with liberty and justice for all," has, thus far, only ever worked for people who are "White" (Ignatiev, 1995).

WHY DOES RACE MATTER? UNDERSTANDING RACISM

Race is a messy concept with a long and complicated history. Some people believe it would be easier to just reject the whole notion and have every-one identify as one race—the human race. In fact, lots of people, especially White people, have taken this approach in their efforts to divorce them-selves from the sordid history of race in America. We have frequently expe-rienced White students and teachers boldly declare that they are "human" when asked their racial background. While it is true that biologically there is only one human race, this "colorblind" approach ignores that the social construction of race has very real consequences for all of our lives. Race matters because of racism.

Racism is a *system* in which White people in our society have unearned advantage because of their race, while People of Color (Black, Latinx, Asian, Pacific Islander, Indigenous, Multiracial, Arab, MENA) have un-earned disadvantage because of theirs. *Privilege* is the term used to talk about unearned advantage, and *oppression* or *marginalization* are the terms often used to talk about unearned disadvantage (see Chapter 3 for more information about terminology). When it comes to race, we would say that White people benefit from *White privilege*.

Often when people use the terms "racism" or "racist" in casual conversation they are talking about how one person consciously feels about and treats someone from a different racial group. In contrast, we (and many other people who do work similar to ours) think about racism as manifesting at three different levels: [5]

- **Individual:** What we personally think, believe, and feel about racial groups. We may be consciously aware of these feelings (explicit bias), or they may be unconscious (implicit bias). And these feelings may be about others, or about our own group (internalized racism).
- **Interpersonal:** How we treat and interact with others as a result of these feelings, thoughts, and beliefs, consciously and unconsciously.
- **Institutional/Systemic:** How our various social systems (education, criminal justice, healthcare, laws, etc.) are designed to privilege some and oppress others.

The *individual* and *interpersonal* levels of racism are what we call *prejudice*. Everyone has some form of prejudice or bias, even those of us who identify as People of Color. The *institutional/systemic* level is what we call *power*. These levels are relegated exclusively to White society.

All of our institutions in the United States are set up to privilege White people over People of Color (and men over women, rich people over poor people, straight and cis people over LGBTQ+ people, people without disabilities over people with disabilities, etc.). While a Black person may have biased feelings about someone who is Latinx (individual) and may even say hateful things to them (interpersonal), Black people do not have the power to create policies that would systematically discriminate against Latinx people as a whole (institutional). They do not, for example, have the power to create discrimination in the housing or banking industries against Latinx folks. People of Color might have prejudice, but they do not have power.

In contrast, even if a White person works really hard to interrupt their personal biases and prejudices (individual) and treats People of Color fairly, even building close and mutually affectionate relationships with them (interpersonal), these efforts are not enough to transform the larger system. Even the most conscientious White person benefits from White privilege, whether they want to or not. For example, White people, regardless of their personal biases, beliefs, political leanings, or social networks, are less likely to be stopped, ticketed, searched, and arrested by the police when driving than their Black friends (Pierson et al., 2017).

Often, when advocates for racial justice use the term *racism* they mean it in the way that Beverly Daniel Tatum (2004) defines it: "prejudice"—individual and interpersonal racism—"plus power"—institutional racism. In contrast, when the average student or teacher uses the term "racism" or "racist" they are almost always only talking about the individual and interpersonal levels—that someone did or said something mean or biased to someone else because of their race. This is an important distinction for two reasons. First, in dialogue, it is imperative to clarify terminology because the words "racism" and "racist" often cause defensiveness on the part of participants, especially those who are White. Recognizing that racism is not just about an *individual* being a good or bad person (DiAngelo, 2011) but rather about how our entire society is structured, allows for participants to be less defensive and more open to seeing how racism plays out in our society.

Second, framing racism as a largely individual failing ignores the fact that we *all* hold prejudices and biases that we are working to overcome—albeit some much more overt, conscious, intentional, and bigoted than others. Even People of Color who do not have institutional or cultural power and privilege can have implicit and explicit bias. It is nearly impossible to live in a society, watch the news, read books, or go to school and not develop biases based on the dominant culture of White privilege.

People who do not understand privilege and oppression when it comes to race might turn on the news and assume People of Color are not doing as well as White people in education, healthcare, and criminal justice because of some inherent (biological) deficiencies. Students of color often buy into negative racial stereotypes about themselves (internalized racism) and others. But the truth is, we see disparities by race in these areas because all of the major institutions in our country have been designed in ways that that unfairly and disproportionately punish People of Color and unfairly advantage people who are White.

RACIAL INEQUALITY IN EDUCATION

The United States education system has systematically advantaged white people throughout our history. Over the course of over 300 years of chattel slavery in the continental United States, laws were passed banning enslaved Africans from learning to read out of fear that if they became literate, they would use their knowledge and skill to more effectively fight for their freedom (Banks, 1996). This foundation of racially inequitable education continued even after the Emancipation Proclamation outlawed slavery in 1865.

The first public schools in the southern United States, established after the end of slavery, were racially segregated—a practice that was upheld in the 1896 U.S. Supreme Court case *Plessy v. Ferguson*, which declared the doctrine of "separate but equal" constitutional. In the south, Black and White students were segregated, and in the west, Mexican and White students were segregated. Despite the Plessy ruling, these segregated school systems were anything but equal. Black and Latinx schools were severely underfunded and under-resourced (Ramsey, 2016).

Black and Latino Americans are not the only racial group who have been historically targeted by discriminatory educational practices. In the mid to late 1800s, Native American children were also being sent to segregated schools. These schools were often church-run boarding schools that had the explicit goal of erasing all traces of Indigenous culture. Students were not allowed to speak their native languages, were forced to cut their hair and dress in European clothing, and even had to change their names. As Captain Richard H. Pratt, the founder of one of the most famous schools, the Carlisle Indian Industrial School, said in an 1892 speech, his goal was to "kill the Indian, and save the man" (Stout, 2012).

The journey toward reversing a nationwide and pervasive pattern of school segregation has been long. In 1954, the U.S. Supreme Court found that racially segregated schools were inherently unequal in the *Brown v. Board of Education*, decision and mandated that schools in the United States desegregate "with all deliberate speed." However, changing the law was not enough to change the hearts and minds of individuals. Not only were efforts to integrate schools met with violence and pushback from many White people, students and families of color had to do the physically and emotionally dangerous work of integrating majority White schools.

Over 6 decades later, it is virtually impossible to find a school whose student body reflects the racial (and economic) diversity of our country, or even the city where its located. At present, schools in the United States are more segregated than they have been in decades, in part because of increased choice policies that allow privileged, largely White, parents to opt into schools they deem better (Hannah-Jones, 2016). Even in instances in which children attend their neighborhood schools, housing segregation in the United States, which was institutionalized with the redlining policies of the Federal Housing Administration in the 1930s (Oliver & Shapiro, 2006) and continues in the real estate and banking industries even today (Bonilla-Silva, 2018; Dymski, Hernandez, & Mohanty, 2013), means that most of those schools, like the neighborhoods where they are located, are also racially segregated.

Segregation has not only affected where students from different racial backgrounds attend school, it is also linked to the resources available at those schools. School funding in the United States has historically been closely attached to local property taxes. This means that majority White neighborhoods, with homes that have historically been valued higher due only to the Whiteness of the homeowners, are likely to have better-resourced schools than neighborhoods that are majority Black, Latinx or Native American (U.S. Commission on Civil Rights, 2018).

Who Are Our Teachers?

Prior to the *Brown* decision, Black students were much more likely to have teachers from their own racial backgrounds. After its passage, Black students began attending historically White schools and the majority of their Black teachers, unwelcome in these new districts, were left jobless (Lutz, 2017). Integration meant that Black students were spending their days in schools that were not designed for them, with hostile White peers, taught by educators who did not connect with them and who likely held deeply entrenched racial biases, led by administrators who did not see fit to hire Black teachers. Sadly, not much has changed since that time.

Currently in the U.S. public school system, 80% of public school teachers are White (National Center for Education Statistics, 2017). For students of color these numbers do real harm. A 2017 study found that Black students are significantly more likely to graduate from high school if they had a Black teacher between 3rd and 5th grade—an experience that was all but lost with national integration and the reduction in teachers of color (Gershenson et al., 2017). Just like the Black students of the postintegration era, students of color today are almost always spending their school days navigating cross-racial interactions with educators who have likely not given much thought to how race matters in their lives, in their classrooms, or for their students.

What Are Students Learning?

Take a look at your curriculum. What are students in your school learning? What books are they reading? What is covered in the units you are teaching this year? Our guess is there is not much that reflects the experiences, histories, writings, or contributions of Black, Latinx, Indigenous, Asian, Pacific Islander, or Middle Eastern populations. Despite decades of efforts, led largely by People of Color, to make our curriculum more diverse, most of what students in U.S. schools learn, even today, centers around White men. Moreover, we bet the majority of learning about People of Color is happening in the context of our histories of discrimination—short sections on slavery or the Civil Rights Movement, maybe a line or two about the internment of Japanese Americans during World War II, but likely little content that reflects the experiences, accomplishments, achievements, cultural knowledge, or values of People of Color in historic or contemporary society. Rather than starting the history of Africans and Native Americans with their flourishing societies prior to the arrival of Europeans, many textbooks teach about People of Color largely through the lens of oppression.

In the 1960s and 1970s, university students of color advocated for the creation of Chicano, Native American, Asian, and Black Studies programs to address the Whitewashing of school curriculum (Hu-DeHart, 1993; Joseph, 2013). In 1980, the first edition of the seminal text *A People's History of the United States* (Zinn) was published, which shifted the narrative of U.S. history from the perspective of European colonizers to that of People of Color. In the 1990s, Native American groups began protesting against the teaching of Columbus and Thanksgiving in public schools and asked that these portrayals be more accurately told from the perspective of the Indigenous populations already here (Dunbar-Ortiz, 2014). Yet the overwhelming majority of schools have not shifted course. In fact, just the opposite has happened. In *Lies My Teacher Told Me: Everything Your American History Textbook Got Wrong*, author James Loewen (2007) reviews history textbooks, the majority of which are published in Texas, and found that they remain biased in favor of White perspectives.

Who Is Achieving? Who Gets in Trouble?

The 2002 No Child Left Behind Act, a reauthorization of the 1965 Elementary and Secondary Education Act, mandated that schools begin disaggregating their achievement data by race. Since that time educators have paid significant attention to what is commonly called *the achievement gap,* the finding that Black, Latinx, and Native American students underperform on standardized tests when compared to White and Asian students; are less likely to be enrolled in advanced and STEM courses, such as calculus and physics (Sparks & Klein, 2018); and have lower rates of graduation and college attendance (U.S. Department of Education Office for Civil Rights, 2016). There is now a growing body of research attempting to make sense of these disparities. Studies have found that standardized tests are often racially biased and that Black, Latinx, and Native American students are likely to go to the least resourced schools with the least qualified and least experienced teachers (U.S. Department of Education Office for Civil Rights, 2016). For this reason, some researchers refer to this gap as an *opportunity gap,* rather than an achievement gap, in order to indicate that Black and Latinx students actually have fewer opportunities to succeed academically than their White and Asian counterparts.

More recently, racial gaps in discipline have also been getting attention. The Civil Rights Data Collection 2015–2016 Report from the U.S. Department of Education tracked all 96,300 public P–12 schools in the country and found that Black, Latinx, and Native American students remained overrepresented in out-of-school suspensions, school arrests, and police referrals (Sparks & Klein, 2018; U.S. Department of Education Office for Civil Rights, 2018). The same report found that these disparities in school discipline referrals begin in preschool. Although Black children made up only 19% of all students enrolled in preschool, they accounted for 47% of those who received out-of-school suspensions (U.S. Department of Education Office for Civil Rights, 2016). Studies have found that these disparities in discipline are not because Students of Color are more likely to misbehave. Rather, the implicit racial bias of teachers means that Black, Latinx, and Native American students are often punished more harshly than White students for the same offenses (Quereshi & Okonofua, 2017). Gaps in achievement and discipline have a trickle-down effect. They determine who is likely to graduate from high school, who will go on to college and graduate, and ultimately who is likely to be employed in some of the highest-earning careers in our country.

CONCLUSION

The United States has a long and sordid history of racism rooted in White privilege. This history starts with the genocide of Native peoples and theft of their lands and manifests currently in every major institution in our country and in the hearts and minds of many. Any educator or young person paying attention to the stories they see in the news, the people they interact with, or the content they are learning in schools can clearly see disparities in the experiences of people from different racial groups. And yet they likely have very little understanding of why the lives of White Americans and People of Color look so starkly different because we still fail to tell or teach the truth about who we are as a country.

A brief overview of history reveals that the racial disparities we observe in our daily lives were baked into the system at the individual, interpersonal, and institutional levels from the very first moment Europeans stepped foot on these lands. As a country, we have done very little to repair this national tragedy. Progress is born from waking up to the realities of our inequitable system and making concerted efforts to educate our communities and actively foster change. Picking up this book today is an admirable and important step in the right direction.

NOTES

1. When Shayla presented to a group of White K–3 teachers and asked them to estimate what percent of the country is Latinx and what percent is Black, they guessed 35% and 50% respectively. According to the 2017 U.S. Census Estimates, the country is 13.4% Black/African American, 1.3% American Indian/Alaska Native, 5.8% Asian, 0.2% Native Hawaiian or Pacific Islander, 18.7% Hispanic/Latino, 60.7% White/non-Hispanic, and 2.7% two or more races. There is no category for people who are Middle Eastern, Arab, or North African (U.S. Census).

In 2013, the U.S. student population was 16% Black, 1% American Indian/Alaska Native, 5% Asian/Pacific Islander, 25% Hispanic/Latino, 50% White, and 3% two or more races (NCES, 2017).

2. This is one reason why we use the word "White" when talking about people of European descent rather than the world "Caucasian." For more on this see "The Surprisingly Racist History of 'Caucasian'" from MTV News' *Decoded* with Franchesca Ramsey (www.youtube.com/watch?v=GKB8hXYod2w).

3. In its over 220-year history, there has never been a census category for Americans of Arab or Middle Eastern descent. Instead, these groups are currently classified as White. For over a decade, there have been campaigns to add MENA— Middle Eastern or North African—to the census in order to be able to better document the experiences and discrimination these groups face. When we fail to provide communities with a racial label recognized by the government, we are unable to track things like where they attend school, how they are achieving, and whether or not they are graduating and going on to college. The remainder of this chapter has virtually no data on how MENA populations are doing in our society because it simply does not exist (Lo Wang, 2018).

4. Latinx identity further complicates the conversation about race and ethnicity. Most people who identify as Latinx come from countries in which there was historically an Indigenous population that was then colonized by Europeans (Spanish or Portuguese) who often brought with them enslaved Africans. In turn, Latinx identity is already one of "racial" mixing. And yet, Latinx is also not quite an ethnic identity because there are so many cultures and nationalities represented under this umbrella. Some Latinx people consider their racial identity to be Mestizo, others identify as Black, White or Indigenous, and still others use Latinx as their racial group. Currently, the U.S. Census asks people to pick a "race" of which Latinx is *not* a choice, and then identify if they have "Hispanic" (i.e., Latinx) heritage.

5. We sometimes also talk about the cultural level of racism, which determines what is considered "beauty," "truth," "right," or "normal." We have left this level out for the purposes of this book because we do not provide a specific lesson about cultural racism in our curriculum.

CHAPTER 2

What Is Intergroup Dialogue?

> To engage in dialogue is one of the simplest ways we can begin as [people], teachers, scholars, and critical thinkers to cross boundaries, the barriers that may or may not be erected by race, gender, class, professional standing, and a host of other differences. (bell hooks, 1994, p. 130)

As we saw in Chapter 1, racial divisions in the United States remain a pressing and intractable issue. At the same time our ability to have conversations and develop understanding across racial differences remains limited. Dialogue provides one way to have these much-needed conversations.

When scholars and practitioners talk about *dialogue* (also called sustained dialogue, intergroup dialogue, or intercultural dialogue), we are referring to a very specific set of practices developed to facilitate conversations between people who have antagonistic sociohistorical legacies due to unequal social power, stereotypes, implicit and explicit bias, and values (Schoem & Hurtado, 2001). David Schoem posits that though intergroup dialogue will not solve all our nation's problems, "open and honest exchange and serious face-to-face engagement that represents good dialogue provides the best opportunity to engage in the practice of deliberative democracy in order to address our institutional and national concerns" (2001, p. 5).

Intergroup dialogue (IGD) is an evidence-based form of dialogic (dialogue-based) educational engagement, which has evolved over the last 3 decades as a set of educational practices used to address social justice issues in educational and community settings (Adams, 2007). Though dialogues will look different depending on facilitator and participant composition, local needs, time availability, and content, there are eight common characteristics that often constitute intergroup dialogue in its various settings. We briefly discuss the common core aspects of dialogue facilitation in this chapter and go into greater depth about various aspects of dialogue facilitation in the subsequent chapters of this book.

Dialogue is about listening. Dialogues are about generously listening to others. It is about turning off one's own internal conversation and listening with curiosity and genuine intent to learn. (See Chapter 3 for more detail on generous listening.)

Dialogue is about learning. Dialogue is about adding to the common pool of knowledge. Like the ancient Buddhist parable (Ireland, 2007) of blind people trying to determine the nature of an elephant by feeling different parts of the animal (see Figure 2.1), facilitators recognize that only by sharing everyone's individual perspective and lived experience can we deepen and expand our understanding across difference.

Dialogue is face-to-face. Because dialogue is predicated upon developing relationships across difference, dialogue takes place face to face, and when possible, is limited to between 9–18 participants. Dialogues can also take place in larger classrooms where care is given to developing brave spaces for participants to share stories, listen deeply, and be vulnerable (See Chapters 3 and 4).

Dialogue is sustained. Intergroup dialogue does not take place in an afternoon workshop or a one-off professional development session. Dialogue takes place over an extended period of time, often 6 weeks to 6 months. This allows participants the opportunity to work through a set of scaffolded learning experiences with the same group that builds trust between participants. Trust allows participants the space necessary to build relationships across difference, generously listen to one another, challenge one's own previously held beliefs, and add to one's own knowledge base.

Dialogue is facilitated by trained facilitators. Because dialogue is predicated on surfacing differences and commonalities between historically conflicting groups, dialogues are led by facilitators who are specifically trained in leading dialogues across difference. When possible, dialogues are co-facilitated by individuals who represent the social groups of the participants. Peer or near-peer facilitation is often used. (See Chapters 4–7.)

Dialogue surfaces conflict. Because the premise of dialogue is to bring historically divided groups together and provide participants space to share their lived experiences which sometimes diverge significantly, conflict often emerges. Dialogue is a space where participants can engage bravely with conflicting ideas. Trained facilitators and thoughtful participants view conflict as learning opportunities. Facilitators know how to use hot moments to deepen participant understanding across difference. (See Chapters 8–9.)

Dialogue is about deepening understanding of shared reality. Dialogue uses a series of activities, reflections, and conversations to move participants into deeper understanding of our society. Dialogue uses both affective and

Figure 2.1. Elephant Drawing

Illustration by Andrew Kaplowitz.

cognitive methods to engage participants in deepening their understanding of others' perspectives. Dialogue facilitators use both content—learning new information—and process—attending to feelings and emotions—to help participants expand their knowledge base.

Dialogue is based in human dignity. Dialogue is predicated on the notion that every human is born with inherent dignity (and should be treated as such). In our dialogic interactions, we treat fellow participants with dignity. When we learn to treat people with whom we disagree with dignity, we often develop deeper, more empathetic dialogues and mutual learning opportunities. Noted conflict mediator Donna Hicks (2011) developed a "dignity model" to address "a missing link in our understanding of conflict: our failure to recognize how vulnerable humans are to being treated as if they did not matter." Hicks writes:

> The primal desire for dignity precedes us in every human interaction. When violated, it can destroy a relationship. It can incite arguments, divorces, wars and revolutions. Until we fully recognize and accept this aspect of what it means to be human—that a violation of our dignity feels like a threat to our survival—we will fall short in understanding conflict and what it takes to transform it to a more fruitful interaction. (Hicks, 2011, p. 14)

Dialogue often leads to action. Though dialogue across difference is, in and of itself, a form of action, dialogue often leads participants to take action to promote equity and justice within their spheres of influence.

WHERE DID DIALOGUE COME FROM?

Theoretical Foundations

Intergroup dialogue, as it is presented here, is a 35-year-old research-based social justice education program that was initiated at the University of Michigan and is now implemented on hundreds of college campuses and additional educational, extracurricular, professional, and classroom spaces around the country.

Dialogue is theoretically grounded in the critical pedagogy of Paulo Freire (1970), the critical multicultural education model (Banks, 2017), and critical race theory (Delgado & Stefancic, 2012). Freire's problem-posing model posits that when participants are treated as co-learners who possess their own lived experiences, rather than as empty vessels waiting to be filled with information from educators, they are able to develop a critical consciousness of their own and other's lived experiences. Through reflection and dialogue participants can move toward praxis (action) in order to create a more just society (Freire, 1970).

Critical multiculturalists extend Freire's work and focus on combating structural inequality (Banks, 2017). They seek to incorporate culture into the classroom to educate citizens to "know, care, and act" rather than "regurgitate information" (Banks, 2017; Lynch, Swartz, & Isaacs, 2017).

Our work on race dialogues in particular is informed by critical race theorists (CRT) who center race as a primary prism through which we understand our reality. CRT theorists believe that racism is not just pervasive, but is *built into* the U.S. social system, including the system of public education (Bonilla-Silva, 2005; Ladson-Billings & Tate, 1995; Leonardo, 2013). CRT theorists assert that the racialization of education is so complete that race is not one of many variables, but the core dynamic that affects the entire education system. Zeus Leonardo writes that "race and racism are implicated in every aspect of education" (Leonardo, 2013, p. 3). Gloria Ladson-Billings and William Tate (1995) believe that the inequalities inherent in our educational system are a "logical and predictable" outcome of our racialized society where we continue to silence discussions of race and racism.

WHAT THE RESEARCH SHOWS

As educators, practitioners, and researchers, we have explicitly chosen to use intergroup dialogue methodologies to address the proverbial racial "elephant in the classroom." We have selected intergroup dialogue because it works. Our own research into participant outcomes from dialogic experiences mirrors similar research done across the country. The largest research project on intergroup dialogue was initiated in 2006 and completed in 2009 through a consortium of nine universities across the United States. The research involved 52 parallel field experiments including 1,463 participants and looked at whether participation in intergroup dialogue about various social identities, including race, has educational impacts not attributable to predisposition to participation in diversity programs. The results are convincing. The study found that participants increased their understanding of race, gender, and income inequality, and they increased intergroup empathy and motivation to connect with members of other groups (Gurin, Nagda, & Zúñiga, 2013). Further, longitudinal research into IGD shows these gains persist for many years after students have participated in the dialogues (Gurin et al., 2013).

INTERGROUP DIALOGUE MODELS

Near-Peer Model

Over the last 8 years, we have developed a model of near-peer intergroup dialogue that has formed the basis for much of the work in this book. We use specifically trained college students as near-peer facilitators embedded within high school English classrooms. Every high school freshman English student (and half of the sophomores) in our collaborating district participate in an 11-week (one time per week) race dialogue program. It is known as ICD or Intercultural Dialogue.

The idea of integrating dialogues directly into public school classrooms using college student "near-peer" facilitators originated with a group of parents whose children had been participating in a voluntary after-school extracurricular diversity and leadership program that Donna and her colleague Dr. Dorinda Carter Andrews sponsored through outreach and civic engagement courses at their university. On anonymous end-of-year evaluation surveys, a majority of parents indicated their frustration that the material covered was relegated to an after-school program. They voiced a strong belief that the content of the diversity and leadership program was both so important and so neglected in curricular programming that it merited inclusion as part of their children's school day curricula.

In response to the after-school program parents' request, university collaborators approached the school district administration to ask if they were interested in collaborating in a race dialogue curriculum that was integrated into the high school curriculum and facilitated by near peers (college students) within classrooms. The administration was enthusiastically on board and initiated a collaborative project between the university faculty member

(Donna) and the high school English Department chair (Sheri) that resulted in the development of a comprehensive program that fit squarely within the state and local curricular requirements, accommodated university requirements for teacher education student instruction, and fit in with teacher and faculty time and resource constraints.

The ICD program that we use is an 11-session curriculum in which pairs of college students facilitate race dialogues in all freshman and honors sophomore English classes at our collaborating school. The near-peer facilitators are all students in the college of education studying to be teachers themselves. They are trained in dialogue facilitation during the fall semester and then lead dialogues during the spring semester. We also introduce dialogue concepts to classroom teachers who support the dialogues and are present and participatory throughout the near-peer dialogues.

University-Based Dialogue Programs

Intergroup dialogue is also common on many university campuses, though it looks different in each setting. Some universities offer credit-bearing classes on dialogues and dialogue facilitation, and others mandate participation in dialogues. Some universities offer intergroup dialogue in extracurricular, student-run programs. Over the past several years, Donna directed a university-level dialogue program at Michigan State University (MSU) that trains paid graduate and undergraduate students to facilitate dialogues on race and gender with peers. Hundreds of university students participate in the free, 8-week extracurricular program each year.

OUR RESEARCH FINDINGS

Our own research resembles the national findings. We conduct annual evaluations of both the near-peer high school level and the college level peer-facilitated dialogue programs discussed above. For both the high school and the college dialogue programs, in every area that we empirically tested, respondents showed a statistically significant positive change from their pre-dialogue measures to their post-dialogue measures.

College Student Outcomes

To assess whether our program achieved its goals, we used a mixed-method approach with both a quantitative component (retrospective pre/post survey with 86% response rate, N=71) and a qualitative component (focus groups with a 30% response rate).

To measure our first goal, increase personal awareness about privilege and oppression, one of the items we asked participants to respond to is the statement, "I understand systems of privilege and oppression." Twenty-seven percent of respondents indicated they "strongly agreed" with the statement prior to participating in MSU Dialogues, while 65% of respondents "strongly agreed" after participating in MSU Dialogues.

One way we measured our efficacy in achieving our second goal of improving intergroup understanding was to ask participants to respond to the statement, "I listen actively to others." Prior to participating in dialogue, 35% of respondents "strongly agreed" with this statement as compared to 89% of respondents after participating in dialogue.

We asked our respondents 10 questions to measure our third goal of exploring ways to work together toward greater equity and justice. For example, one statement they were asked to respond to was: "I have developed concrete strategies to work toward greater justice." Prior to MSU Dialogues, 9% of respondents strongly agreed with this statement, while after dialogues 46% of respondents strongly agreed. Similarly, another item said, "I intervene when I hear or see bias." We saw significant changes from before MSU Dialogues to after MSU Dialogues. Prior to MSU Dialogues, 7% of the respondents strongly agreed with this statement, and after MSU Dialogues, 49% reported they strongly agreed with this statement.

High School Student Outcomes

Similarly, we conducted a 45-question retrospective pre/post survey of high school students (N=281) immediately following their participation in our intergroup dialogue program in the high school. With a 72% response rate, the survey found that there was statistically significant growth on all questions asked to the entire group.

In terms of our first goal, promoting deeper awareness of racial identity issues, students reported major growth in understanding institutional racism, microaggressions, implicit bias, and how to be an ally, among other concepts. For example, prior to dialogue, 16% of respondents said they strongly agreed that they knew what a microaggression was, and after dialogue, 41% of respondents strongly agreed with this statement. Similar growth was seen in other areas tested.

In terms of the second goal, high school students indicated they deepened their understanding of the history of racism in the United States, moving from 34% who strongly agreed with this statement prior to dialogues to 62% after participating in dialogues.

In terms of the third goal of advancing strategies to interrupt bias, we saw similar results. For example, students indicated that prior to participating in dialogue, 13% strongly agreed with the statement that they know how to be an ally, compared to 44% who strongly agreed with the statement after dialogue. Similarly, to the statement, "I know what to do when someone tells a racial joke," 16% of students strongly agreed with this statement prior to dialogue and 43% strongly agreed after dialogue. After dialogue, 95% of the students strongly agreed or agreed with the above statement.

We were also interested in how students felt about being taught by near-peer facilitators. Seventy-seven percent of the respondents indicated they enjoyed learning from their facilitators. One student noted: "They were very encouraging and were able to bring out thoughts in me which I had never considered before." Another student wrote: "They were extremely careful about topics that were very sensitive and really help us become more open about these topics" (Kaplowitz, Lee, & Seyka, 2018; Kaplowitz, 2018a, 2018b).

CONCLUSION

Intergroup dialogue is a research-based educational methodology that helps participants deepen their understanding of self, develop relationships across difference and engage in action to move toward equity and social justice in our communities. It is based upon face-to-face sustained contact between participants working with trained facilitators who know how to surface conflict and use it as a learning opportunity. The research on dialogue is replete with evidence that it is effective in helping participants increase understanding across different identities and intergroup empathy.

We have had a meaningful experience using intergroup dialogue in our own classrooms, professional development series, and extracurricular efforts. Our results show that dialogue alumni have the skills to reduce race-based misunderstandings and the strategies necessary for productive engagement in our increasingly racially diverse world. Scores of university, school district, business, and nonprofit leaders have asked us to share our formula for creating and leading intergroup dialogues on race. In the following chapters, we share the concrete techniques developed through trial and error (lots of error!) that we have used to teach facilitators how to sharpen their craft and to lead thousands of participants in dialogues designed to dismantle entrenched systems of race-based oppression in our society.

CHAPTER 3

Setting Up an Inclusive Dialogue Space

> Human conversation is the most ancient and easiest way to cultivate the conditions for change—personal change, community and organizational change. (Wheatley, 2009, p. 3)

Though race dialogues can take place in many different settings, there are some commonalities across most dialogue settings that work. In this chapter we share explicit actions facilitators can take to create inclusive spaces that are conducive to constructive dialogues across and about race. The practices we outline are fundamental for creating educational settings where participants suspend their own judgment, actively listen to one another's lived realities, and cocreate a more robust, complex, intersectional, and innovative understanding of the social systems in which they live.

DIALOGUE NUTS AND BOLTS

Room Setup

Setting up the room so that participants and facilitators sit in a circle is the best way to ensure equitable participation during dialogue. We prefer using chairs without desks because we want to break down barriers, real and imagined. We have found that when desks are removed from dialogic circles, participants report feeling more vulnerable but also more willing to share their stories. Desks can feel like physical barriers behind which participants are protected from deep introspection.

We recognize that it is not always possible to set up a room in a circle, or to remove desks and tables. Many of our high school dialogues take place in classrooms with desks set in small groups, or even in rows, and we have been successful using those spaces as well. Occasionally, for certain dialogue activities, we use space in hallways or courtyards, or reserve a room for specific lessons that require more open space.

Group Size

A successful dialogue can have a variety of group sizes. We have facilitated
effective race dialogues in groups as large as 35 in some of our high school
classrooms. However, the optimal size for dialogue groups is between 9–18
participants. This is small enough to ensure verbal space for all participants,
and yet is large enough to attain a diversity of ideas. We have found that often when the group size is large, there are fewer active participants. Hence,
with larger groups it is important to offer more opportunity for pair-shar-
ing and small group activities so reluctant or shy participants can speak in
smaller group settings.

Participant Selection

Though we know that in many settings we have no ability to predetermine
the social identities of dialogue participants, when we can, we strive to create dialogues that are racially balanced. For example, in Donna's application for dialogue participation at Michigan State, she explicitly asks potential dialogue participants to share their racial identity. Then, when her team
constructs the dialogue groups, they can attempt to create groups that have
an even distribution of White students and Students of Color. There are
inherent issues in grouping all participants of color into a single category
because it falsely presumes there is a singular experience of being "of color"
(i.e., that an Asian student's experience is similar to a Black student's experience). Hence we are careful to ensure, when possible, that there is racial
diversity *within* the Student of Color group. Since we know that our country
is highly segregated, most dialogue organizers will not have the luxury of
ensuring racially balanced participation. In those cases, it is incumbent on
the facilitators to raise the experiences of those not present in the room. (See
Chapter 4 section on multipartiality and counternarratives.)

Accessibility

It is important to plan in advance to accommodate a variety of abilities. We
try to ensure inclusive spaces for all participants, and we prepare materials
that meet a variety of ability needs. For example, we have created reading
material in large font size, sent materials in advance to those who needed
them in order to best learn, included closed captioning of videos, and considered the possible need for interpreters. Our dialogues all take place in
wheelchair-accessible locations.

   One way to make sure everyone has equal access to participation is to
proactively survey participants and invite them to let you know in advance of
the first meeting what types of support they need to successfully participate.
Shayla and Donna both send out presurveys to attend to individual needs.

Dialogue Structure

We begin and end every session following a predictable format. You might use a "quick check around the circle" as a good beginning for each session. Doing so allows facilitators to get a pulse on what people are bringing into the space on any particular day. Examples of an opening question might be: "What is one positive thing that happened to you today?" or "If your feelings were the weather, what is the weather report today?" or "What are you bringing to our space today?"

Closing each session should also follow a predictable, familiar format. Facilitators may ask a clarifying question that provides each participant an opportunity to reflect on the shared experience. Some examples of "closing round questions" are: "What is one word for how you feel leaving today?" or "Share one sentence on something new you have learned from someone in the circle," or "What is one thing you are going to think about before we meet again?" or "What important questions remain unanswered for you?" See Appendix C for more ideas.

Time Management

It takes experience to know how to navigate improvisational activities with large or small groups and how to move some conversations along without making the participants feel rushed. Pre-thinking each part of the dialogue lesson and keeping careful track of time are ways to ensure that you cover what you plan to accomplish. Good facilitators are familiar with their lesson plans, the expected length of activities, and the overarching arc of each dialogue session. It is essential to be aware of how much time you have throughout the session, so you can pace yourself accordingly, communicate with your co-facilitator during the dialogue, and adjust as you go.

Monitor your own speaking time during dialogue sessions. Ensure that you are not taking up more time speaking than is essential. While facilitators do need to share their own stories, respond to participant comments, and make connections during dialogue to tie individual experiences to structural and institutional oppressions (see Chapter 6), it is their role to keep the dialogue among participants moving along.

PREPARING FOR DIALOGUE: KEY CONCEPTS AND ACTIVITIES

The following are concepts and terminology that guide dialogue. We share these concepts with participants in nearly every dialogue we develop. Activities that facilitators can use to illustrate all of the concepts below can be found in Chapter 11, Lesson 2.

Dialogue vs. Debate

In our culture, debate is often the most common form of communication between people who disagree. Many of us have been socialized to deal with conflict by competing to prove that someone else is wrong and that we are right. The goal of debate is to win an argument. In contrast, the goal of dialogue is to add to the common pool of knowledge. See Figure 3.1 for key differences between debate and dialogue. Krista Tippett (2016), a noted author and radio personality, writes:

> Our cultural mode of debating issues by way of competing certainties comes with a drive to resolution. We want others to acknowledge that our answers are right. The alternative [is]: to invite searching—not on who is right and who is wrong and the arguments on every side; not on whether we can agree; but on what is at stake in human terms for us all. There is value in learning to speak together honestly and relate to each other with dignity, without rushing to common ground that would leave all the hard questions hanging. (pp. 30–31)

Helping participants understand the key differences between dialogue and debate not only helps dismantle combative communication patterns, but also contributes to developing deeper understanding across difference.

Generous Listening

Though active, deep, and generous listening skills might seem like something we all should have been taught in kindergarten, in our experience, dialogue participants (and facilitators) are often unfamiliar with and unpracticed in generous listening. Dedicating time to explicitly think about generous listening yields positive results in dialogue. Tippett (2016) explains generous listening:

> Generous listening is powered by curiosity, a virtue we can invite and nurture in ourselves to render it instinctive. It involves a kind of vulnerability—a willingness to be surprised, to let go of assumptions and take in ambiguity. The listener wants to understand the humanity behind the words of the other, and patiently summons one's own best self and one's own best words and questions. (p. 29)

There are three levels of listening:

1. *Internal listening:* Listeners are focused on their own internal voice and are thinking about their own response to the speaker. Most of us listen at this level. At the internal listening stage, a listener might interject a comment like: "I had an experience just like that. . . . " The internal listener wants to center themselves in the conversation. Some

Figure 3.1. Dialogue/Debate

Dialogue	Debate
Goal: Grow together/add to the common pool of knowledge.	Goal: Win an argument/prove the other person is wrong.
A form of communication between two or more people that is directed toward common understanding.	A form of communication between two or more people where an issue is discussed and opposing arguments are put forward.
Assumes many people have the answer and that only together can people find the solution.	Assumes there is one right answer and that you have it.
Is collaborative. Participants work together toward a common understanding.	Is individualistic. Is about proving someone else is wrong and winning an argument.
Is about learning through listening to other people and discovering new ideas.	Is about listening to find flaws and weaknesses in other people's ideas.

Adapted from University of Michigan, Program on Intergroup Relations, 2013.

internal listeners, accustomed to our combative speech patterns, listen just long enough to find weakness in the speaker's arguments, so they can debate the speaker. Sam Killermann and Meg Bolger who wrote a very useful primer on facilitation called *Unlocking the Magic of Facilitation* use the term "predatory listening" to describe the phenomenon of people just waiting for their turn to attack an idea that has been offered instead of considering it for its merits (Killermann & Bolger, 2016, p. 60).

2. *Generous listening:* Listeners focus their attention entirely on the speaker using authentic curiosity. This requires turning off our own internal voices and leaning in to what the speaker is saying with genuine interest. This is where we want participants in dialogue to be. It is a skill that facilitators should share with participants and invite them to practice in and out of dialogue settings.

3. *Global listening:* Listeners are aware of everything in the room, notice how others respond, and pay attention to verbal and nonverbal cues and engagement. This is a skill that we explain to participants and that we expect our facilitators to develop.

Perhaps the most important skill a facilitator needs to incorporate into facilitation practice is *listening*. Facilitators need to know both how to be generous and global listeners and how to inculcate those skills in their dialogue participants. As the late U.S. diplomat and founder of the D.C.-based Sustained Dialogue Institute, Harold Saunders, once said, at its core "dialogue is about *listening* to each other deeply enough to be changed by what we hear" (Saunders, n.d.). In her Ted Talk, 10 Ways to Have a Better Conversation, Celeste Headlee (2016), journalist and public radio host, offers specific techniques to practice and develop good listening skills that we have found useful. Headlee says good listeners are brief, focused, use open-ended questions, are honest when they do not know something, center others' stories, and maintain an eye on the larger goals without getting bogged down in details.

As we noted in Chapter 2, our research confirms that listening skills are among the most profound lessons participants develop in dialogues. One dialogue participant put it this way:

> For me, active listening was [the] most meaningful [part of dialogue]. Before dialogues, I would just get frustrated with people when they made racist or discriminatory comments. Now, I am thinking about ways (using the tools provided by my facilitators) to challenge people in their thinking in a productive way. I don't want to shut people down for what they say, but rather challenge them to think in a different way. (Kaplowitz, 2018b)

Brave Learning Space

We introduce our participants to the concept of *brave spaces* and *learning edges* at the outset of dialogues. A learning edge is a space where we challenge ourselves to get out of our comfort zone. We share the concept of growth mindsets with participants to encourage them to view mistakes as learning opportunities (Dweck, 2016). We do not use the term "safe space" in our dialogues because we cannot guarantee that every utterance that comes out of each person's mouth will be safe for every other participant (Arao & Clemens, 2013). Framing the dialogue space as a *brave space* invites participants to take risks, expect discomfort, and view conflict as a learning opportunity.

Triggers

Sometimes, when we are pushed beyond our learning edge/brave space we can feel unsafe, emotionally hooked, or "triggered." Brené Brown (2018) calls this response being "snagged by emotion." A trigger is something that an individual says or does, intentionally or unintentionally, that makes us feel offended, threatened, stereotyped, discounted, or attacked (Obear, 2013).[1] Triggers do not necessarily threaten our physical safety, but our psychological safety may be at risk. We can also be threatened on behalf of another person or social group if our sense of justice feels violated. When we are triggered, our limbic system fires up, our amygdala is activated, and we enter into our ancient fight, flight, or freeze response. We stop learning.

It is important for facilitators and participants to be aware of their typical emotional hooks so they can recognize them, name them, and practice effective responses that help them remain in dialogue when experiencing a hot moment. By pre-thinking how we would like to respond in those conflictual moments, and practicing responses, we can override our natural fight/flight/freeze inclinations and instead respond with mindfulness and intention.

We lead all participants through an activity (see Chapter 11, Lesson 2) to help them identify their typical trigger responses and pre-think responses that are conducive to remaining in dialogue. The key, however, is paying attention to our emotional reactions and *practicing* responses to them. Our natural instinct to these difficult emotional hooks is to "offload" them onto others by blaming someone else. Brown (2018) writes, "Instead of feeling our emotions and getting curious, we offload them onto others. We literally take that ball of emotional energy welling up inside us and hurl it toward other people." We need to mindfully pay attention to those moments and intercept the gut response to volley back at the source of the trigger, which rarely ends well.

There are several techniques that facilitators can try when they themselves are triggered during dialogue. First, when facilitators recognize that they have been triggered, they can mentally use a previously determined mantra, like "This isn't about me," or "I'm triggered because I really care," or "Other people may be feeling the same thing so it is good that this is now out in the open for us to address." Second, facilitators can adjust their physical response. They can place both feet firmly on the floor, take deep breaths, count to ten, re-center themselves, and calmly respond. Third, facilitators can suggest the group write a reflection to a specified prompt and then ask them to share. Fourth, the facilitator can release themselves from the pressure to respond and instead ask the group to do so verbally by saying, "Does anyone have thoughts on this issue?" Finally, we always find that getting really curious about an issue and asking open-ended questions is helpful.

If you trigger someone or make a mistake during facilitation, it is important that you apologize. We discuss how to apologize in Chapter 8, but briefly, a good rule of thumb is to reflect on what you did wrong, acknowledge that you made a mistake, apologize, state what you will change in the future, and thank the person for bringing the mistake to your attention.

Group Norms/Ground Rules

One of the most important things we do when establishing a brave dialogic space is to create group norms. The act of working together as a community to establish community norms in advance of a difficult moment is helpful when hot moments occur. Group norms are living documents that can be altered if necessary and referenced regularly. In general, there are a variety of ways to create group norms. One common way is to let the group develop their own set of norms from scratch. When we choose this option, facilitators can have their own list of non-negotiable group norms that they can introduce if need be. The second way is to share a list that has already been created, such as the one we use below, and allow the group to add or delete. Regardless of how you set up group norms, make sure you display them during each dialogue session. We have found that the act of talking through group norms can be as important to the participants as the actual list itself.

Some of our group norms typically include:

1. Take the learning, leave the stories.
2. Be present and engaged. Avoid technology distractions.
3. Share airtime.
4. Speak from your own experience.
5. Be aware of intent and impact.
6. Listen to learn, not to respond; listen harder when you disagree.
7. Do not freeze people in time.
8. Expect discomfort and joy; we are on our learning edge.
9. Anticipate unfinished business.

See Chapter 11, Lesson 3, for an activity on group norms and more detail on each norm.

Understanding Social Group Identities

Understanding our own various social group identities is paramount in facilitation. Social group identity refers to a group of people who belong to a broader social group that grants or denies them access to power and privilege. Often, though not always, these group identities are things you are born with or that are immutable. Social group identities affect the opportunities to which you have access, the ways you are expected to behave, the official and unofficial rules you must follow, the resources available, and the way you are treated in our society. In this way, they are different from personal identities (such as being a person who really loves pie). Common social identities include race, gender, sexual orientation, social class, and ability. In every dialogue group we facilitate, and in our facilitator training, we make sure the members of the dialogue community are familiar with their own multiple social identities and the relative power/privilege (or lack thereof) their identities confer. In the United States, the following are examples of those who hold power and privilege: White people, men, people without disabilities, and straight people.

We use an identity chart (see Chapter 11, Lesson 5) that lists some of the major social identities. We invite participants to identify which identities give them power/privilege and which do not. This particular activity is a cornerstone for much of the other work we do. Oftentimes, people are acutely aware of their marginalized or oppressed identities and less aware of the privileged identities they carry.

Similarly, Beverly Daniel Tatum (2000) asks her students to complete the sentence "I am ____" in 60 seconds, and in general, she finds that students record their marginalized identities far more often than their privileged identities. Privilege often goes without notice. This is because our privileged social identities are considered "normal" by the dominant culture. We have found that participants rarely note their privileged identities as those they think about frequently. Instead, when asked which identities they think about the most, we see identities like: "woman," "gay," "Black."

Although this book is written to help you facilitate dialogues about race, there are many social identities around which people experience privilege and oppression, and many of the techniques and skills we share would apply to dialogues about other identities as well. In fact, it is impossible to talk about race without discussing our other identities in conjunction with race. Hence, we introduce the concept of *intersectionality*, coined by critical race theorist Kimberlé Crenshaw. Crenshaw posits that we experience our lives through all of our various social identity groups—our race, class, gender, sexual orientation, religion, and ability status, among others. Our different social identities do not act independently of one another, they overlap. For those of us who have multiple marginalized social identities, this means we experience multiple levels of social injustice that cannot be reduced to just one identity (Crenshaw, 2003).For example, Black women have a different set of lived experiences due to their multiple intersecting marginalized identities (gender and race) than Black men or White women have.

Additionally, it is important to note that no one's understanding of or response to race is determined by their racial identity alone. Each of us bring our own lived experiences, our own private histories, and our own social experiences to bear, and these all work together to shape our racial awareness.

Understanding Values

Brené Brown (2018, p. 186) writes, "A *value* is a way of being or believing that we hold most important." Being in touch with our values, naming them, and sharing them are part of our facilitator training. We provide our facilitators with a list of 100 values (see Appendix D) and we ask them to identify their top five values and write a paragraph sharing why they selected that particular value. Many people have never been asked to think about what they hold most important, but we have seen over and over again that when we are clear about our values, many other things fall into place. Brown (2018, p. 186) continues,

Living into our values means that we do more than profess our values, we practice them. We walk our talk—we are clear about what we believe and hold important, and we take care that our intentions, words, thoughts, and behaviors align with those beliefs.

Margaret Wheatley (2009), a writer and management consultant who studies organizational behavior notes that she wants to publicly describe her beliefs because she wants to be held accountable. "I want my beliefs to be visible in my actions," Wheatley writes (p. 18). Facilitators who live their values and beliefs find it easier to facilitate uncomfortable situations with dignity and compassion.

Developing a Sense of Community

The better you know your participants, and the more they know one another, the richer the dialogue. Spending time getting to know one another will allow dialogue members to view each other as whole people with dignity, as opposed to single-identity or single-issue people. This is helpful when conflict emerges. To facilitate community development, we do several things:

Introductions. At the beginning of a new dialogue group, welcome everyone to the dialogue space. Greeting participants at the door is a warm beginning. Once everyone is assembled, co-facilitators model introductions starting with themselves and sharing enough information to be a little vulnerable, thus setting a tone for others. We also use tent cards or nametags with each participants' name, and we ask participants to use them every time we gather.

Ensure everyone has a voice. Go around the dialogue circle and ask everyone to share early on in each session. This gives even the quietest members a chance to hear their voice in the dialogue space. It is often hard for participants to enter a dialogue later on if they have not yet participated. There are a variety of techniques to ensure everyone finds their voice. Some common strategies include opportunity for private reflection or journal writing followed by pair/share in duos and group work in triads or foursomes. These activities offer reflection in smaller spaces that are more conducive to opening up. Then move to full group sharing thus allowing the cross-pollination of ideas between small groups.

Icebreakers/community builders. Use icebreakers throughout the dialogue sessions to help participants continue the process of developing a sense of community. We adhere to Margaret Wheatley's philosophy, "You can't hate someone whose story you know" (Wheatley, 2009). There are many icebreakers detailed in Appendix B from which facilitators may select.

Extracurricular dialogue communities. Although not formally part of the dialogue curriculum, our experience is that many groups value the sense of community formed in dialogues and create additional ways for group members to extend their time together. Participants can create Facebook pages, Instagram, or other social media meeting spaces. It is important that such virtual groups adhere to the same inclusive values and group norms of the dialogues. Our participants also report organizing pizza parties, going to the movies together, or participating as a group in social justice activities as a result of their dialogue group experiences.

Group dynamics. Familiarize participants with Bruce Tuckman's stages of group development (Figure 3.2). As Tuckman (1965) posited, most groups go through five stages of development in their work as a group. Stages may vary in duration and may not be linear, but many productive groups face challenges, tackle problems, and find solutions in a similar pattern. It is useful to share the model with dialogue participants because when groups hit various stages (especially the "storming" stage) it is helpful to remind participants that what they are experiencing is typical in most groups and that facilitators are trained to navigate the stages.

Terminology and word choice. There are many terms in social justice work that are often used and yet misunderstood. Taking time each week to collectively define social justice terms and concepts is beneficial. We have provided definitions in Appendix A for many of the terms we use throughout the book. At times, despite our best efforts to develop a shared vocabulary, there are participants (often well-intentioned) who misuse words. It is good practice to address such an issue when it arises both because other participants in the dialogue may be uncomfortable about a specific word, and also because dialogue is a learning space.

For example, we often encounter participants who use the word "colored" when referring to People of Color. A good response can be, "Many people continue to use the word 'colored.' Language and terminology change rapidly, and it can be hard to keep up with all of the changes. Today, it is more appropriate to use the term 'People of Color,' which refers to all racial groups who are non-White. 'Colored' is a term that was historically used to describe Black people in particular, and that is now commonly seen as offensive. If you are talking about a specific racial group, you could also just use that term, such as saying 'Black people' or 'Asian Americans.'" You might also add: "We suggest that you ask a person how they like to refer to themselves when appropriate." This response enables the facilitator to address the issue immediately without making the participant who used the term feel spotlighted. Most people are grateful to learn appropriate terminology, and the entire group relaxes when the facilitator is able to use a tense moment as a "teachable moment."

Figure 3.2. Tuckman's Model of Group Dynamics

Stage	Experience
Forming	Teams get to know one another. Participants are typically excited to begin working together and are often on their best behavior. Bonding occurs.
Storming	Disagreements and personality clashes emerge. Participants question each other's actions, intent or participation level. Facilitators should not attempt to avoid this stage, as surfacing differences are key to our work. How facilitators manage this stage is key to the group's future work together. Teams may get stuck at this phase if not managed carefully. Noting that tension is expected as part of normal group development can be helpful. Referring to group norms and meeting with individuals can help deter escalation of issues. See Chapters 8 and 9 for more information on managing hot moments in dialogue.
Norming	Disagreements are resolved, and intergroup intimacy develops, often as a result of weathering the "storming" phase. Team members share responsibility and respect one another.
Performing	Once the group has advanced through the previous stages, they can better focus on achieving common goals, often reaching high levels of success. The group is knowledgeable and motivated. Conflict is used as way to improve performance.
Adjourning	The group completes the task and thoughtfully moves on. It is important to end the group in an intentional way that allows all participants to carry on the work in their own spheres of influence.

Source: Adapted from Tuckman, 1965.

Privilege and oppression. Social justice educators have considered and sometimes disagreed about appropriate terminology to discuss groups with more power and groups with less power. The language around these issues is contested and continually changing because words can mean many different things.

Figure 3.3 lists alternative ways to refer to groups with more and less power. Introduce this list to participants and invite the group to discuss together language that they feel is most appropriate.

CONCLUSION

In this chapter, we have provided some of the fundamental building blocks that go into creating inclusive dialogue communities. We have discussed the basics, from how to set up a room to group size, participant selection,

Figure 3.3. Privilege and Oppression

Oppressor	Oppressed
Privileged	Marginalized
Group with more power	Group with less power
Agent	Target
Group with unearned advantages	Group with unearned disadvantages
Dominant group	Minority group or Minoritized group

and physical accessibility, to how to structure a well-planned dialogue. We have also explored the most important key concepts in dialogue process including the fundamental differences between dialogue and debate, the core value of generous listening, navigating triggers, establishing group norms, understanding identity, and the mechanics of developing a strong dialogue community to best serve group dynamics.

While these strategies might sound simple in writing, in fact, when facilitators root their practice in these vital principles, they are creating a sound framework from which to launch the dialogue journey. If the basic structure of setting up a dialogue space is missing, then when the going gets tough, it is nearly impossible to retroactively develop a strong dialogic space. In the next chapters we are going to explore in greater detail various aspects of facilitation practice.

NOTE

1. In recent years there has been concern about using the word "trigger" to identify the feeling of having your buttons pushed in a social justice setting for several reasons: (1) it borrows from psychology, and some people feel it is overused and diminishes a trigger response for people who suffer from PTSD; (2) others object because of the recent increase in gun violence and synonymous meanings of the words; (3) youth have pushed back on the word "trigger" because it is associated with memes that demean folks who have experienced triggers in social justice settings. We have decided to use the word trigger here because it is still generally accepted in the social justice education community, though we continue to look for a new word to describe this experience.

Dialogue Facilitation

A Science and an Art

Facilitators play the single most important role in creating an effective dialogue experience for participants. Good facilitators gently guide the dialogue by asking thoughtful questions and sharing relevant content material in a non-didactic way. Facilitators drive the dialogue experience by crafting meaningful interactions among participants within and across groups (Landreman, 2013; Nagda & Maxwell, 2011).

Facilitation is both a science and an art. We will discuss below what more than 30 years of research has revealed about specific steps facilitators can take to enhance the dialogue experience. We will also look at the improvisational nature of facilitation. No matter how well versed in the scholarship a facilitator might be, the very nature of dialogue means that a facilitator cannot possibly predict every participant's utterance. Facilitators need to cultivate a willingness to suspend control and go with the flow.

Facilitators make split second decisions every time they facilitate. They make decisions each time they introduce a new definition, activity, or concept, when they respond to a comment, hold space for silence and reflection, or select how to connect different comments and personal stories to larger systems of privilege or oppression. Facilitators make decisions about where, and if, they stand or sit, how they employ eye contact and how they hold their bodies. When working in pairs, co-facilitators learn the impromptu dance of co-facilitation. Like good dance partners, good facilitators can often anticipate their co-facilitator's next move. Facilitators make decisions about how and when they manage conflict between dialogue members and develop productive ways to respond to discord in the heat of the moment. For some facilitators, these actions come fluidly and intuitively, and for others, they are learned through premeditation, practice, and experience.

This chapter and the subsequent four chapters present skills that facilitators can incorporate into their own "facilitator's tool box." Some of these skills can and should be developed in advance. Facilitators should understand the subject matter content of their material (see Chapter 1 for basic content background specific to race dialogues), the mechanics of activities, and the strategies they might use to achieve their goals in advance of beginning a dialogue. Those elements should be refined in collaboration with a co-facilitator. Doing so will help each facilitator know exactly which parts of the dialogue they are leading, and how their partner needs them to respond in a variety of anticipated conditions. Planning is useful, but there is no substitute for experience. Facilitators will learn some of the skills below through practice, making mistakes, and reflecting on how to do better the next time. Working well, in a supportive partnership with a co-facilitator or coach, or reflecting alone can help a facilitator immeasurably in developing their own "tool box."

FACILITATING A DIALOGUE VS. TEACHING:
A FREIREAN MODEL OF EDUCATION

Facilitating dialogues is different from what we think of when we think about the traditional "banking model of education" where students are viewed as empty receptacles waiting to be filled with the teacher's knowledge. Facilitation is based on what Brazilian educator Paulo Freire calls the "problem posing" model of education in which participants are themselves educators of their own experiences and co-learners who share in understanding society. Freire (1970, p. 80) explains:

> In the banking concept of education, knowledge is a gift bestowed by those who consider themselves knowledgeable upon those whom they consider to know nothing. . . . Through dialogue . . . [t]he teacher is no longer merely the-one-who-teaches, but one who is himself taught in dialogue with the students, who in turn while being taught also teach. They become jointly responsible for a process in which all grow.

Freire's educational theory forms the basis for many social justice education programs. These social justice education models are not commonly used in traditional U.S. school systems where classrooms are often designed for the teacher to be the expert and "deposit knowledge" into students.

It can be difficult for people accustomed to traditional "sage on the stage" learning experiences to embrace the concept that their dialogue participants have important funds of information that contribute to the common pool of knowledge. At the same time, many facilitators report feeling liberated knowing that they do not have to pose as "experts" and relieved that they can seek support and information from every person in the dialogue space. Ultimately, in developing inclusive learning spaces conducive to dialogue, facilitators need to deconstruct their traditional concepts of "teacher" and "student" and learn to trust in the process of shared learning. The feedback from our facilitators has shown us that this is possible and that it is rewarding to do so.

THE ROLE OF THE FACILITATOR

According to University of Michigan dialogue pioneer Mark Chesler, the facilitator's role is to create an environment where participants bravely share their personal stories, challenge previously held assumptions, break down stereotypes, and develop new, more complete understandings of our shared reality. Facilitating dialogue is *not* about ensuring that everyone feels comfortable. It is about helping participants experience discomfort in a way that leads to growth (Chesler, n.d.).

The role of the facilitator is to keep the dialogue focused on the topic by practicing global listening, guaranteeing that the group norms are attended to and ensuring that all participants feel they can participate effectively. Facilitators do this by asking thoughtful questions, connecting responses, linking ideas to larger cultural and institutional issues, building trust among the group members, and ensuring that everyone feels as though their dignity is honored.

Research conducted by Patricia Gurin and a team of scholars across nine different universities (Gurin et al., 2013) reveals that the most effective facilitators engage in a set of specific actions that result in fruitful dialogues. Facilitators who *support, redirect,* and *guide* dialogues rather than teach didactically are more successful. Rephrasing a participant's comments, making a responsive comment, or redirecting the flow of the dialogue are important elements of skilled facilitation. Good facilitators also ask clarifying questions, probe for elaboration, and inquire why participants think and feel as they do. Posing the right question at the right moment in dialogue is at the core of master facilitation and so we have devoted the entire Chapter 6 to asking good questions.

Facilitating dialogue most often entails engaging participants in an activity geared toward experiential learning about an abstract concept and then reflecting on the activity collaboratively to solidify learning. Occasionally facilitators need to incorporate mini-lectures into dialogue where the facilitator spends a few minutes introducing a new term or concept. While we differentiate between lecturing and facilitating, we incorporate some mini-lectures in our facilitation as well. Similarly, we encourage educators to incorporate facilitation into their teaching tool box.

FACILITATION TRAINING AND FACILITATOR MODELS

Facilitator Training

Facilitator training and preparation looks different in different contexts. Some training programs like at Michigan State University select facilitators from among past dialogue participants and provide a 3-day training program. Some universities offer a semester-long course on facilitator training. Other institutions, like school districts, offer facilitator training opportunities as well. Many of our readers may not have training programs available to them and may choose to dive in and facilitate after reading this book and consulting other resources. What we know is that even with the most extensive facilitator training programs, there is no substitute for practice, experience, self-reflection, calling upon other facilitators, and humility. Though we have facilitated dialogues about race for years, we are constantly learning new aspects of facilitation. Dialogue facilitation is an art form that is developed only through continual practice and learning from mistakes. Take heart if you are just starting out. The best training is just diving in and doing! If you wait until you are totally prepared, you will never start.

Dialogue Facilitation Models

Below we outline four different dialogue facilitation models (instructor as facilitator, near-peer facilitators, peer facilitators, and outside consultant facilitators) that draw upon different facilitator constituencies. Regardless of the model, in race dialogues we advocate using a co-facilitation model in which there are at least two people, ideally from different racial backgrounds, facilitating the group rather than just one. (See Chapter 7 for more information on co-facilitation.) It is not always possible to have two facilitators, or two facilitators of different racial identities. We have successfully navigated both of these scenarios. When facilitating alone, or with a co-facilitator who shares the same race, use multipartiality techniques discussed below. Research shows that well-prepared individual facilitators, regardless of race, can successfully lead dialogues (Thakral et al., 2016).

Instructor as Facilitator

In this model, a classroom teacher or professor assumes the role of facilitator and sets up a dialogic space (an environment conducive to promoting the principles of dialogue) in the classroom. To most successfully navigate shifting from a didactic (teacher-centered) classroom environment to a true dialogue experience, educators should first participate in a dialogue experience or facilitation training themselves or educate themselves about facilitation through reading and practice. The challenge of this model is that if students are accustomed to the educator teaching in a traditional method, shifting to a dialogic environment where all participants and the facilitator are true co-learners can be difficult. If dialogue is just one part of a larger course, it is important for the facilitator/teacher to be explicit about when the group is shifting to dialogue, and to closely follow strategies for creating an inclusive space illustrated in the previous chapter. Another option is for educators to incorporate dialogue methods into all aspects of their practice. This may require rethinking how they have historically led their classrooms.

Near-Peer Facilitators

In a near-peer model, university students serve as facilitators in 3rd–12th grade classrooms or extracurricular spaces, or high school students serve as facilitators for younger students. These facilitators have taken or are simultaneously taking a dialogue facilitation course. Preservice teachers may be particularly interested in participating in facilitation courses because they can learn both the content and process of facilitation as well as practice their skills on "real students."

The challenge of this model centers on identifying appropriate university–school district partnerships. School officials who are interested in developing a collaborative relationship with a local college or university could contact the school of education or the center for service learning and civic engagement on campus. Both of the units might have an interest in developing a collaboration. Some universities also have dedicated units focused on intergroup dialogue which could potentially provide resources for a near-peer relationship. A partnership could also develop between a school district and a community youth organization training young people to lead dialogues.

Another challenge to this approach is finding racially diverse facilitators. At Michigan State University, preservice teachers can opt into a race dialogue lab course. Hence, they attract students who *want* to learn how to facilitate race dialogues. However, because the college of education, like most in the country, is predominantly White women, they are often forced to have two White people, often White women, co-facilitating dialogues about race. While we recognize the inherent problems in this model, we try to manage the situation by (1) training our facilitators to be multipartial (see below) in their facilitation techniques and (2) naming the fact that there is no racial diversity in the co-facilitation team with participants. This often precipitates important conversations about systemic and cultural racism.

Peer Model

Peer facilitation is another option. This could be college students facilitating other college students, faculty or teachers facilitating their colleagues, or even high school students facilitating other high schoolers. While the challenges of this model center on the fact that sometimes people do not respect their peers in the same way they might respect a facilitator they perceive to be more "authoritative," we find that the peer model has significant positives. In our experience, peers facilitating peers has allowed for genuine open dialogue precisely because peers understand exactly where participants are coming from. Shayla has trained peer facilitators selected from previous dialogue participants to facilitate peers in extracurricular settings. She has also co-facilitated dialogues for educators with teacher–leaders she has chosen from previous cohorts. In both instances peer facilitators had unique insights that other facilitators did not.

At Michigan State University, dialogues are free extracurricular opportunities open to all undergraduate and graduate students. Donna recruited paid facilitators from among past dialogue participants and used an intensive application and interview process to select facilitators. Faculty facilitate faculty dialogues; graduate students facilitate graduate students; and undergraduates facilitate undergraduate dialogues. This approach allowed her to recruit a diverse pool of peer facilitators who had prior experience with our dialogic method. Donna has found that participants are remarkably willing to open up in peer-led groups.

Other universities use the peer facilitation model where prospective facilitators sign up for credit-bearing facilitation courses, then lead their peers in specific dialogues. At the University of Michigan, for example, students can sign up for a sequence of dialogue courses: (1) a dialogue course in which they participate; (2) a facilitation course where they learn how to facilitate; and (3) a practicum where students facilitate their peers (college students) under the supervision of faculty. This model allows faculty to help students develop facilitation skills while also helping to build a selective and diverse facilitator base.

Consultant as Facilitator Model

With the recent surge in hate incidents in our schools and on college campuses (Bauman, 2018; Smith, 2017), there has been an upsurge of interest in dialogues for teachers, faculty, staff, and administrators. Without trained facilitators available within the organization or institution to meet the demand, most schools hire outside consultants to facilitate dialogues. While the challenge of this model is that the facilitator is not intimately familiar with the group they are facilitating, we have found that with sufficient preparation, outside facilitators can be quite effective. Donna, Sheri, and Shayla do facilitation on a consulting basis and the results have been positive. In fact, one of the incentives for us to write this book is that we are stretched beyond our capacity to meet the growing demand for dialogue facilitators. It is our hope that this book includes many of the tools we have learned over decades of practice to help others develop the art of facilitation.

WHAT GOOD FACILITATORS DO

There are some specific skills and practices in dialogue that years of research and practice have shown are key to ensuring that participants grow bravely in dialogue space. We examine some of the specific tools facilitators should be aware of in the following pages.

Content and Process Knowledge: Doing Your Own Work

Facilitators need to have a firm command of content knowledge. They gain this by having participated in dialogue groups that address the content material and by, as Melanie Morrison, executive director of Allies for Change has put it, constantly "doing their own work" of learning and self-reflection by seeking out opportunities to deepen their knowledge (Morrison, 2014). In order to successfully lead dialogues about race, it is imperative that facilitators have significant content knowledge about race and racism, that they understand race through an intersectional lens, that they have had ongoing and sustained conversations in their lives and work about issues of race and racism, that they keep up with current events and debates related to issues of race and racism, and that they are deeply honest about their own biases and shortcomings. Facilitators must do this so that they can provide context and content information to participants. They also must be familiar and comfortable with the process. They must understand specific activities they are going to facilitate, as well as the basics of group dynamics. As facilitators, they attend as much to the learning process within the dialogue as they do the content covered.

Self-Aware and Committed to Learning

Facilitators know themselves, their values, their various identities, and the power that accompanies those identities. They know their relative strengths and weaknesses as a facilitator and are self-reflective and committed to continuous growth. Brené Brown (2018) writes, "All of the work leads back to self-awareness and personal accountability" (p. 229). Researchers at the University of Michigan have developed a tool called the PASK that allows facilitators to honestly assess their skills in terms of four key facilitation areas:

- Passion, energy, and commitment to doing social justice work;
- Awareness about their identities, values, personal style, and triggers;
- Skills related to working with different groups, ability to take risks, work with others, give and receive feedback;
- Knowledge of content related to topic area (Beale, Thempson, & Chesler, 2001).

A blank facilitator's PASK personal assessment chart is located in Appendix G. Working through the PASK gives facilitation partners a structured opportunity to discuss their relative strengths, concerns, and areas for growth as facilitators.

Prepared but Flexible

Facilitators need to come to dialogue spaces well prepared in both content and process, and with a detailed agenda in hand. Co-facilitators should meet prior to the dialogue sessions to plan the agenda and assign roles. Some activities might take longer than expected, and others less time. While it is most often our experience that we run out of time rather than have too much, it is important to be prepared for the unexpected when you are a facilitator. It is always good to have an additional activity or two for those instances when you cover planned material in less time than anticipated. Learning to be flexible in the facilitation space is important. If an issue emerges that needs to be attended to it is okay to abandon plans and deal with the matter at hand.

Name Race

In mixed-group settings, it is often comfortable for the dominant group to use terminology that weakens the meaning of the topic (Singleton, 2015). An example of this is the use of the word "diverse" as a way of avoiding naming race. Notice the difference in meaning when we say, "Our group is diverse" versus "We notice that we have many Students of Color present." Or when we say, "Professors/teachers don't reflect our student body," we avoid the uncomfortable specifics that the following statement amplifies: "All of our teachers are White and 40% of our students are Black and Brown." Surfacing those realities is one of the goals of dialogue. Therefore, facilitators should model appropriately naming and labeling racial realities so that racial vocabulary becomes the norm for the group and its participants.

Do Not Avoid Conflict

Many dialogue participants (and facilitators) want to avoid conflict and will agree with people in order to be polite or to avoid an issue. However, the goal of dialogue is to surface disagreements, biases, stereotypes, and prejudices in order to learn deeply from one another (Knauer, 2011). Because it is so complicated to facilitate conflict—the essence of what a good dialogue is about—we have devoted three chapters to conflict and resistance (see Chapters 8–10).

Make Room at the Table

It is the facilitator's job to ensure that everyone has an opportunity to speak. Most dialogues include a mix of people who are very comfortable speaking and others who are reluctant. If you notice that someone (or a group) is quiet, there are strategies you can use to encourage them to share: "I'd like to hear from someone who has not spoken yet." Or (privately): "I've noticed you have been quiet today, Sam. Would you like to contribute to the conversation?" You can also remind people of group norms which should include some form of "share airtime." You can encourage those who are more talkative to hold back and let others speak up, by observing that, "I've noticed that some of you have contributed multiple times, but that I haven't heard from everyone. Let's remember our group norm of hearing from everyone." Or "At this time, I think it important that I hear from some of you who haven't shared your points of view." In the end, it is the facilitator's job to create an environment where all participants actually participate by speaking their truth and sharing their stories.

Ask Probing Questions and Use Silence Effectively

Asking the right questions is a core element of successful dialogue. Facilitators often worry about what to do when their participants do not respond to their questions. If we are met with silence, it may mean that our question or prompt does not work for some reason. Sometimes the prompt or question as phrased during the dialogue may simply be too vague, broad, confusing or uninspiring. If your prompt is met by silence, first reflect on what it is you are trying to ask and rephrase your prompt in terms that are clearer and easier to understand. Instead of saying, "What do you all think about the video we just watched?" you can say, "The video discussed microaggressions. What is an example of a microaggression you have experienced?"

Second, recognize that sometimes silence is a chance for people to think. We look at silence as an integral part of the dialogue space. Giving participants a chance to reflect helps them formulate their ideas. One of the common challenges for facilitators is being comfortable with silence. It can feel like an eternity to wait for someone to speak up, when in fact it might only be 30 seconds. Dialogue challenges people's previously held beliefs, and there is a lot of internal work that happens during silent periods. We encourage facilitators to allow room for participants to be silent.

Third, in the event that it appears that something beyond wording choice or reflection time might be at play, you may choose to ask meta-cognitive questions in order to "dialogue about the dialogue." Ask participants why they are reluctant to participate. You may want to do this anonymously in writing so that reluctant participants can share privately. Perhaps you need to create a new group norm to ensure brave space for participants. Perhaps something was said previously that needs attention. Probe to see why people are being quiet.

Appropriately Share Stories

Although we have cautioned facilitators against talking too much, research on intergroup dialogue facilitation has found that when facilitators purposefully and mindfully use themselves and their experiences in dialogues, they can model how to speak from a personal perspective, deepening others' willingness to be vulnerable, and normalizing dialogue about different identities (Maxwell, Nagda, & Thompson, 2011).

Contrary to popular norms in many classrooms that intentionally demand teachers be impartial, neutral, and withhold their personal stories and experiences from discussion (see more information on neutrality below), good facilitators understand that *vulnerability enriches the dialogue*. This is especially true when the dialogue is facilitated by individuals who come from different identity groups. This productive use of self is a way of interrupting traditional/hierarchical power dynamics and offers learning opportunities for all.

Equalizing Power Dynamics in Dialogue

An important part of the role of the facilitator in dialogues is to ensure that societal inequalities are not re-enacted within the dialogue space. For many participants, dialogue space may be the first time they are having open conversations with people from another racial identity group, and there are a few common trends in cross-racial dialogue that facilitators should be aware of. The following six ideas help ensure that power dynamics are balanced in race dialogues.

1. Resist exploiting the lives of oppressed groups for privileged learning. In our experiences, people from privileged and oppressed groups have different expectations of dialogue. Participants from oppressed groups often hope the dialogue space is a place to talk about social inequalities, while members of privileged groups are often looking to find common experiences in ways that downplay, avoid, or ignore differences, or to make new friends of color. Members of privileged groups may also hope or expect that the members of oppressed groups will educate them, without understanding that it can be very painful for People of Color to share their stories. For example, one White dialogue participant in a dialogue Donna was facilitating asked a Black participant to share more stories about what it is like to go shopping while Black. Though the White participant believed her colleague's stories helped deepen her understanding of his reality, it was extremely painful for the Black participant to recount stories of being followed and having his bags checked. In this case, Donna needed to step in and suggest to the White participant that she search elsewhere (books, movies, articles) for stories without further burdening her Black co-participant.

2. Share air time. Another common dialogue pattern that emerges is that privileged group members often unconsciously dominate the airtime in the group. If a facilitator notices that privileged groups (men, White people, straight people, Christians, etc.) are dominating the conversation space, it is important to name this and invite everyone to the conversation. Sometimes reminding participants of the "group norms" is sufficient to halt re-creating systemic inequalities in dialogue spaces, and sometimes facilitators need to be more direct.

In one race-based dialogue that Donna facilitated, the White participants talked more often, and occasionally over the People of Color. Referring to group norms was not sufficient for the participants to understand what was happening. Donna needed to point out what was happening quite directly to the full group by saying, "Remember our 'share air time' group norm?" "Have you noticed who is doing most of the talking in this group?" "Why do you think the White folks are talking about People of Color's experiences for them in our space?" Only after it was gently but explicitly brought to the attention of all dialogue participants did the dialogue participation shift towards a more equitable balance and power dynamic.

Facilitators might also encourage reluctant participants to engage in dialogue with phrases, prompts, and questions like: "Please say more." "Can you help me/us understand your thinking?" "It seems like this resonated with (or triggered) you. Can you share more?" "I'm curious about what you are thinking now?" "I'd like to hear from some of the participants who have not yet shared."

3. Debunk the master narrative. The master narrative is the dominant story that our society has developed to make sense of our shared history. Though the master narrative is commonly accepted as fact, it is often inaccurate. One example of a master narrative in the United States is the myth of meritocracy. This narrative posits that if you just work hard enough in the United States, you can make it. It presumes that anyone can earn wealth or power through hard work, and if you have not "made it" it is your own fault. An example of this might be: "My grandfather came to this country from Ireland with just the coat on his back, but he worked hard on his own. He didn't have any handouts, but he made it." Not everyone in the United States has the same access to resources, and People of Color face oppression at the individual, interpersonal, and institutional levels that prevent them from having an even starting line.

robbie routenberg (routenberg, Thompson, & Waterburg, 2013) writes that with the master narrative it is assumed that all people's experiences resemble those of the privileged group. The master narrative helps those in positions of privilege justify and maintain their status. Participants whose lived experiences fit within the particular narrative are advantaged. So, in this example, if your grandfather came to the United States from Europe with only the coat on his back and made it, he likely was not forced on slave ships against his will to come here and did not face segregation in the housing market, predatory lending in the banking sector, segregated and unequal schooling, and so on. The dominant group has the privilege of not seeing or believing there is a master narrative that advantages them. This is often expressed when privileged group participants express surprise, doubt, or disbelief about the experiences of marginalized groups.

4. Multipartiality and the counternarrative. One way for facilitators to help dismantle the master narrative is through being *multipartial*. As Roger Fisher, University of Michigan Associate Director of Intergroup Dialogue, explains: "Multipartiality is a 'power-balancing' approach to intergroup dialogue that supports and sustains all voices, especially the minoritized voices, or the concerns and needs of those with less power (i.e., oppressed groups)" (Fisher & Petryk, 2017, p. 5). Multipartial facilitators assume that the master narrative is present in every setting and that it is up to them as facilitators to balance power in the dialogue. This may involve bringing forth narratives from marginalized groups when others do not, either because those voices are not in the room, because participants do not know them, or because they cannot yet articulate them.

Another way for facilitators to dismantle the master narrative is to introduce the counternarrative. A counternarrative is a perspective that contradicts the presumed order in society. This is an especially important tool for White facilitators when there is no co-facilitator of color involved in the race dialogue. An example of a White facilitator using a counternarrative to contradict the master narrative is when a White facilitator acknowledges that their family benefited from the Federal Housing Loans offered to White veterans but not to Black, Latinx, Asian, or Indigenous veterans after World War II. The home loan enabled their family to purchase a home that, decades later, continued to propel their family's economic stability. In sharing this counternarrative, they challenge the master narrative that White people have money because they work harder.

Multipartial facilitation challenges the master narrative, amplifies the counternarrative and invites the privileged group's experiences to be a participatory element, not the defining story, which creates a more robust and healthy dialogue environment (Maxwell, Fisher, Thompson, & Behling, 2011).

5. Neutrality and bias. The title of Howard Zinn's 2002 book is *You Can't Be Neutral on a Moving Train*. Some people erroneously assume that facilitators should be "neutral," and while this may be appropriate for certain kinds of facilitation, it is not true for dialogue facilitation. Being "neutral" may appear appealing because it seems to be a middle ground representing some abstract absolute truth. But in fact, attempting to be neutral is both unrealistic and unhelpful for a variety of reasons. First, neutral or impartial facilitators do *not* counter the master narrative but may reinforce it by allowing it to remain central in the dialogue. Because power is unequally apportioned in our country, a neutral facilitation style results in perpetuation of the master narrative, the privileged perspective. For example, a neutral approach allows for false equivalencies, such as the idea that there were "very fine people on both sides," during the march of White nationalists and neo-Nazis in Charlottesville, Virginia in 2017. Dialogue facilitators *do* have an agenda that includes surfacing all voices in ways that get all dialogue participants to think, grow, and learn (Fisher & Petryk, 2017).

If we are honest, all of us have biases. It is more useful to be transparent about our biases than to pretend we do not have them. As Killermann and Bolger (2016, p. 29) write, "By openly and honestly naming our biases, and the cultural biases we've unknowingly internalized or brought into the space, we are most able to create a space where folks are genuinely able to share their perspectives, explore difficult subjects, and be honest themselves." Killermann offers several tips on being honest instead of neutral including: (1) Allow all participants to share their opinions even (and especially) if they are different from your own; (2) Call out your own bias when you have it; (3) Know that your voice carries weight every time you speak, so use it sparingly.

6. Surface both dominant and counternarratives. Good facilitators need to take care *not* to silence privileged group members for articulating a dominant narrative. Novice facilitators may want to bend over backwards to ensure that marginalized voices are heard. It is important to surface *both* the dominant and counternarrative. If we silence White voices in race dialogues, we actually stifle the depth of critical analysis that goes on and can cause the White folks to withdraw from the conversation (routenberg, Thompson, & Waterburg, 2013). Moreover, when facilitators are perceived to push a particular opinion, participants demonstrate resistance (Gurin, Nagda, & Zúñiga, 2013). (See more on this below.)

The key to good facilitation is conveying empathy, dignity, and respect as you challenge some presumed truths about race in U.S. society. Some basic strategies that help cultivate surfacing everyone's story in facilitation include asking someone who has shared the dominant narrative *where* they learned this perspective; inviting responses from others in the group; and challenging the group to think about an alternative perspective (routenberg, Thompson, & Waterburg 2013). Finally, if participants fail to do so, facilitators should themselves introduce counternarratives not previously mentioned.

WHAT GOOD FACILITATORS *DO NOT* DO

We end this section with three notes about what good facilitators *do not* do.

Do Not Use Dialogue Space for Personal Reasons

Because of the structure of dialogue and the powerful role of the facilitator(s) in directing the conversation, a common pitfall for facilitators is to use the dialogue space to work through their personal issues. It is one thing to mindfully share one's experience in a facilitation practice in order to model vulnerability and personal sharing, or as a way of introducing new content. It is quite another to use the group to do one's own therapy. For example, Donna attended a workshop where the facilitator spent a large chunk of time recounting her reaction to President Trump's election. She shared details about how her alcoholism was ignited after Trump's victory with the dialogue group. Though she was clearly in pain and wanted to process her reaction to the 2016 election with the group, her focus on her own issues undermined the work she was trying to facilitate.

Do Not Push Too Hard

One of the most compelling research findings about facilitator effectiveness is that when facilitators clearly advocate their own agenda, their participants do not show significant growth in understanding across difference (Gurin, Nagda, & Zúñiga, 2013). Although we know it is important for facilitators to participate as co-learners in the dialogue setting and to share their own lived experience, when facilitators attempt to *convince* participants to change their minds, their effectiveness declines. For example, a facilitator who consistently focuses on trying to prove to White folks that reverse racism doesn't exist is going to be less effective than asking probing questions and assisting the dominant group in uncovering historical and structural roots of White supremacy.

Do Not Spotlight or Ignore

Participants from groups with less power are often spotlighted in certain situations and ignored in other situations. Both of these circumstances can be harmful. It is the job of the facilitator to remain conscious of the potential of both of these situations and to work to avoid them. For example, often participants from marginalized groups are asked to speak on behalf of their group. Black feminist writer bell hooks (1994) describes this type of situation as a time when individuals are problematically objectified and cast in the role of racial spokesperson. On the other hand, some facilitators bend over backwards in an attempt to avoid spotlighting and actually end up ignoring certain individuals. Critical Race Theorist Dorinda Carter Andrews points out that each participant is unique, and facilitators must be highly attuned to each individual's needs in a particular situation. One participant might be comfortable sharing racist experiences while another might feel spotlighted in the same situation. Being aware and flexible will help facilitators monitor and correct these situations when they occur (Carter, 2008). Brené Brown suggests that we need to be "mindful" or "pay attention" to what is happening in these dialogues because every person has a unique need. Brown points out that if we are sharing something difficult with someone, there are a multitude of ways we might want the person to respond: eye contact, look away, hug, give you space, respond quickly, listen and be quiet. The only way to know what is right in each unique situation is to pay attention (Brown, 2018).

CONCLUSION

Facilitation is both a science and an art. We learn how to facilitate both by studying what good facilitators do, and by practice, feel, intuition, and critical reflection. We began this chapter by looking at the difference between facilitating and teaching. We noted the biggest difference is that when facilitating we assume everyone has an important piece of the learning puzzle as opposed to having one expert who deposits knowledge into all participants. We also shared that facilitating is not predicated on making everyone feel comfortable in the experience, but it is about helping participants feel brave with the discomfort that arises when we dive deep into complicated issues around race. We also introduced the pros and cons of different models of facilitation including teacher as facilitator, near-peer, peer, and outside consultant facilitator. The model you select will be unique to the facilitated situation you are creating given your resources, stakeholders, and opportunities.

We took a deep dive into aspects of what good facilitators do, including being knowledgeable about both content and process, being self-aware and committed to doing one's own work, and being prepared but flexible as facilitation is improvisational in nature. We also pointed out that facilitators cannot shy away from talking directly about race and using language around race even though it may be uncomfortable in many mixed-race spaces. Good facilitators also welcome conflict as a learning opportunity and ensure that everyone has a voice at the table. Effective facilitators know the power of asking probing questions and sharing their own stories appropriately. When we interview potential facilitator candidates, we always end the interview by asking if they feel comfortable sharing their own stories because it is important for facilitators to model vulnerability in order for their participants to feel comfortable doing the same. It is essential that facilitators be willing to share themselves with the group.

Good facilitators are constantly aware of their key role in ensuring equal power dynamics in dialogue and are hypervigilant about not exploiting the lives of oppressed groups for privileged learning. Strong facilitators look out for the master narrative and ensure that counternarratives are represented, especially when participants do not surface them. We cautioned against neutrality because neutral facilitators do not counter the dominant stories in our society, but simultaneously, we pointed out that it is important for facilitators to allow privileged voices to be heard. Facilitation *is* a science and an art!

We ended with a review of some specific things to avoid in facilitation: do not use dialogue space to work out your own problems, do not push your participants so hard that they dig their heels in and push back, and do not spotlight or ignore group members. In the next few chapters, we are going to unpack some of the subtleties we introduced in this chapter by looking deeply at the power of sharing stories, asking good questions, and working in co-facilitation teams.

CHAPTER 5

The Power of Sharing Stories

The courage to be vulnerable is not about winning or losing, it's about the courage to show up when you can't predict or control the outcome. (Brené Brown, 2018, p. xviii)

THE IMPORTANCE OF STORYTELLING

Anthropologists, marketing experts, scientists, and educators have known for centuries about the power of a good story to change people's opinions, determine what people purchase, and ignite passion for learning (Yong, 2017; Zak, 2014). Storytelling and listening to others' stories is at the heart of dialogue. While facilitators should be comfortable and confident in the skills and methods identified in Chapters 3 and 4, we know that ultimately good dialogue outcomes occur when facilitators create a space where participants feel brave enough to share vulnerable stories about their lives. Research shows that deep personal sharing among dialogue participants is an important factor for breaking down unconscious and conscious bias, stereotypes, entrenched prejudice and discrimination (Yeakley, 2011).

As scholars have pointed out, using storytelling and activating empathy often does more to surface and counter implicit bias and to challenge previously held beliefs than cognitive learning (Broockman & Kalla, 2016; Maxwell, Nagda, & Thompson, 2011; WNYC, 2018). Facilitators who use activities that involve feeling and doing, not just thinking, are often more productive in moving participants to deeper levels of understanding identity, power, and privilege. Moreover, research on storytelling reveals that in the long run, people are more likely to remember a personal story than data. For example, Stanford marketing professor Jennifer Aaker (2014) has found that stories are remembered up to 22 times longer than facts alone.

VULNERABILITY

Everyone in a dialogue, participants and facilitators alike, carries shared responsibility for contributing to the common learning of all. As Fisher &

Petryk (2017) notes, dialogue "is a participatory sport, a contact sport. No one gets to be a passive observer."

One of the tools that we use to help facilitators and participants develop their ability to share meaningfully centers on deepening their appreciation of the power of vulnerability. The Brené Brown quote we opened this chapter with perfectly summarizes the importance of vulnerability to this work. Vulnerability is not necessarily about disclosure. Brown talks about vulnerability being "based on mutuality and requires boundaries and trust. It is not oversharing, it's not purging, it's not indiscriminate disclosure and it's not celebrity-style social media information dumps. Vulnerability is about sharing our feelings and experiences with people who have earned the right to hear them. Being vulnerable and open is mutual and an integral part of the trust-building process" (Brown 2018, p. 45). We invite our participants and facilitators to embrace courage and to be vulnerable even when we cannot control or predict what will happen. Our facilitators watch a TED talk called "The Power of Vulnerability" by Brown (2010). Brown's seminal work on the importance of vulnerability has provided many of our facilitators with a powerful foundation for understanding vulnerability, empathy, belonging, love, and human connection. Watching Brown's TED talk collectively during facilitator training, and then debriefing the experience in a dialogic setting, creates a great shared learning experience on the power of vulnerability that facilitators carry with them and use in their dialogues.

MULTIPLE WAYS OF KNOWING

Like many people, especially those in academic settings, we are socialized to believe that good academic and professional work is focused on intellectual ways of knowing: data, hypotheses, theories, truth. We are taught that interjecting emotion into academic work is a liability. This is not true in dialogue. In dialogue we invite participants to use multiple ways of knowing, ways that include feelings and beliefs, in addition to data and content knowledge, to deepen their understanding of our shared reality.

Encouraging participants to use both their brain and their heart when they share their stories will deepen participants' understanding across difference and help create stories they can use to remember ideas, messages, and insights for a longer time.

EXPECT AND NAME EMOTION

If facilitators are doing their job, participants are learning about power and privilege, race and racism on both an intellectual and emotional level. Because this work *is* emotional, participants and facilitators will experience a variety of gut reactions, or triggers, ranging from ambivalence and fear to dissonance, discomfort, anger, shame, and guilt. There are also positive emotions that result from this work. Even though learning about oppression is difficult, there can be joy, relief, hope, passion, and commitment associated with knowledge. When facilitators help participants recognize and name their emotions, normalize them, and talk about them, participants can more deeply engage in the work. When facilitators have a good command of vocabulary for emotions, they are more fluently able to guide participants in discussions about how they are feeling.

Because so many of us are trained to check our emotional lives at the door in academic and professional settings (and sometimes at home as well), it is important for facilitators to specifically name the fact that emotions are welcome in the dialogic space. From the outset, facilitators should communicate directly that the topics covered in dialogue are emotional and that it is both okay and necessary to experience those emotions to get the most out of the experience. Share with participants that emotional reactions to the content are *normal* reactions and are a starting point for deeper cognitive learning. Recognizing when strong emotions are present is typically not difficult, but for the newly initiated facilitator, reading body language, subtle changes in tone of voice, and change in vocabulary can be clues to the presence of emotions.

When emotions do occur, there are several useful ways to respond. First, help your participants *name the emotion*. Howard Stevenson's (2014) racial literacy work is very helpful here. He asks that we name what we are feeling, where we are feeling it in our bodies, and rank it on a scale of 1–10. This might sound like: "I noticed that you got really quiet during that conversation, Sheila. What is it that you are feeling? Where are you feeling that in your body? On a scale of 1–10, how acute is it? Do you want to share more about what you were feeling?"

Second, *validate the emotion*. If you let emotions go unattended, participants may feel invalidated. Something you can say here is: "I can tell that sharing the story about the police action made you feel very vulnerable. I appreciate that you took a risk and shared your emotional vulnerability. Thank you."

Third, *explore the emotion*. Rather than spotlighting the participant who just shared something vulnerable, it can be useful to ask the group, "When did you feel something akin to what Dionte just shared?" This allows others a venue to enter the discussion as well.

Fourth, *integrate the emotion* into the larger societal/structural context of the dialogue topic. For example: "Lucia shared that she feels as though she has been passed up for promotions because she is an immigrant and speaks with an accent. Others of you have also shared similar experiences. This is rooted in structural racism in the United States that often prioritizes

White native English-speaking people for promotions. It is really important to be aware of these policies, so we can help dismantle them when we see them."

FIND LEARNING EDGES

Sharing personal stories, being vulnerable, and listening deeply across different identities is often uncomfortable and unpredictable (Gurin, Nagda, & Zúñiga, 2013). As discussed in Chapter 3, facilitators are not supposed to eliminate discomfort, but rather facilitate it in a way that yields the most productive learning for all involved. Social justice educators (indeed most educators) recognize that being uncomfortable often indicates that one is on a *learning edge*. Brené Brown (2018) writes that learning needs to be *effortful*. The key here is what Brown calls *desirable difficulty*. Brown points out that the brain is a muscle and just like other muscles, it burns when it is being strengthened. This is where growth takes place.

It is the job of the skilled facilitator to invite people to their learning edge—the place just beyond what they currently think they know—but not to push dialogue participants so far into their "trigger zone" that they resist new ideas. It is a fine balance. We are often conditioned to avoid conflict, and as facilitators, it is our work to reveal conflict and work through it. By learning how to deal with conflict, participants can deepen their awareness of the full picture of our social experience, discover common ground within our differences, and practice being allies for each other. (See Chapter 11, Lesson 2, for more information on activities about learning edges and establishing brave spaces in dialogue.)

CONNECTING PERSONAL EXPERIENCES
WITH STRUCTURAL INEQUALITIES

Participants in dialogues come from very different lived experiences and bring unique perspectives as well as various implicit and conscious biases to the conversation. Because good facilitation invites participants to share personal stories, it is vital for facilitators to locate those stories within the larger context of structural inequalities. Facilitators can help surface those conversations by asking participants to share stories and then moving from deeply listening and appreciating lived experiences to contextualizing societal inequalities and encouraging group participants to see how the experiences are informed by a larger social structure (Maxwell et al., 2011). Some probes and questions that can be used to link personal stories to structural inequality include: "Are there larger societal norms at play that might impact how different individuals experience the same event?" "How is this example of interpersonal racism related to institutional forms of racism?"

During one of Sheri's high school dialogues, a Black student shared his experience of getting stopped by police on his way home from school for no apparent reason. Having not experienced a similar situation, many of his White classmates were surprised and troubled by his story. Some tried to look for alternative reasons why their classmate was stopped: Did he have a broken tail light, they wondered? Was the license plate expired? The master narrative that most of the White students grew up with was that the police are fair arbiters of legal situations. Sheri was able to introduce a counternarrative and link the participant's personal experience with police to local and national data on police stops of People of Color. In doing so, Sheri was able to help participants see the structural inequalities that led to their classmates' lived experience and give them new insight. Sheri was also able to point out to the White students that their first reaction to disbelieve their classmate's story was invalidating to him.

In another instance, one of Sheri's Black high school participants shared his grandparents' story of being denied the right to buy a home in the town where her high school is located. The story was painful and uncomfortable for many of the White participants who had no previous knowledge of the local history of housing discrimination. Sheri was able to incorporate the student's personal story into a historical read-around activity (see Chapter 11, Lesson 4) that includes the history of housing discrimination in U.S. history. Dialogue participants in this case were able to develop their general knowledge of how People of Color were denied housing opportunities in the United States through federal and local policies and laws that excluded them from purchasing homes due to redlining. Participants were also informed and moved by the tangible story of a classmate's familial experience with those discriminatory policies in their own town. Undoubtedly, the combination of data and personal story will stick with those participants far longer than simply relying upon intellectual ways of understanding the historical context.

In a third instance, a White-identifying student was sharing how hard it is for him to observe his Jewish religious holidays in the local town. He shared that he did not have his holidays off from school because they were not part of the school calendar, that teachers assigned tests and field trips on his most important holidays, and that he was often forced to choose between his family's holiday observances and crucial school experiences. The near-peer facilitator was able to add some data and information about religious observance as well as local school district and state-wide policies that limited non-majority religion adherents' ability to fully practice their traditions. In response, a Student of Color commented that he had never realized that he had certain privileged identities (like being a part of a religious group that has his holidays guaranteed off from school) because he never had to think about it.

In a final example, a White student shared how, after participating in dialogues about race, she was struggling with how to talk to family members who espoused racist beliefs, and though she tried to interrupt their racist ideas, her tactics to date did not result in her desired outcome of getting her relatives to re-think their biased ideas. The near-peer facilitators adeptly handled her comments by acknowledging the complexity of her situation, and also by tying it to data showing that her experience was not singular—31% of White Americans believe that the United States should protect its White European heritage (Ipsos, 2017). They were able to give her specific strategies to engage in conversations with her family that she subsequently reported using with some success.

In all of these examples, participants were willing to share their lived experiences, facilitators were able to introduce links between those personal stories and structural inequalities, and everyone was able to deepen their understanding of U.S. social structures in ways that simply introducing statistics and data would not have accomplished.

Guilt

White people often experience feelings of guilt when they first engage in race dialogues. When White people begin to see their unearned advantages through the dialogue experience, they often feel as though they are somehow responsible for racial inequality in the United States. Brené Brown (2018) writes that guilt is actually adaptive and helpful. Unlike shame, which says, "I am bad," guilt says, "I did something bad." Guilt lets us know that we have done something that is not in sync with our values. For example, one of Donna's students shared in a race testimonial that her great-grandfather was a member of the KKK. While she felt guilt over the revelation and originally resisted sharing it with her classmates, she understood that sharing her stories of growing up in an environment that encouraged her to "be a little bit racist" would provoke deep conversations about how we are socialized, and ultimately, how we can break away from our socialization. Effective facilitators know how to help White participants understand the institutionalized origins of racism in the United States. Pointing out that none of us are directly responsible for the predicament we are in can be an important way to help participants learn how to channel feelings of guilt into deeper learning, listening, and ultimately, into action directed at dismantling systems of oppression. This conversation comes up in nearly every race dialogue we have run. Normalizing the emotions, naming them, and then channeling guilt into more productive outcomes is paramount in dialogue facilitation. We introduce ways to be effective allies in different spheres of influence in the final lessons of our curriculum. (See Chapter 11, Lessons 10 and 11.)

White Women Tears

There is a growing body of literature (Accapadi, 2007; Hamad, 2018) on the experience of White guilt in the form of White women weeping when doing social justice work. This also applies to men, though they are less apt to express their emotional response to racial awakening with tears. While this work is emotional, and open displays of emotion are expected, welcomed, and normalized, care should also be paid to ensure that the facilitators do not center White peoples' emotions at the expense of the People of Color. Many Participants of Color have felt as though the pain they convey when they share their lived experiences is superseded when White people break down and command center stage at these vulnerable moments. It is useful as facilitators to remember to focus on the marginalized individual who has shared the story first and foremost. Acknowledge to White participants that it is painful to learn about social injustice but that channeling their pain into productive action is far more useful. Share that People of Color can experience the centering of White emotion as yet another example of marginalization and oppression. Sometimes we have had private conversations with White people to let them know that their emotions can be perceived as a form of oppression and that it might be useful for them to do their own processing in a separate space.

Facilitators Are Not Therapists

Though dialogues can be an intensely emotional experience for participants as they venture into deep-seated work on personal values and beliefs and mine their own lives for racialized personal experiences, it is important to remember that most facilitators are not trained as therapists and that dialogues are not group therapy. Be clear about this with participants, and make sure that you know in advance where to refer participants for support if you think they may need psychological or professional help. In our practice, we include lists of support networks in the materials we provide to our participants and facilitators.

Mandatory Reporting

In many settings where our facilitators work (public schools, universities), they are considered mandatory reporters. Because this work is emotional, participants occasionally share past traumatic experiences within the confines of a dialogue. Facilitators should share from the outset of a dialogue that they are mandatory reporters and should be familiar with mandatory reporting responsibilities associated with the organization where they are facilitating.

CONCLUSION

In this chapter, we have discussed the importance of facilitators engaging participants in multiple ways of knowing in order to break down bias, stereotypes, entrenched prejudice, and discrimination. We believe that creating the right conditions for vulnerability and storytelling is a key component of facilitation. Creating an environment where participants feel brave enough to share their vulnerable ideas is what dialogue is all about. We have demonstrated methods facilitators can use to connect personal stories with larger structural and institutional issues. When facilitators create that magical space where participants are willing to share their vulnerabilities, like "My grandparents are outright racists and everybody just ignores it"—a common trope in many of our dialogues at the college level—we, as facilitators, can begin to frame those experiences in ways that participants can understand and perhaps eventually help dismantle. We discussed the difference between guilt (which can be productive) and shame, which usually is not, and we provided some ideas about managing emotion and channeling it in productive ways. We also reminded facilitators to abide by the mandatory reporting obligations in their institutions because oftentimes heart-wrenching stories require institutional follow-up. In the next chapter, we are going to examine the role of creating good prompts and asking probing questions that help facilitators develop the framework to advance vulnerability and share stories.

CHAPTER 6

Asking Good Questions and Responding to Participant Comments

If I've learned nothing else, I've learned this: a question is a powerful thing, a mighty use of words. Questions elicit answers in their likeness. . . . It is hard to resist generous questions. We all have it in us to formulate questions that invite honesty, dignity, and revelation. There is something redemptive and life-giving about asking a better question. (Tippett, 2016, pp. 29–30)

ASKING BETTER QUESTIONS

If the goal of dialogue is to help participants dig deeply into their own experiences, share with one another, listen to each other, and work together to create equity and justice, one of the principal tools of a facilitator is asking good questions that prompt reflective responses. We define a "good question" as one that prompts the respondent to reflect on their experience(s) and previously held beliefs, and in the process learn something new. In this chapter, we explore a variety of methods to formulate the kinds of generative questions that produce transformative dialogue.

Practicing Affirmative Inquiry

Roger Fisher has written about a dialogic practice called *affirmative inquiry*. Fisher (Fisher & Petryk, 2017) identifies three basic elements of affirmative inquiry practice in dialogue facilitation. Affirmative inquiry:

- Involves mutual risk taking or vulnerability. It asks all participants to share in the learning process. One person/group cannot ask another to be transparent without doing so themselves.
- Is mutually beneficial. No one identity group can benefit disproportionately. Dialogue does not exist just to educate groups with more power or to empower groups with less power. While both goals are important, facilitators need to ensure that both groups can grow from the experience.

- Attends to both groups. One group's questions are not more important than the other's agency in deciding to respond. Because of the asymmetric way that power exists, we need to avoid creating situations where one group's desire to know comes at the expense another. This is particularly relevant in race dialogues where White participants often expect to learn about race from Participants of Color. Facilitators need to be aware of this common dialogue detour and ensure that there is equal participation on the part of both the dominant and the oppressed groups. Questions that help privileged participants dive deeply into their own racialized experiences, such as, "What does it feel like to be White?" or "When did you first realize you had a race?" or "How does racism harm you?"or "How has your life been shaped by race?" help advantaged group members understand their own race-based experiences and see themselves has having a race. (pp. 9–10)

Asking Open Questions

In 1929, the poet Ranier Maria Rilke wrote: "Be patient toward all that is unsolved in your heart and try to love the questions themselves. . . . Live the questions now. Perhaps you will then gradually, without noticing it, live along some distant day into the answer" (Rilke, 2004). Almost 100 years later, we still think this quote is pertinent. Dialogue is more than an attempt to *answer* questions (Knauer, 2011). It is an exploration of questions that challenge participants to think deeply about what they think they know, and how they know it. Brené Brown (2018) writes, "A brave leader is not someone who is armed with all the answers. A brave leader is not someone who can facilitate a flawless discussion on hard topics. A brave leader is someone who says '*I see you. I hear you. I don't have all the answers, but I'm going to keep listening and asking questions.*'" The goal of dialogue is to challenge previously held beliefs and to learn through listening. Some participants may be uncertain about what they believe, especially those who may be hearing ideas that are counter to their socialization, or who have not previously been asked to think deeply about identity.

When encountering dialogue about race for the first time, it is not uncommon for individuals to feel defensive about messages they received during their upbringing. Gordon W. Allport, a noted social psychologist and the precursor to intergroup dialogue theory, writes: "In every society on earth, the child is regarded as a member of his parents' groups. . . . The child is ordinarily expected to acquire his parents' loyalties and prejudices" (1979, p. 31).

Facilitators should be aware of how difficult it is for individuals to challenge their socialized beliefs. (For more on the cycle of socialization, see Chapter 8.) Facilitators can address this resistance by gently encouraging participants *not* to be defensive, but to turn toward one another to help deepen understanding. It is useful to specifically articulate how difficult this work is, and to acknowledge that for some folks the risk of questioning their previous beliefs can be significant. Treating people with dignity will do more to help them remain in dialogue than forcefully challenging them.

Using open-ended questions places the respondent in a position in which they can formulate their own response; they do the work of reflecting, articulating, and taking ownership of their contribution to the discourse. Questions like: "Tell me where that notion originated?" "I'm curious to hear you say more about that," and "I wonder if you have ever thought about what it might be like to walk in their shoes?" can help people parse out their own beliefs, discern their beliefs from those acquired through socialization, and develop perspective-taking ability.

Sometimes an open-ended question as simple as "Why is that?" is effective to create change. One participant in a recent dialogue reflected on her facilitator's ability to help her dive deeply into her own beliefs. She wrote on an anonymous evaluation form:

> I had an "aha" moment. It was with a facilitator and we had been talking about intervening when bias occurs, and she just asked me, 'Why is that?' And as I was explaining it to her and it was coming out of my mouth, I suddenly saw what was wrong with my logic. . . . She kind of just continued to question me and asked me to explain why I had thought that. She helped me think things through. (Kaplowitz, 2018b)

Shifting Away from Experts

As we saw in Chapter 4, facilitators do not need to be experts in everything. In fact, it would be impossible. You gain credibility as a facilitator if you acknowledge what you do not know. Facilitators should have general content knowledge, but their value in a dialogue is helping surface everyone's contributions. Moreover, facilitators who model continuous learning rather than being all-knowing experts on everything are far more valuable in the long run to participants.

Because facilitators do not know everything, they should encourage participants to ask questions of one another, and redirect questions that appeal for "expert" answers toward the entire group, asking all participants for their ideas on the issue. This ensures inclusion and challenges the "facilitator as expert" assumption. Some useful questions to elicit input from the group include: "What do others think about _____?" "How does _____ make you feel?" "How does this link to what we know about racism?" and "What are some questions you have about _____?"

Asking Meaningful Questions

Effective facilitators ask probing questions without pushing participants too far. Meaningful questions are those that help participants get to deeper understanding of themselves and their beliefs, as well as shed light on ways to grow and make positive change.

The following list of 10 ways to generate questions is designed to lead participants into deeper understanding across different identities, thereby adding information to their knowledge base. Many of these concepts and examples were developed by the Sustained Dialogue Institute (2017–2018) and modified by us to fit our purposes.

1. **Share experiences, not opinions:**
   Do: "What have your experiences been with immigrants on campus?" (If you are not an immigrant.)
   Do not: "What do you think about immigration?"

2. **Share participants' backgrounds, not just concepts:**
   Do: "You mentioned equity. What is an experience that makes you care about equity?"
   Do not: "How do you define the concept of equity?" (Unless you are discussing definitions of terms.)

3. **Evoke feelings and experiences leading to dialogue, not to debate:**
   Do: "Where have you seen the division between domestic and international students?"
   Do not: "Don't you think international students should spend more time with domestic students?"

4. **Invite personal reflection, not "answers" or philosophical postures:**
   Do: "Share a story of a time when you needed more support from your community."
   Do not: "What do we need to do to eliminate racism?"

5. **Do not use the word "Why?" when trying to understand other's behaviors, thoughts or choices:**
   Do: "What are reasons that you've heard that #blacklivesmatter are protesting on campus?"
   Do not: "Why do #blacklivesmatter protest here?"

6. **Focus on your sphere of influence:**
   Do: "What can we as a group do to learn more about multiracial students' experiences before next week?"

Do not: "How could the administration better support multiracial students?"

7. Simple and easy to remember:
Do: "Tell us a little more about that."
Do not: "You have just been talking about your experience with Greek life, and I'm wondering if anyone here has a similar experience or maybe a different experience or could you share a little more about your experience with Greek life on that day or in general?"

8. Open-ended, not yes or no:
Do: "Please share what led you to decide to join a dialogue group?"
Do not: "Did you know about dialogue before you came?"

9. Practice global listening:
Do: "I'm noticing a lot of energy in the room. I'm wondering if someone who has not spoken yet can share what they're thinking?"
Do not: Ignore an issue or pretend it is not happening.

10. Do not try to demonstrate subject matter expertise unless you DO know:
Do: "Where or from whom have you learned about the situation of Native Americans on this campus?"
Do: "So here are a couple of things to know about Native Americans before we move on." (If you know!)
Do not: Make up information.

Check Your Tone

How we say something often matters even more than *what* we say. The *tone* of how you ask a question could mean the difference between drawing in a participant or shaming the same participant. When facilitators ask questions out of genuine curiosity, rather than with some particular goal in mind, participants are often more interested in responding.

Consider this example: A participant reveals that their parent regularly uses derogatory terminology to refer to Black people who live in Detroit. A facilitator who responds by asking in a direct and leading tone, "How does that make you feel when your father says that?" is going to elicit a different response from the participant than a facilitator who uses the same words with genuine compassion and curiosity. These tonal changes may seem minor, but to the wary participant, they can be the difference between deepening commitment to dialogue and being triggered into a fight, flight, or freeze response.

Use of Silence

As many new educators know, silence can feel awkward in a classroom or group setting, and yet we also know that it is crucial to offer participants a quiet opportunity to digest new material. Allowing for silence can be a gift that allows participants the opportunity to think deeply about the question and to build up the courage or find the right words to talk. We encourage our facilitators to be up front about silence from the beginning of dialogue and let participants know that they, as facilitators, are comfortable with silence and that they will offer the participants opportunities to reflect without rushing them to answers. We have found that using quiet writing time sometimes allows us to break the awkwardness of verbal silence while engaging those participants who think better through writing.

Sequencing Questions

Just like tone may send very different messages for questions worded the same way, so, too does question order. It is important to think about the best way to order your questions to help participants move towards deeper ways of knowledge. We use a 5-stage question sequencing model: Experience, Process, Content, Connect, and Apply (Killermann & Bolger, 2016). You will note that our lesson plans in Chapter 11 generally follow this model.

- Experience = Do an activity, watch a video, read something.
- Process experience = Talk about your emotional reaction to the activity. "What was it like to do the activity? What did you feel?"
- Content = Reflect on new content. "What did you learn from the activity that is new to you?"
- Connect = Connect learning to greater content knowledge, structures of privilege and oppression, institutional racism. "How does this connect to what we learned last time about housing discrimination?"
- Apply = How do you plan to integrate the new knowledge into your life/work/relationships? "How do you think you can use this knowledge to create change in your office?"

RESPONDING TO PARTICIPANT COMMENTS

One of the challenges for new facilitators is learning how to respond effectively after participants have shared something with the group. There are a variety of moments that occur in dialogue that can easily be missed, ignored, or, worse, responded to in a way that silences people or perpetuates systems of oppression or bias. In this section, we are going to examine a few scenarios to help facilitators think through how they respond to participant comments in advance of the critical moment.

Responding to Opinions

As a novice facilitator, Donna had the experience of facilitating a dialogue about social class when one of the university participants shared that she thought people who were poor were lazy and that if they just worked hard enough, they could move out of poverty. In the heat of the moment, Donna, flustered, ignored the comment and quickly moved on to a new topic because she felt awkward and unsure how to handle the situation. She wanted to protect those students who identified as low-income from feeling shame or embarrassment about what the participant said, and she wanted to protect the speaker from being publicly humiliated for her position in front of the group. But her action of burying the comment only perpetuated the master narrative and failed to help any group member deepen their understanding of the structural nature of poverty in the United States. Diving in when the situation is messy and uncomfortable is not something most of us are programmed to do. It takes intentionality, premeditation, reflection, and practice.

Therefore, it is important for facilitators to pause when someone has shared a perspective, even if it perpetuates a master narrative. Do not move on to the next comment. In the anecdote above, it would have been better for Donna to respond, "I'm really curious about why you think poor people are lazy. Can you share more about this?" Or perhaps Donna could have introduced a counternarrative such as, "Thank you for voicing your perspective because a lot of people share your beliefs that if poor people just work harder, they could get out of poverty. What do we know about poverty and mobility in our country?" Donna might also offer her own perspective by sharing, "In my experience the poorest people I know work the hardest and often have two and three jobs." With further probing and input from others, participants gain new perspective. At the very least, responding with follow-up questions asking for more clarity will prevent the propagation of the master narrative.

Courageous Compassion

Oftentimes if the dialogue is doing what it is supposed to, and participants are sharing deeply from personal experiences, they reveal sensitive or even traumatic stories. This is a part of facilitation that requires concentration, deep listening, and compassion. We have heard participants share stories about sexual assault; horrendous acts of racism, sexism, and heterosexism; family trauma; food insecurity; police violence; and more. When people are brave and vulnerable enough to share a story that is personal, they merit a thoughtful response from a facilitator that helps the sharer feel heard, and that may encourage other participants to take risks and share. Killermann and Bolger (2016) call this type of response *courageous compassion* which they define as a response that validates overcoming fear, anticipated danger, or pain, or empathizes with another's suffering. Rooted in empathy, this type of response is as much an action as a mindset.

Because as a culture we do not have a great deal of practice listening to one another's pain, it is not always natural for facilitators to know how to react when someone reveals a raw personal story. Sitting with the pain, acknowledging it, and not rushing to the next comment or activity is key. Here are some specific things a facilitator can say in such a situation:

- Thank you so much for sharing that with the group. That took a lot of courage.
- I am so sorry that that happened to you. Nobody should go through that.
- (To the whole group) Isabel just demonstrated exactly what dialogue is about. She was brave enough to share her story with us. We will hold her story as a gift.
- Thank you for your courage in sharing that story. We know it is not easy to share personal stories like that. Have others in the room experienced something similar? Why or why not?
- Do others have thoughts about what was just shared?
- Isabel has just shared something really powerful. How do others connect with her sharing?

We have witnessed traumatic revelations in many dialogues that we have participated in over the years. Remembering in the heat of the moment to stay with it and not quickly sweep the pain or shock under the rug is something that often takes premeditation and practice. That being said, it is also true that you as the facilitator do not want to spotlight the sharer beyond their comfort zone.

Picture this moment: The facilitator has successfully created a space where participants feel brave enough in the group to share their personal stories. A participant has gone out on the proverbial limb and is vulnerable. The moment is tense, and emotion is high. Because we so rarely have experience with public vulnerability, it is understandable that facilitators might feel uncomfortable and want to hurry away from the moment. And yet, this is this precise moment of bravery and vulnerability that dialogue is about. Skilled facilitators can use these moments to move the dialogue even deeper.

For example, in one race dialogue Donna facilitated, a participant shared that she had been raped. (Race dialogues often uncover other issues.) It took a tremendous amount of courage for the participant to share her story. Donna took a moment to acknowledge her pain and reflect with the group about what had just been shared. It was clear, however, from the participant's body language that she did not want to spend more time with the story. Donna noticed that, moved the dialogue along, and checked in with the participant after the dialogue session. (As a mandatory reporter, she also had to report the incident.) Taking a moment to recognize what has happened may be all that the speaker wants or needs. This is where facilitation is an art. Facilitators need to *feel* out the most appropriate response(s) in real time and appropriately guide the discussion.

Sometimes, it may be appropriate in these moments to allow for silence and reflection. You may ask dialogue participants to take out a piece of paper and free write, or give them a prompt like, "When I heard this story, it made me _____."

If someone has shared something traumatic during a session, it is appropriate to reach out to that participant after the dialogue session and make sure they are okay. It is also useful to have a list of mental health and other support resources available to share with anyone who might need it.

Connecting Comments

Most comments and personal stories shared by participants are not as emotional as the situation described above, and yet it is still important that facilitators mindfully respond to participants' comments. We have previously discussed how important listening is to good facilitation outcomes. And yet, as facilitators we need to do a number of things nearly simultaneously: (1) we need to listen generously and globally; (2) we need to mentally organize participants' comments in order to make connections among what people are saying; (3) we need to connect comments to larger structural or institutional issues; (4) we need to summarize specific points; and (5) as noted above, we need to respond to painful or traumatic comments appropriately.

If we fail to make connections between what participants say to larger structural issues, and simply affirm each person's comment or fail to respond at all, facilitators will not effectively assist participants' understanding of the interrelated nature of identity and power relationships. Missing opportunities to connect participants' comments may make participants more hesitant to share their stories, and opportunities for transformative learning will be lost.

Some ideas for connecting comments include: "What accounts for the similarities and differences in people's lived experiences?" "Both ___ and ____ share a common experience and yet they experienced it entirely differently. How does this relate to larger systems we have discussed?" "How are these stories connected to the definitions/activity/reading we did?"

The ideas here give you a glimpse of possible responses to comments that connect them within dialogue settings. The most important takeaway to remember as a facilitator is that when people are willing to share something in dialogue space, it is important to honor that courage.

Creating Space for Critical Reflection

A lot of the transformational growth done in dialogue, both by facilitators and participants, is not visible. Intentionally inviting participants to critically reflect on what happened in dialogue is useful. You may do this by providing time and space within the dialogue setting, or by offering prompts for participants and facilitators to contemplate on their own outside of the dialogue setting. Asking participants to think or write about personal motives, reactions, skills, and experiences can help participants continue their own internal work of consciousness-raising and can help facilitators improve their practice. Facilitators who try to imagine their participants' experiences, as well as their co-facilitators' experiences, can deepen their facilitation practice by using input from others' critical reflections to reflect upon the dialogue and improve upon their skills.

One brief activity that both gives participants the opportunity to think reflectively and gives facilitators a glimpse into participants' experiences is to invite participants to respond to a simple reflective prompt at the end of a session as part of a closing activity. Facilitators can reflect on the feedback and modify their practice mid-dialogue. Participants may be asked to anonymously hand in their reflections, so facilitators can get an honest snapshot of what is working and what needs to be tweaked. Some potential prompts for such an exercise include meta-cognitive reflections about the dialogue process itself: "What is working for you in this dialogue?" "What can facilitators do to improve your experience?" Other critical reflection prompts may focus on the specifics of a particular session: "What was an 'aha' moment you had today?" "What is something someone said that might have shifted the way you see things today?"

CONCLUSION

In this chapter, we have looked at both the importance of generating good questions and the significance of responding to participant comments with sensitivity and meaning. A good question prompts the participant to critically reflect on their experiences or beliefs and as a result, to think about the experience or value in a new way. Open-ended questions do not necessarily seek answers but invite participants to unpack their thinking on an issue or an event so that it shines with new light. Facilitators are aware of how hard this work is because it often challenges participants' family beliefs or their own deeply held values. Asking good questions retains the dignity of the individual, while inviting them to gently but honestly question previous assumptions.

Responding to participant comments also takes thought and finesse. We recommended that facilitators honor the individual who has shared a comment, even if they do not agree with the point of view. Using courageous compassion—validating the participant's experience from an empathic perspective—can do more to help the participant and group grow than nearly anything else that happens in dialogue.

Both parts of dialogue facilitation (asking good questions and responding to participant comments) are extremely important in creating a learning environment where participants can fully experience the impact of dialogue. A better question, asked with appropriate tone, sequence, and opportunity for reflection, invites participants to delve into their assumptions and question their own previous thinking. Connecting participant comments to one another and to larger systems invites participants to continue to do the hard work of unmasking larger systems of racism. Many facilitators (both novice and experienced) report being exhausted after a facilitation session, and for good reason. Responding to comments, making connections between comments and connections to larger systems in place, is one of the most active and demanding parts of facilitation, and it may take you a lot of practice before you feel confident with it. However, the joy that comes from being a party to those transcendent moments when things "click" for a participant is, according to many of our facilitators, the best part of facilitation.

CHAPTER 7

Co-facilitation

Research on dialogue facilitation indicates that there is considerable value in having two facilitators for each dialogue group. We define *co-facilitators* (or "cos") as two facilitators with equal power who share responsibility for everyone's learning in the dialogue. Dialogue is an active process that demands facilitators do multiple things at once: listen globally, connect comments, link comments to institutionalized bias, lead and debrief activities, respond to emotion, empathize, and so on. Having two facilitators in dialogue helps attend to the variety of facilitation responsibilities. It is even better if the two facilitators come from two different backgrounds, one facilitator with the historically privileged identity and one facilitator with the historically marginalized identity (Gurin, Nagda, & Zúñiga, 2013; Maxwell et al., 2011; Schoem & Hurtado, 2001). For example, if the dialogue being facilitated is about race, it is helpful to have a co-facilitator who is White and one who is a Person of Color; if the dialogue is about sexuality, it is useful to have a facilitator who is straight and cisgender and another facilitator who identifies as LGBTQ+. In such cases, facilitators from the different identity groups can, among other things, model equal power relationships across difference.

A caveat: Grouping all Facilitators of Color into one category and grouping White facilitators into another category implies that Facilitators of Color are interchangeable regardless of their race, which of course is not the case. People of Color have very diverse life experiences. An Asian American facilitator has had very different experiences than a Black American facilitator, for example. Even if we were able to match participant and facilitator racial identity, this *still* would not address the variety of experiences participants bring with them to race dialogues because no two people, even of the same race, share identical racial experiences. Openly acknowledging this dilemma at the start of a dialogue session, and reminding participants that we are all co-learners, including the facilitators, helps bring the issue out into the open and validates that everyone's story is crucial.

Another common issue in creating co-facilitation teams is that we may not have control over who the facilitators are. This is especially likely to be the case if facilitators are coming from colleges of education or the teaching ranks, as most educators in our country are White women. In such a situation, it can be a good idea for facilitators to begin the dialogue session openly discussing the inherent race problem in public education: White women remain 80% of the nation's teaching force, while almost 50% of students are of color. Using multipartiality and counternarratives discussed in Chapter 4, White facilitators have been able to address the problem openly.

SELECTING CO-FACILITATORS

In addition to trying to select co-facilitators with different identities relevant to the dialogue topic(s), it is good practice to select co-facilitators with compatible but not necessarily identical facilitation styles. Everyone brings something unique to their facilitation. Modeling different leadership practices can benefit the participants. When possible, we have found that interviewing potential co-facilitators with an eye on creating balanced and compatible co-facilitator teams may ward off problems in the future. For example, place an experienced facilitator with one who is developing skills; place an extrovert with an introvert. We also try to mix other identities when possible, so we prefer mixed gender or mixed sexual orientation facilitators, along with different race facilitators for race dialogues.

In general, whether we have the luxury of selecting co-facilitator teams or they are assigned more randomly as in the case with our near-peer co-facilitators in high schools (co-facilitation teams are assigned based almost exclusively on the times they have available for dialogue), we have found that facilitators really appreciate being able to work in pairs or trios. And despite what we write above about intentionally mixing facilitators, in fact, we have found that even when we randomly assign facilitators, we have had good luck when we provide both proper facilitation training, *and* we give facilitators a chance to get to know one another in advance of dialogues.

Our anonymous facilitator evaluations forms are replete with positive feedback about the co-facilitation experience. Our co-facilitators have shared with us comments such as:

- "Having a co-facilitator of a different race was so helpful. We worked well in that we usually deferred to each other's strengths."
- "We had a great balance and flow to our planning and engagement."
- "I honestly appreciated my co-facilitator. Because when I wouldn't say something, she would say something. And we just filled each other's blanks which was really helpful for me."

Facilitation Team Size

In general, we recommend that dialogues be co-facilitated by two individuals. On occasion, however, we have used co-facilitation teams of three individuals. We find that three facilitators can work well together, especially when they are college students facilitating race dialogues with high school students. This is because average high school class sizes (about 30) are much larger than our optimal dialogue groups (9–18). We also use three facilitators occasionally in our college dialogues to give a novice facilitator the time to develop their facilitation skill set. Having three facilitators helps ensure that nothing is missed or that when one facilitator is ill or otherwise unable to attend a session, their co-facilitators do not have to facilitate a session alone or postpone the session. Resource and other constraints often dictate decisions about dialogue format. However, we believe that the value of using co-facilitation merits prioritizing the use of co-facilitators over other programmatic trade-offs whenever possible.

Benefits of Interracial Facilitating

Co-facilitation with mixed-race facilitators allows facilitators to demonstrate shared power and ensures that participants from different identity groups are represented by individuals in leadership roles. Kelly Maxwell, the former co-director of Intergroup Dialogue Program at the University of Michigan, points out that co-facilitators can sometimes support and challenge participants from their own identity groups more easily than facilitators with different identities (Maxwell et al., 2011). For example, a White participant might be able to learn about White fragility more openly from a White facilitator. Similarly, a Participant of Color might be more willing to share their story after experiencing a Facilitator of Color modeling vulnerability. In Donna's race dialogue program, a Black participant was frustrated with her initial engagement in the dialogic process which she felt was too mild given her feelings of urgency around her experiences with racism. This participant forcefully advocated for more assertive forms of dismantling systemic racism during dialogue sessions. The group's Black facilitator created space to identify with the participant's frustration and share her sense of urgency while at the same time pointing out that dialogue is one form of addressing racial inequity, not the only way to do it. In this case, the White facilitator of the group likely would not have been able to convey the same shared understanding.

Similarly, Shayla has found that when she works with a White co-facilitator, they are able to name and talk about Whiteness in a way that she cannot do as a Black woman and be as well received. This is not only beneficial for White participants, who have often commented on the power of seeing someone from their own racial group talk about themselves as "White" so openly, but also for Participants of Color. In one dialogue, a middle-aged Black man approached her White co-facilitator after the session, almost in tears, and exclaimed with admiration that he had never heard a White person talk with such passion and honesty about racial justice. Seeing her do so reignited his hope for the future of our country.

Facilitators can also use their own identities to help group members understand differing perspectives and model ways of connection across different social groups. In one dialogue co-facilitated by Donna (White) and Tama Hamilton-Wray (a Black colleague), they began by openly discussing what they wanted their college students to call them. Tama preferred the use of formal titles like "Professor" or "Dr." and Donna was more comfortable having her students use her first name. There were strong socio-historical and racial reasons for the preferences. Because there are long-standing stereotypes about Black people not being qualified for positions of authority, it was important for Tama to confront those negative racist stereotypes, and using a proper title helped address that issue. Moreover, in the Black community it is often considered impolite and even disrespectful to call authority figures or elders by their first names without any title. In Donna's White community, however, she was taught that people who demanded titles were attention seekers. Having the open, planned, but unrehearsed dialogue about the roots of why each facilitator was comfortable or not with titles in front of the participants was revealing to everyone. The co-facilitators modeled in an authentic way how two people can have a meaningful dialogue across racial differences and deepen their understanding of one another, even when their opinions differ.

BEST PRACTICES IN CO-FACILITATION

While there are good reasons for including two co-facilitators in a dialogue, it is not always easy to facilitate deeply personal topics with someone who, by design, comes from a different identity group. In fact, as many educators have experienced, collaborative teaching in general is much more complicated and time consuming than teaching alone. It is therefore important to make sure from the very start that the co-facilitation team members develop a strong, honest, and balanced working relationship.

Get to Know One Another

Co-facilitators should meet together prior to facilitating and get to know one another. Some teams have the luxury of working together multiple times which allows them to streamline their practice. Both Donna and Shayla have facilitated with a specific partner for a number of years. In these cases, the facilitation teams know what to expect of one another. This is especially helpful when hot moments arise. We know, however, that the luxury of working with the same co-facilitator over time is unusual, and that is why we advocate structured time dedicated to co-facilitation team development.

Co-facilitators should reflect on the type of issues that trigger them and how they typically respond. They should discuss in advance how they will let one another know if they need the other to step in during the course of a dialogue. For example, in one high school race dialogue, one of the participants said something extremely homophobic. One of the facilitators was a lesbian, and she froze in response to the assault on her identity. Her co-facilitator, familiar with this potential trigger was able to take over that section of dialogue, address the comment, and allow her to collect herself and return to facilitation.

Here are some useful prompts to help new co-facilitation teams get to know one another:

- What do I need from my co-facilitator when I am planning for sessions?
- What do I need from my co-facilitator if I get triggered by a participant comment or by my co?
- How will I let my co-facilitator know if I am triggered?
- How do I want my co-facilitator to let me know when they see room for improvement?
- What are my hopes/fears for this dialogue?
- What do I want to do when a participant is resistant?
- What do I anticipate as a member of my racial group?
- What is a good time for me to meet regularly?
- What do I want my co-facilitator to know about me prior to facilitating?
- What are my pet peeves when working with others?
- How will we distribute the workload evenly?

Open and Honest

Because of the deep personal nature of this work, we have found that co-facilitation teams work best when they are clear from the start about their expectations; they share openly, honestly, and regularly; and they develop specific communication plans, such as when they will plan the dialogue sessions and when they will reflect together on issues that have arisen during the facilitation process. Co-facilitation teams typically break down over lack of communication or different work styles. Some folks are detail oriented and others are more improvisational. Both styles have advantages in dialogue. What is most important is that co-facilitators communicate directly with one another about their expectations.

We have navigated co-facilitator teams through some challenging moments. For example, Shayla coached a team where one of the co-facilitators wanted to prepare what was going to happen in dialogue down to the minute while the other co-facilitator was willing to facilitate more flexibly. The co-facilitators differed in approach so drastically that communication broke down between them. Shayla met with the team individually and collectively throughout the dialogue sessions to try to bridge the difference in styles. She helped them learn how to articulate their different approaches to facilitation with one another, and each facilitator was able to modify their style enough to work effectively together. The facilitator who preferred to approach the dialogues with more flexibility was willing to meet and plan ahead. The facilitator who wanted everything planned ahead learned to let go a little bit and allow time in the agenda for flexibility. After all, even the most detailed plans are often just a template once dialogue begins and participants start sharing. The team ultimately finished the dialogue series together and though the participants were largely unaware of the backroom negotiations between the co-facilitators, everyone, including the facilitators, learned from the experience.

Assigning Roles

Co-facilitators should be explicit in going over the agenda for each dialogue session and decide who leads each part of the dialogue. Co-facilitators should share equally in all tasks and responsibilities. This can be especially important when an extroverted facilitator and an introverted facilitator are matched as it can be very easy for the facilitator who is more comfortable processing out loud and speaking in front of large groups to dominate.

Reflection

Reflecting on the dialogue process is an essential element of facilitation whether you work alone, in duos, or in triads. There is so much that happens in each session that it is important to unpack everything that might have arisen, preferably immediately following dialogue or soon thereafter. Regular reflection check-ins allow co-facilitators to address any issues that need to be attended to. When we coach multiple facilitation courses in a semester, we require facilitators to email us with a brief synopsis of what happened in the dialogue (see Facilitator Feedback Form in Appendix E) and to attend a weekly group reflection to unpack the week's session and help one another navigate complicated dialogue moments. Facilitators report that these weekly meetings are extremely important for improving their practice. When we lead dialogues as facilitators, we often plan to stay an hour longer than the session in order to debrief on site and read through any evaluations or feedback forms we have collected.

Below are some questions that can help with co-facilitator reflection meetings. Many of these debrief prompts come from the Sustained Dialogue Institute (2017–2018).

DEBRIEF PROMPTS FOR FACILITATORS

Content:
- Was the content interesting and thought provoking for the participants?
- What went well? What could have gone better?
- Are there topics we should further explore with the group as a result of the dialogue?

Method/Process:
- How could we as facilitators do better next time?
- How well did we follow the group norms?

Participation:
- Did all the attendees participate? If not, what can we do differently to address that?
- Which perspectives were not represented today?

Next steps:
- What can we talk about next time to further the dialogue?
- Moving forward, what should we do differently as a result of what happened in this session?
- What do we need from each other as facilitators next time?

Many of the above prompts can be tweaked to be used with participants as closing prompts.

CONCLUSION

There is significant value for participants and facilitators alike when dialogues are co-facilitated. Facilitators benefit from having another responsible party in the space who can help navigate the complex journey of dialogue. Participants benefit from having two different individuals, from different racial backgrounds if possible, model equitable leadership and attend to differing participant needs. Working closely with another person—even someone you know well—can be difficult in the best of circumstances. In dialogue facilitation, the challenges are great, tensions run high, and minor differences can escalate quickly.

The best defense to ward off major co-facilitation problems is open communication. As outlined above, co-facilitation teams should work together to anticipate possible triggers, and regularly check in with one another so that they can address dialogue challenges before they escalate. In our facilitator trainings we give our co-facilitation teams time to meet and get to know one another by working through a list of questions provided in this chapter. The more time co-facilitators spend getting to know one another, the more successful the dialogue experience. Many dialogue programs also include group reflection circles. This dedicated time allows all facilitators to debrief together thus providing support and opportunity to address issues before they escalate. Despite the challenges, many co-facilitators have expressed that working with a co is the best part of the facilitation experience.

CHAPTER 8

Encountering Conflict and Resistance

Dialogue is predicated on the concept of surfacing conflict and managing it in a brave way that honors the dignity of all parties. In turn, conflict is bound to occur if the facilitators are doing their job well. Managing that conflict is core to effective facilitation.

Donna, Shayla and Sheri have all had to facilitate through their fair share of unforeseen conflict that threatened the health of a dialogue group. In one example, Shayla and her colleague were midway through a 15-week race dialogue. They had built a strong rapport among participants, and group members were willing to speak bravely and vulnerably with one another. At the tail end of a session when participants were invited to share their racial testimonials, Mark (names have been changed), one of the Black participants, discussed how difficult it was to be a gay Black male growing up in Detroit. His story was painful, and participants were quite moved. One Black participant, Lila, shared that though she cared deeply for Mark whom she considered a close friend, she did not support same-sex marriage and "would never be able to attend his wedding." Many of Mark's peers expressed distress and outrage over their colleague's homophobic comment. Others indicated they understood where Lila was coming from. Her comment was so incendiary and hurtful to some group members, especially Mark, that as facilitators, Shayla and her colleague realized that they needed to immediately address the issue at hand or risk the viability of the dialogue. In the few moments they had left for that session, they assured participants that the conflict would be addressed at their next meeting, and they asked both Mark and Lila to meet with them individually. In so doing, they were able to (1) guarantee to the entire group that the conflict would be dealt with collectively; (2) check in with the two principal parties in conflict; and (3) use the intervening time to develop a strategy to move forward.

Before the next meeting of the dialogue, the facilitators checked with seasoned colleagues, spoke at length together as co-facilitators, met individually with both Mark and Lila, and listened deeply to their perspectives, treating each participant with dignity. Ultimately, they developed a plan to use the conflict for deeper learning and hopefully move the group from the heights of storming to a semblance of norming (see Tuckman's group dynamics in Chapter 3).

When they next met as a full dialogue group, they replaced their original lesson plan for that entire session and introduced the group to the cycle of socialization activity (see below and Chapter 11, Lesson 7) centered on sexual orientation. They explained that a lot of folks shared Lila's sentiment that gay people should not be allowed to marry, and so it was important to delve more deeply into why people feel that way. In so doing, they were able to unpack the intersectionality of oppression as well as the lessons people learn about sexual orientation, while directly addressing the conflict. The fact that they were flexible and willing to devote time to the conflict eased the tension considerably. Participants learned that conflict could be managed in an effective way, and they were able to use the new activity around socialization to deepen their learning about another social identity. Ultimately, the group was able to return to their robust race dialogue at the next meeting. In fact, the group "storming" led to a much stronger "norming" and "performing" phase. Conflict had, in fact, brought the group closer.

Nearly all facilitators encounter conflict in dialogues. While these conflictual moments can be some of the most difficult parts of dialogue facilitation, they can also be the most transformational. Facilitators can respond to conflict in ways that will improve the quality of learning that participants experience and set the course of the dialogue toward deeper understanding across difference. Conflict often occurs when participants are on their learning edge (Chapter 3), and are confronted with new ideas that may be in discord with their previously held beliefs. Changing deeply held beliefs doesn't come easily to most of us, so the way facilitators frame those learning edge moments is critical.

There is a difference between genuine conflict, which we view as potentially productive and resistance, which is not useful. Diane Goodman has studied privileged groups' resistance. In her book, *Promoting Diversity and Social Justice* (2011), she concludes that resistance is not typically about people's specific views, but rather about people's openness to consider other perspectives. At its core, dialogue is about facilitating participants engagement around conflicting beliefs. Resistance, on the other hand is an unwillingness to engage in the challenge of dialogue. In the rest of this chapter we are going to examine why resistance exists, and then look at how to prepare in advance for pushback. We end with a deep dive into how to apologize, because even when we are doing this work well, we will make mistakes.

WHY IS THERE RESISTANCE?

It is virtually impossible to do social justice education work without encountering resistance. People understandably want to push back when they feel their deeply-held beliefs are being challenged. Listening to other people's stories often contradict messages of various master narratives and socialization experiences, creating cognitive dissonance in some participants. In many of these narratives, members of privileged groups are conditioned to: (1) not see their privilege (*I've worked hard for everything I have*); (2) deny there are differences (*"colorblind" mentality*); and (3) blame the victim (*if People of Color only worked harder, they would make it*). Many people respond to challenges to a master narrative with defensiveness and resistance. Goodman (2011) notes that resistance is often an expression of fear, anxiety, and discomfort. When people feel resistant, they are not open to listening to alternative viewpoints or to exploring societal biases. Brené Brown also notes, in her book *Dare to Lead* (2018), that "people are opting out of vital conversations about diversity and inclusivity because they fear looking wrong, saying something wrong, or being wrong." It is the facilitator's job to recognize when and why people are feeling resistant and manage resistance in such a way that encourages participants to push through their resistance and stay in dialogue.

Cycle of Socialization

Our beliefs and ideas about race stem largely from our socialization—what Bobbie Harro describes as, powerful external forces that are pervasive, consistent, and often invisible in our lives (cited in Adams et al., 2010). We all take lessons, overt and covert, conscious and unconscious, from our families, our institutions, and the larger society that teach us the official and unofficial rules of how the world works, how we should behave, and how we should make sense of what we observe and experience. We internalize the messages gained through our socialization as "normal," "right," and "true." Unless this cycle of socialization is directly revealed to us (often in dialogue for the first time), we are likely unconscious of how we know what we know or why we think what we think.

Some of our socializations are positive, like treat people the way you want to be treated (or better, treat people the way *they* want to be treated). But many are designed to maintain the status quo that supports the maintenance of power of privileged groups. When participants begin to understand the invisible systems in place to ensure that advantaged groups maintain their supremacy, previously held core beliefs, stemming from this socialization, are often challenged.

Our socialization experiences become our implicit biases—our unconscious stereotypes, attitudes, and biases that affect our understanding, actions, and decisions. Implicit biases are activated involuntarily and without our awareness or control as a direct result of our socialization process, and we all have them. The good news is that we can change our implicit biases (see Chapter 11, Lesson 7, for information on implicit bias).

Harro identifies five stages in the cycle of socialization (see Chapter 11, Lesson 7 for an activity on the cycle of socialization):

First socialization. When we are born, we do not have stereotypes, biases, or prejudices. In the first stage of socialization (our earliest experiences), we learn lessons about our own identities through listening and observing our families, caregivers, and peers. Oftentimes these messages are not articulated in words but are learned through actions. For example, a family that only has friends of a certain race is socializing their child into thinking that "friends look like me."

Second socialization. These early messages about identity are reinforced through contact with institutions including the media, school, religious organizations, the judicial system, and even sports teams. In this second stage, we learn from authority figures like police officers, teachers, judges, and TV personalities, and we internalize those messages. For example, we might notice that when Black people are portrayed on television they are often depicted as criminals, or we may hear that the president thinks some Mexicans are "illegal" people or rapists, or we might notice that in our schoolbooks we are not learning anything about Asian Americans. We begin to assimilate these messages as truth.

Third socialization. The attitudes and beliefs conveyed in the first and second stages of socialization are reinforced all the time in a variety of ways, especially if we try to challenge them. Advantaged groups and marginalized groups can both be punished for not going along with the "norm." For example, White people who publicly support #BlackLivesMatter may be ostracized as "race traitors" by other White people.

Fourth socialization. The fourth part of the cycle attends to our feelings about how the socialization has impacted our lives. We may feel confusion, guilt, anger, shame, fear, resistance, love, or even inspiration. Participants may question why people they trust tell them something that is at odds with their own experience.

Fifth socialization. In this final stage, individuals have given thought to their socialization and may want to do something about it. For example, folks might want to deepen their understanding of the cycle, speak out against stereotypes, or challenge friends who make racist jokes. Or they may choose to do nothing and thus continue to perpetuate the cycle when they raise their own children or lead their own classrooms.

In dialogue, when people begin to see some of the messages they received from birth, it is often natural for them to want to defend their ideas. These are dearly held beliefs, and it is normal to want to protect both the beliefs themselves and the people close to us who taught these things to us. Once the cycle is unveiled, however, dialogue participants are often forced to consider what they want to do about it (fifth stage). Challenging these core beliefs can be confusing and even frightening because understanding systems of oppression is incredibly complex. Confronting what we always believed to be true (like White people believing that White people are successful because they work harder) can challenge people both intellectually and emotionally. Participants might be forced to think about what they say to the people (or even harder—how to think about the people) who taught them these messages. It is really hard work, and it is natural that people want to push back.

Understanding White Fragility

Sociologist Robyn DiAngelo has coined the term "White fragility" to describe this phenomenon of White people who resist acknowledging the advantages that their Whiteness confers. Because so many of the master narratives in the United States elevate and normalize Whiteness, White people live in a social environment that insulates them from race-based stress. (This is true of all privileged groups. In general, people from groups with more social power enjoy the privilege of being able to ignore their advantaged social positions.) As DiAngelo (2011) defines it, *White fragility* is:

> A state in which even a minimum amount of racial stress becomes intolerable triggering a range of defensive moves. These moves include the outward display of emotions such as anger, fear, and guilt, and behaviors such as argumentation, silence, and leaving the stress-inducing situation.

Below are four examples of typical manifestations of White fragility, and some responses for facilitators to consider when facing resistance in the form of White fragility (Olsson, 2011).

1. "Colorblind" master narrative: "I don't see color, we all bleed red." This master narrative negates the cultural values, norms, and dreams of People of Color and erases their lived experiences of racism. In our society, people are treated differently because of their race. Facilitators should assure participants that being conscious of race does not equate to racism and that seeing race is important.

2. Blame the victim narrative: "It's their fault if they can't get a job. I worked hard for everything I have." This master narrative erases the fact that institutional racism exists in a variety of ways that prevent People of Color from being treated with equity in the job market, as well as in education, housing, and other institutions, which impact a variety of opportunities and outcomes.

3. Racism is not my fault: "*Don't blame me, my family came to the United States after slavery ended.*" While it is true that systemic racism is not the fault of any individual White person, White people still reap the benefits of a *system* of White supremacy in the United States—even those who only migrated to the United States this year. Facilitators can respond to this narrative by pointing out that regardless of when you arrived in the United States, White people still have unearned advantages that they can and should work to dismantle. These advantages are not reserved for the descendants of slave owners, just as experiences of racism and discrimination are not reserved only for those people who had enslaved ancestors.

4. Reverse racism: "*Nowadays, White people are the ones being discriminated against.*" Racism is racial prejudice (individual and interpersonal) plus institutional power. People of Color can be prejudiced against White people, but they do not have the institutional power to inflict systemic harm on White people. You can respond to this narrative by saying: "There is not any evidence to back this up. On a national scale, there is still preference for White people in every institution in our country, including criminal justice, health care, housing, employment, and education. Some People of Color may be prejudiced, but they don't have the institutional power to oppress White people" (Olsson, 2011).

Recognize Signs of Resistance

As global listeners, facilitators need to pay attention to participants' communication styles to detect when a participant may be resistant to a presented idea. Being alert to both verbal and non-verbal cues is important. Paying attention to tone of voice, body language, withdrawal of engagement, written responses, or overt verbal participation will help facilitators recognize when a participant is struggling with the material. It is always good not to make assumptions, however, so checking in with participants is a good rule of thumb.

PREPARING FOR PUSHBACK

It is often easier to prevent pushback than to manage it after it surfaces. Therefore, in this section, we will discuss ways to prepare for resistance in dialogue. Below, we identify two major strategies that facilitators can incorporate into their practice that allow for challenging conversations while minimizing the potential for participants to engage in resistant behavior that gets in the way of learning: (1) building deep relationships and (2) using emotion effectively in dialogue.

1. Create the Stage to Build Deep Relationships

So much of dialogue and social justice work is based upon developing relationships across difference. The more facilitators can develop authentic relationships among and with their participants, the easier it is to avoid resistant behavior and to manage conflict when it occurs. Using icebreakers regularly can help participants develop a sense of belonging in a group. We have found that sharing testimonials as icebreakers are effective in helping participants see one another as fully human (see icebreakers in Appendix B).

In some of our dialogue groups, the facilitators offer participants multiple ways of getting to know each other outside of the dialogic space, like pizza parties, movies, and social justice-oriented group activities, as we discussed in Chapter 3. These relationship-building opportunities help participants cross identity divides and get to know each other in deeper ways, thereby creating authentic relationships that can ease tensions when they arise in the dialogue.

Use "I" stories. It can be helpful to judiciously locate yourself in the story. Glenn Singleton (2015) points out that locating topics in the local, personal, and immediate sphere is key to engaging people. Linking personal stories to institutional racism helps situate the stories in the larger picture. Building trust with your reticent or resistant participants through personal sharing will go a long way to keeping them involved in the dialogue. Make sure, however, *not* to make the dialogue all about you. Your goal in sharing your story is to model for others the courage it takes to get "real" with one another and invite others to do the same. Be brief. For example, Donna often shares a personal anecdote about when she was 16 in her first job as a receptionist at a hospital. Her boss told racist jokes when her Colleagues of Color were not in the room. When Donna brought the situation home, her parents encouraged her to gently let her boss know she was not comfortable with the jokes. Donna did so, and then became the butt of her boss's jokes—her boss would say, "I can't tell this joke because *Donna* is in the room." When Donna brought this home to the dinner table, her parents told her she had succeeded in letting her racist boss know that not all White people are comfortable with racism, and that was a first step. When facilitating, Donna ties her personal story to systems of oppression in employment and shares how scary it was to confront a person of authority, and yet how satisfying it was to take her first step in dismantling racism. The story takes less than 3 minutes to share, but participants have come back years later to say that the story was a roadmap for their own action.

Be clear about expectations. Participants may enter the dialogue with pre-existing concerns about what is considered "politically correct," participating in embarrassing activities, or being asked to reveal more about their identities than they are comfortable with. Being up front about the material and nature of the activities at the outset of your work together, and also at the beginning of each dialogue session, can help allay participants' concerns and anxieties about the experience. Sharing the agenda on the board or in a PowerPoint is an easy way to do this.

Avoid personal blame. Part of this work is unveiling invisible systems of power and oppression for people with privileged identities. This is eye-opening, heart-rending, and emotional work. If you couple the *systems* of oppression with the reassurance that you understand that the individuals in the room did not invent these systems, and that it is not their fault that they benefit from them or hold biased views, you can help alleviate participants' fears of being publicly humiliated. Refocus participants' feelings of personal blame or guilt on systems of oppression they did not create, and channel their feelings toward action. In our curriculum, we provide two sessions dedicated to the types of actions people can take in various spheres of influence (see Chapter 11, Lessons 12 and 13).

Meet with potential resisters in advance. If you know or believe that you have a particular participant who is pushing back against specific material, meeting with them outside of a session to provide them with an opportunity to be heard can be useful. Near-peer college facilitators do this often in high school classrooms to help develop relationships with their students prior to facilitating. This allows the facilitator to listen to potential resisters and learn about what their core values are. The greater rapport you have with participants, the more likely they will be open to listening to new ideas.

Provide opportunity for feedback on dialogue. Participants often need to be listened to. Building in opportunities for feedback *on the dialogue itself* can help dismantle feelings of resistance and build a better dialogue. This might take the form of offering participants the opportunity to provide anonymous written feedback on both content and process at regular intervals during the dialogue. It might take the form of an exercise in a closing circle where each participant shares a word or phrase that captures their impressions from the day's experience, or it might take the form of a survey. We have found that this type of continual feedback is valuable for informing and improving our practice and for making participants feel heard and valued. We have done mid-dialogue surveys that have helped correct course partway through a dialogue. For example, in one formative survey that Donna conducted, her participants indicated that she and her co were dominating the dialogue space with their preplanned agenda. In response, Donna publicly acknowledged the negative feedback and created a major structural change in how the dialogue was managed. As Donna Hicks points out in her seminal book

Leading with Dignity (2018), receiving negative feedback enables the facilitators to (1) acknowledge they valued the feedback; (2) adjust course mid-stream; and (3) honor participant needs. It also models how to receive negative feedback for everyone involved in dialogue.

2. Work with Emotions

Acknowledging the affective part of this work up front and regularly throughout the dialogue helps normalize participants' emotions around this work. Share with participants that they are likely to feel anger, guilt, shame, and sadness as they go through the dialogue, and invite them to think of ways to stay engaged *before* they experience those feelings. There are also positive emotions that come out of this work like understanding, empathy, passion, hope, and support.

When feelings arise, it is useful to name them, and get curious about them. In his book *Promoting Racial Literacy in Schools,* Howard Stevenson (2014) shares the insight that becoming "racially literate" is useful not just to doing social justice work, but to fully function in society. He defines racial literacy as the "ability to read, recast, and resolve racial stress in social encounters," and suggests that racial literacy, though primarily aimed at People of Color, is a core competency for anyone navigating a wide array of social contexts. Racially literate individuals are able to (1) be aware of their own and others' racial stress; (2) prepare for racialized situations; and (3) develop healthy responses to racial insults.

Acknowledge individual pain. It is often impossible for us to take on the deep and troubling pain of systems of bias and oppression that impact others while we carry our own sources of pain and discrimination. Providing space for participants to do their own work and uncover the ways in which they have personally been victims of bias can provide them the space to bear witness to others' pain. For example, disabled people might be hesitant to talk about racism until their own ability-based experiences are recognized. Reminding participants that there is no "oppression Olympics" and that most of us have experienced some form of bias can create space for reluctant participants to empathize with others.

White people are often more open to engaging in dialogue about race when they are given some space to acknowledge that they too might be experiencing oppression around another identity. In one of our race dialogues, a White participant lashed out about Christianity, calling belief in a higher power "ridiculous," thus insulting members of her dialogue group. It was not until the facilitators probed a little to discover that she had been ostracized from her church because of her sexual orientation that they could help her navigate her own pain while leaving space for dialogue around racism. When we leave space to explore areas of individual pain, we are mindful not to co-opt the focus of the dialogue about race, but we have found it to be a useful piece of participants' openness to learning. This can also be helpful to People of Color who have experienced sexism, homophobia, or classism within their own groups and are then expected to discuss "race" as though these other identities are not a part of their experiences.

Racism hurts everyone. There is a popular but false master narrative that suggests that if a marginalized group is treated with more equity, the privileged group loses something. We need to reframe this mindset. Multiple studies have shown that having a diverse employee pool leads to better productivity and a better bottom line which benefits everyone (Phillips, 2014; Rock & Grant, 2016). Schools that pay attention to diversity issues create a welcoming climate for all students, not just the historically marginalized (Gurin, Nagda, & Zúñiga, 2013). Everyone benefits from the elimination of bigotry.

One useful activity that gets at this asks participants to respond to the prompt, *"How does racism hurt me?"* For example, having White students think about the ways they have been negatively impacted by racism is useful in helping White participants internalize why they may want to participate in its dismantling. Responses from White participants to this prompt typically include: "I didn't know People of Color; I was afraid of people I didn't know;" "My history books denied me an opportunity to know the real story of our country;" and "I did not realize how much I benefit at the expense of others." Having people identify their self-interest and their role(s) in the status quo and in this work will help them more deeply engage. This is true for groups with more power as well as groups with less power across many kinds of difference.

Foster empathy and perspective-taking. Empathy and perspective-taking are cornerstones of dialogue. Participants, especially resistant ones, who get to know fellow participants from different social identity groups more deeply can begin the hard work of imagining what it is like to walk in someone else's shoes. Social scientist Daniel Goleman (1995) defines empathy in three ways: *knowing* (cognitively understanding) what others are feeling; *feeling* (experiencing) what others are feeling; and *responding compassionately* (acting) to another's distress.

Brown (2018, p. 140) writes that empathy is taking the perspective of someone else: "Empathy is not connecting to an experience, it's connecting to the emotions that underpin an experience." Empathy is about feeling *with* someone. Brown continues: Empathy is not about fixing someone's problems, but about "the brave choice to be with someone in their darkness—not to race to turn on the light so we feel better."

Sharing stories (see Chapter 5) helps foster emotional growth. Dialogue participants from privileged groups are often moved to act when they hear specific stories from members of marginalized groups in their dialogue settings. Some participants from oppressed groups have also been moved when listening deeply to their dialogue-mates' stories with newfound empathy for those whose lives they assumed were uniformly privileged. When responding to really hard stories, empathic listeners know they cannot fix the problem, but that simply listening to the speaker and connecting with the emotion is significant. The beauty of empathy and perspective-taking is that we can honor one another's stories even when we have not experienced them ourselves. We know we are hardwired for connection. Brain research shows that our brains are highly neuroplastic. They can change as a result of mental activity (Hicks, 2018). Empathy is a key component in helping participants grow and change with dignity as a result of dialogue. And, as Brené Brown's most recent research shows, empathy is both infinite and renewable. Brown (2018) writes, "the more you give, the more we all have" (p. 140).

Some things we can say to demonstrate empathy and perspective-taking include: "I'm curious. Tell me more." "I'm not sure how to respond to what you said, but I'm honored that you shared it with me." "It sucks that happened to you. What can we do?" "I'm sorry."

THE ART OF THE APOLOGY

Several years ago, Sheri was in a national 4-day workshop with a skilled White facilitator, Judy (name changed). Sheri was really excited about the opportunity to study under a big name in the field. Midway through the third day of the workshop, Judy publicly and aggressively called out Helen, a participant, for a minor (and debatable) misunderstanding around microaggressions. Helen, publicly shamed, was mortified. Her amygdala fired up, and she immediately stopped participating in the workshop. The other members of the group were puzzled by Judy's response, gently queried her during the break, and expected that when they reunited the following day, Judy would publicly apologize and explain her actions. In fact, on the next day of the workshop Helen did not return, and Judy failed to acknowledge any part of the incident. Sheri did learn a very important lesson from this well-known facilitator: exactly what *not* to do.

As we have already noted, one thing that we can guarantee, whether you are a novice or a seasoned facilitator, is that we *will* make mistakes. It is inevitable. We have learned some of our greatest lessons from those challenges, and we invite you to view those errors as part of learning the art of facilitation. Brown (2018) calls the willingness to lead despite knowing that we will make mistakes "the physics of vulnerability." She writes: "If we are brave enough often enough, we will fall. Daring is not saying 'I'm willing to risk failure.' Daring is saying, 'I know I will eventually fail, and I'm still *all in*'" (Brown, 2018, p. 19, emphasis in original). The most important piece of advice we can give you in those moments when your facilitation skills are stretched, and you make a mistake is to be honest with yourself and with your participants.

We know that when we make a mistake in dialogue (or anywhere else), our limbic system fires up, we go into panic mode and we want to protect our dignity (Hicks, 2018). A natural gut reaction to making a mistake is to pretend it did not happen or to discharge our shame and embarrassment by blaming someone or something else. This is the exact opposite of what needs to happen. Facilitators who demonstrate how to apologize when they make a mistake are gifting their participants with a model that can be followed well into the future. Even further, according to Hicks, leaders who *seek* negative feedback have higher job performance and lead teams who are more effective. This is because, when leaders model how to receive negative feedback, they create environments where others have space to take risks, be vulnerable and brave, exactly the predispositions that lead to the most effective dialogues. When the person who makes a mistake is not defensive and does not give excuses, it has a healing effect on everyone. It takes courage and practice *not* to get defensive and to hold oneself accountable in the heat of the moment. As Hicks notes, "We are moved by such strength" (p. 91).

Brown (2018) furthers this idea: "While some leaders consider apologizing to be a sign of weakness, we teach it as a skill and frame the willingness to apologize and make amends as brave leadership" (p. 58). In fact, Brown teaches new employees how to fail during their "on-boarding" period as a way of saying that they expect risk taking and bravery, and she offers a plan for failure. She suggests to her new employees that when confronted with negative feedback, they can develop self-talk to help them through. Brown's self-talk is: "I'm brave enough to listen. There's something valuable here. Take what works and leave the rest." We believe that our failures have been some of our most important teachers, and we invite our facilitators to view failures and mistakes as learning opportunities—gifts.

We have come up with a really simple method of remembering how to apologize if you are called out or if you make a mistake. Learn it for yourselves and teach it to your participants. We call it Re-AACT. It is an acronym that you can remember in the heat of a mistake when your gut instinct is telling you to fight, flee, or freeze.

> **Re = Reflect.** Listen to what people are saying. In the case above, other people in the workshop tried to bring Judy's attention to her mistake, but she did not want to hear it. She was unwilling to personally reflect.
>
> **A = Acknowledge.** Acknowledge responsibility for your actions.
>
> **A = Apologize.** Say you are sorry. It doesn't really matter what you

intended. If you have made a mistake or violated someone else's dignity, you simply need to address the impact of your actions.

C = **Change your behavior.** Share exactly what you will do in the future to avoid such a mistake.

T = **Thank your participants for helping you learn.**

In the case above, Judy simply should have said, "I hear what you are saying. I made a mistake. In the future, I will be more careful when leading this exercise. Thank you for bringing this to my attention. It will make me a better facilitator." What is key here is not to ignore your mistake, or to double down by trying to defend yourself. The best facilitators are constantly reflecting and deepening their own understanding of their work. Do not get too bogged down by one mistake. Reflect. Acknowledge. Apologize. Change. Move on.

CONCLUSION

In this chapter, we examined the difference between conflict and resistance, and we explored a variety of reasons why resistance exists. Conflict is productive. When conflict surfaces in a healthy dialogue, participants can lean in, question previously held beliefs, and grow. Resistance, however, is an unwillingness to engage in the challenge of dialogue and it is often motivated by fear, anxiety, and discomfort. When people are resistant, they tune out, push back, or are openly hostile. The cycle of socialization, explored in this chapter, is often a gateway resource for helping people understand the epistemological (how they know what they know) basis for their resistance. Deconstructing the master narratives around White supremacy also helps unveil White fragility and White people's resistance to acknowledging the advantages that their Whiteness confers. We provided some common tropes around White master narratives with specific ways facilitators can respond to some of them.

We also provided participants with some concrete strategies to put into place to help resistant participants embrace the dialogue process from the outset of dialogue. It is often easier to prevent pushback rather than respond once it has blown up. We encourage facilitators to build deep relationships with participants and engage in community-building activities so participants see one another as fully human. Moreover, when facilitators are clear from the outset about what to expect, avoid shaming or blaming participants, and provide opportunity for feedback on dialogue, they create an environment that helps break down resistance. We encourage facilitators to be explicit from the outset that the work might be emotional, and we provide facilitators with a toolkit for dealing with emotion which includes acknowledging individual pain, exploring how racism hurts everyone, and fostering perspective-taking among participants.

Finally, we discussed the "art of the apology." It is virtually impossible to facilitate dialogues about race without "stepping in it" at some point. Talking about race can be a minefield, and it is best to prepare participants in advance with a good way to apologize so they have the skills when the moment occurs and they have to apologize. Learning to undo centuries of racism is hard work—some of the hardest work we humans can do. When we engage in dialogues, we are on our messy learning edges, and no matter how skilled we are at facilitation or how eager we are to undo racism, we will make mistakes. Following our "Re-AACT" method provides a concrete strategy to offer a genuine apology.

In Chapter 9, we look at specific actions facilitators can take when conflict arises in dialogue, and in Chapter 10, we share our own experience with resistance on a number of fronts.

Responding to Conflict and Resistance

If you are anything like us, you likely want to run away when you are facilitating a dialogue and conflict emerges. We are often taught to be polite, to downplay difference and quickly move past conflict, sweep it under the rug, or ignore it. In dialogue facilitation, we need to reframe our past association with conflict from something that is negative to viewing conflict as an *opportunity* for participants to grow. As we discussed in Chapter 8, the goal of dialogue is actually to surface conflict so that participants can examine one another's viewpoints and learn from the different perspectives that emerge. If we fail to use conflict as a gift to help participants maneuver disagreement in a way that deepens understanding, then we undermine our own goals of using dialogic space to add to the common pool of knowledge. Moreover, when we avoid conflict, we fail to model for our participants how to lean into difference. In this chapter, we present a variety of tools you can turn to when you are facing a hot moment in your dialogue that will transform conflict into a learning opportunity. Below, we offer six ways to immediately respond within the first minutes of an emerging conflict, and then we provide five additional concrete tools you can use to unpack the disagreement with a little more time.

IMMEDIATE RESPONSE

Consider this example: You are leading a dialogue on race and a White participant, Susan, says that her father has been denied a job opportunity because the company where he works is trying to increase their racial diversity, and several People of Color have been selected for promotions instead of her father. She calls this "reverse racism." Several Black and Latinx participants in the room strongly object and say that reverse discrimination is not real. Tension is high. These are things that facilitators can do immediately when something like this emerges.

Maintain Your Composure

Oftentimes facilitators find their own fight, flight, or freeze response triggered when specific issues come up in the dialogue, especially if the issue involves a facilitator's own identity or area of passion. (See Chapter 3 for managing triggers and Chapter 7 for working with co-facilitators.) Even if the issue does not trigger you, managing a group through the storming stage of development often leads to heightened stress, and some of our carefully developed preplanned skills can fly out of the window. Remembering to breathe, collect yourself, put both feet squarely on the floor, and take a moment to draw upon your toolbox of responses will help you regain or maintain your ability to facilitate thoughtfully.

Acknowledge What Happened

It is important *not* to ignore conflict or a hot button issue when it arises, though your gut instinct may be to brush it under the rug and pretend it did not happen. Many of us react to unpleasant situations by hoping that if we ignore it, it will just go away. It usually does *not* go away, but rather, it festers under the surface and/or explodes. Frame the moment as a learning opportunity. Articulate exactly what is happening. For example, "A conflict has just emerged in our dialogue. I'd like to use this as a learning opportunity. We know that learning can be uncomfortable, but that is when we know that growth is occurring."

Sometimes it is useful to step outside the moment in the dialogue and invite participants to look at the situation as a whole or dialogue about the dialogue. Acknowledge that a conflict has arisen, and that you want to understand more about *why* the conflict arose. Ask them: "What just happened here?" You can talk about dialogue dynamics in general. Ask the question: "How did we get here?" or "What needs to happen to restore learning to our environment?" or "Do we need to add a new group norm?"

There are multiple reasons why you should manage the conflict in some way when it emerges: (1) If you avoid an issue in the dialogue, participants learn that saying problematic things will go unchecked. This allows some individuals to escalate situations and prevents others from fully participating in the learning experience because of fear that their peers will misinterpret or ridicule their words, values, or beliefs. (2) Participants want to know that you, as the facilitator, will honor dialogue group norms. This makes the dialogue space a place where people feel they can bravely participate. (3) When you demonstrate methods to effectively deal with divisive issues, participants learn those skills as well. They may remember your composure when dealing with a hot moment long after they forget the topic. The converse is also true.

PALS

In order to create a simple, easy-to-remember method for participants and facilitators alike to use when a hot moment occurs, Donna developed a technique called PALS.

PALS is a mnemonic device that stands for: Pause, Acknowledge, Listen, and Share your story. This approach allows both parties to pause the action, breathe and respectfully return to the topic with curiosity and dignity. (See Appendix H for PALS Handout.)

P = Pause/Halt/Stop/Slow the conversation. The goal here is to interrupt the flow of the conversation to let the speaker know that you are interested in learning more about something they just said. Use your own instinct and language, but the most important first step is pausing the conversation in a polite way when you hear something you think might need to be addressed further. Some things you can say are: "Wait a second. . . ." "Excuse me, can you share more?" "Um, hold on a second. . . ." "Can we pause for just a minute?" "I want to return to something that was just said. . . ." Sometimes we do not get farther than pausing the conversation. That is a first step, and if that is as far you go, that is okay.

A = Acknowledge. When you acknowledge what the person said, you send a message that you are trying to make meaning out of it, even if their comment is at odds with your own ideas. It shows respect, dignity, and interest in learning more. Ask for clarification, get curious, make sure you understand what the person said, or repeat back what you think you heard. Some things you can say here are: "What I hear you saying is . . ." "I appreciate your thinking on this. . . ." "That sounds important, can you say more?"

There is a chance that you misunderstood the person. Keep your voice calm and repeat back to them what you think you heard. "I think you said that your dad is a victim of reverse racism. Is that what you meant?" Sometimes when you repeat back what you think you heard, and the speaker hears back their own words, they change their position, and you do not need to go further. Sometimes you may have honestly misinterpreted their original meaning.

L = Listen. Though listening may sound simple, it is probably the most important thing you can do to continue to engage the person. Using generous listening skills that we discussed in Chapter 3 can go very far in preventing and addressing resistance. People want to be heard. Treat the other person with dignity. Learn about what really matters to them.

S = Speak your truth/share stories. As we saw in Chapter 5, there is something powerful in storytelling. People remember stories 22% more often than they remember data (Aaker, 2014). We know that people are moved to open up, feel empathy and adopt other perspectives when they hear stories (Broockman & Kalla, 2016; WNYC, 2018).

Our dialogue participants, facilitators, teachers, faculty, and others from across the country have used PALS in a variety of situations over the last 5 years. In fact, PALS is now being translated into Spanish so that our Cuban colleagues can use it there. Our empirical research as well as anecdotal evidence have shown the PALS technique to be extremely useful when encountering resistance and conflict. As a result, we introduce this approach early on in both facilitator training and in dialogue so that both participants and facilitators can use it. PALS provides a structured response to use when we hear someone say something that may be problematic or hurtful to a specific group of people or to oneself. The major objective of this approach is to stay connected with the offending person and to speak our truth clearly. It is designed to be useful precisely in those moments when we are triggered, and our rational response evades us.

It is not uncommon for folks to use PALS, or various parts of it, multiple times in the same dialogue. It is designed to ensure that generous listening with dignity occurs. The goal is to add content information in a way that can be heard and assimilated. When the facilitator conveys a deep sense of empathy and respect, resistant participants often remain in dialogue and continue to listen generously to others' perspectives. Introducing PALS to your participants early in the dialogue gives them a tool they can use within the dialogue and beyond.

As one recent dialogue group participant noted:

> [PALS] is very helpful. I think what it does is it just defuses the hot, immediate reaction that you have when somebody says something incendiary. PALS sort of helps you calm yourself down, count to ten, before you say something that you might regret and might not be productive (Kaplowitz, 2018b).

Another facilitator reported that he uses the PALS techniques with his students in a school where he works in restorative justice, and it has had extremely positive outcomes. Universities across the country are training their students in this method.

Validate and Depersonalize Participant Contributions

It is important to validate participant contributions, even when you strongly disagree with what they have said. Surfacing a variety of opinions is key to helping all participants deepen their understanding across difference. You do not have to agree with the participant when you give them a platform, but treating the individual with dignity is important. It is useful to connect their ideas to a greater community and de-personalize the moment. Returning to the example above, it can be useful to respond to opinions that you strongly disagree with by saying, "Lots of people believe that reverse racism is a thing. I'm glad you raised this, so we can really unpack the issue. . . ."

In the example above, we did not refer to or shame the speaker. We allowed their dignity to remain intact. It is useful to acknowledge that some-one has said something that others (in the dialogue or the greater communi-ty) also believe. You can say: "Many people share your perspective. Why do you think people feel that way? Why do others disagree?" Do not say: "Su-san said reverse racism is real. What does everyone else think?" but rather say, "When someone says they believe in reverse racism, what exactly does that mean?" or "Why do you think some people believe affirmative action is necessary?" It is important to remember that no matter how you feel about what was said, as a facilitator you should model treating participants with dignity and helping them learn from the experience.

Killermann and Bolger (2016) advocate using "both/and" rather than "but" when responding to a participant's comment with new information. When facilitators use "and," we are building upon what they have said. When we respond using the word "but," we are negating what they have said and may shut down engagement. For example, consider the impact of these two statements: "Linda is Greek, but she is very smart." Here the "but" implies that she is smart despite being Greek. In the sentence, "Linda is smart, *and* she is Greek," Linda's intelligence and her ethnicity coexist equally. "And" allows two ideas that have unique meaning to coexist in-stead of putting them at odds with one another.

Know Participant Values

George Lakoff, a Stanford psychologist, has written a book on the impor-tance of framing issues so people with different political perspectives and values can listen to one another. His research is helpful in dialogue as well. In *Don't Think of an Elephant* (2014), Lakoff points out that we should consider the values of the people we are talking to if we want them to hear us better. For example, in response to Susan who believes her father has been a victim of reverse discrimination, a facilitator can say, "I understand that you feel really bad for your dad because he has worked hard and de-serves a promotion. I believe in the value of hard work too. I know a lot of People of Color who work incredibly hard and have not been able to ad-vance in their jobs either." This approach uses Lakoff's insights to appeal to a common value around hard work as a way to share a different perspective on the topic of reverse discrimination with a participant who has strong values around work ethics.

Recently, a high school student in a dialogue of ours with views more conservative than the majority of dialogue participants reported that she felt more comfortable in the dialogue space than in her other classes. She shared that, despite the social justice focus that challenged her worldview, she valued the space because she was encouraged to share her opinion. If the facilitators had silenced her ideas, she may have rejected the majority of the learning that the facilitators were attempting to nurture. By welcoming her ideas into the space with dignity, getting really curious about her position, honoring her values while also presenting her with additional content information, and giving her space to listen to her classmates' stories, the facilitators kept her involved.

Flexibility

Sometimes a conflict requires that we as facilitators abandon our plans and address the issue at hand. We have been in situations where we had to devote part of—or an entire—session to unpacking a hot moment in the dialogue. In the example we presented in Chapter 8 when our race dialogue erupted into conflict over sexual orientation, we chose to respond to the situation by modifying our syllabus so that we could spend the next dialogue meeting devoted entirely to sexual orientation, though our dialogue subject was not that topic. If we had not been flexible enough to abandon our plans, the issue may have continued to distract our participants and hinder our ability to get our participants to deepen their learning on the principle dialogue content. When we gave our participants the gift of time to work through the conflict together in a structured manner, all were able to learn new content and multiple skills including learning how to view conflict as an opportunity for growth.

One of the hardest parts of dealing with conflict is that conflicts often arise when we are least expecting them to come up. It is often the case that you, as the facilitator, need time to think through the best way to manage the issue, and this is especially true if a participant says something that is triggering to you as the facilitator. If you do not feel prepared to respond at the moment, you can acknowledge to the participants that a hot button issue came up and that you will move on, but will plan to return to it at the next meeting. Being honest with your participants is not a sign of weakness. On the contrary, by naming the issue and explaining that you will deal with it later, you allow participants to acknowledge that something happened, and it helps them trust that you will work it through with them the next time you come together. This approach gives you time to design precisely what you think will produce the best outcomes given what you know about your particular setting.

We regularly have had situations arise that challenge us in ways that we cannot adequately resolve alone. Seeking support from another facilitator or a trusted colleague who has done this type of work has proved to be invaluable. Sometimes we are so close to the situation that we cannot see a clear way forward, but the wisdom of some distance and experience has proven to be indispensable.

CONCRETE ACTIONS

The following is a series of specific actions you can take when conflict arises. You have managed the first precarious moments after a conflict emerges by regaining your composure, if necessary, and acknowledging that a conflict has emerged. You may have used the PALS technique to validate and de-personalize the issue, and you might have bought some time with a flexible response to the issue. Now what? The next section looks at some additional tools you can use to address the situation.

Go Back to the Beginning

Refer to group norms that have been violated or that need to be attended to. Point out specific group norms that need to be respected. Remind participants about the difference between dialogue and debate, the goal of staying on a learning edge, and also remind them about trying out a trigger response that is conducive to staying in dialogue. (See Chapter 11 for more about these topics.)

Writing/Journaling

Sometimes it is good to take a moment to have participants think for themselves about what has just arisen. You can have participants respond to the prompt: "What I don't want to say out loud right now . . ." or "What I really want to say out loud right now . . ." Likewise, you can connect a writing prompt to dialogue content material. For example, ask participants to respond to the prompt: "What I know about the history of the job-related racism in the United States . . ." or "This is how we can get past this hot moment." You may choose to have your participants respond anonymously and hand in their written notes so that you can see what participants are thinking about the particular conflict, and you can devise your next session around their responses.

Small Group Discussions

It is usually easier to manage conflict in a small group than in a larger group. If a tense moment erupts during a dialogue session, it can be useful to divide participants into duos or triads and provide them with prompts to help them think through what happened, where they stand, what they know, and/or what they want to know about any given topic. Incorporating small group discussions in dialogues (even dividing small groups into smaller groups) is generally good pedagogy because invariably there are participants who prefer not to speak up in large groups but will share in twos or threes. You can have the small groups report out, or, if the situation is very tense, you may ask each small group to write down what they discussed and what questions they still have. You can address these issues by collecting the comments and reading some aloud for discussion or holding them for consideration after the dialogue session for addressing at subsequent sessions.

Have Participants Do Their Own Research

Sometimes when people push back, they feel as though information is imposed upon them, and they do not trust it. Giving participants space to do their own research sometimes helps to dismantle feelings of resistance. In the example at the start of this chapter, a facilitator might say something like this: "I understand that information about job-related racism seems new and perhaps untrustworthy to you. I encourage you to find your own information from reliable sources." It may be useful to discuss the importance of reliable sources, especially when dealing with high school participants. This type of activity can link well to other high school curriculum objectives around research. When the research and material comes directly from participants, it can be easier for them to trust and internalize the data.

Content/Data Sharing

Depending on the content of the challenging issue, it may be useful to develop a data-based response as a community. You can create a chart on the board like the one in Figure 9.1, and have participants help fill in various areas. If you can connect it to the content of your dialogue, this intervention can be particularly useful. For example, if a student uses "the N-word," or questions why they should not be using it, doing a brief historical review of why the word is problematic can help provide background for everyone. You can also use this task together with a "doing your own research" homework assignment (see Chapter 11 for more information on "the N-word").

WHEN THERE IS DISRUPTIVE BEHAVIOR

While we rarely have to deal with overtly disruptive behavior in our college and professional-level dialogues, we have encountered a variety of disruptions in high school classrooms where students are often participating in dialogues despite resistance. We discuss how to respond to three different kinds of disruptions: overt, disengaged, and humor.

Figure 9.1. What We Know: Chart Example

What we know about this topic:	What is disputed about this topic:	What more we want to know about this topic:

Overt Disruptions

Sometimes a participant will dominate the dialogue and interject their opinions or rebut other people's perspectives. There are several ways to consider intervening. You may set a time limit on responses if they are long-winded, or you may create norms of waiting a certain amount of time/number of people before sharing again. You may ask to only hear from people who have not yet shared. You may acknowledge what the disruptive participants have said, summarize their perspective, and move on. You can simply acknowledge that people have different opinions on this particular issue but inform the group that it is time to move on to the next topic. Finally, when confronting participants who are dominating, disrupting, or disproportionately impacting the group, it is often useful to meet with those individuals outside the dialogue space so that they can be heard, and you can incorporate their concerns into your lesson plans. Often, giving zealous participants your attention outside of the dialogue enables them to become better dialogue participants.

Disengaged Disruptions

Sometimes disruptive behavior can take the form of disengagement. Participants who are resistant to the material check out, put on earbuds, stare at their cell phone, or put their heads down. Your first step is to check in with your co-facilitator and collectively develop a strategy to engage the participant. Perhaps you need to revise your dialogue group norms to incorporate a "no technology" ground rule for dialogue space if it is not already an expectation. Sometimes, given individual circumstances, it is okay to allow a participant to check out. Other times a silent disruptor is disconcerting to the entire group. Checking in privately with the individual, listening to their story, building a relationship with the individual, and creating future lesson plans that engage their particular interests may be ways to engage the silent disruptor. There are times, however, when it is best not to have the participant return for the health of the rest of the group.

When Humor Is a Weapon

Sometimes individuals use humor to couch their offensive statements and contributions. Humor can be particularly disruptive, and people often feel reticent to respond because the typical comeback is something like, "Can't you take a joke?" See Shayla's book, *Those Kids Our Schools* (2015), for an excellent review of the use of humor to couch (sometimes unwittingly) racist sentiments. If someone creates a hot moment or conflict in your dialogue using humor, it is important for you to neither condone nor ignore the behavior. Some strategies for your response might be: (1) Practice PALS. (2) Get curious with the participant and ask genuine questions about why they said what they did and why they found it humorous. (3) You can simply say, "I don't find that to be funny because . . ." (4) You may return the group's attention to the group norms and point out how a norm was violated. We show a video by Franchesca Ramsey about the problem of racial humor, where she outlines options for response including: silence, sarcasm, playing dumb, and being direct. Interrupting offensive comments expressed through humor will allow other participants to see that you do not let offensive humor pass unchecked, and it will model for others a method to interrupt oppressive comments couched as jokes. (For activities around interrupting biased jokes, see Chapter 11, Lesson 12.)

CONCLUSION

It is impossible to anticipate every issue that might arise in a dialogue situation. Facilitators will learn a great deal by doing. This guide attempts to provide facilitators with basic tools to use in a variety of conflictual dialogue situations. In the first moments of an emerging conflict, facilitators need to override their gut response that may be telling them to avoid conflict. We suggest you maintain your composure by acknowledging to yourself what is occurring, grounding yourself, and remembering that you have the tools to navigate troubled waters.

We have found from our research over the years that the PALS technique is probably the most important tool in both facilitators' and participants' toolboxes when dealing with hot moments. We outlined PALS (Pause, Acknowledge, Listen, Share) in this chapter, and offer ways to teach it in Chapter 11, Lesson 6, as well as a handout in Appendix H. In our survey research, participants indicate that PALS is the most-used takeaway from the dialogue experience. It seems so simple and straightforward, and perhaps that is its power. When Uncle Eli says something racist at Thanksgiving and all your buttons are pushed, drawing the simple PALS acronym out of your back pocket to help you to de-escalate the conflict, engage Uncle Eli in a dignified conversation, and create space for growth is powerful.

We also explored a variety of other strategies you can use to de-escalate conflict. Knowing participant values and morally reframing the dialogue in ways that participants can relate to may contribute to growth. Being flexible and abandoning lesson plans when necessary has proved key in some dialogue situations. Reiterating group norms, using a journal to get ideas down, sorting participants into duos to discuss the conflict in more manageable groups, inviting participants to do their own research, and sharing data have all been useful when various dialogues we have facilitated have gotten conflictual. Finally, we shared some techniques that you can draw upon when there is overtly disruptive behavior—something we have experienced more often in high school classrooms than with older participants.

The most important takeaway we can give you is to address conflict when it arises. We have offered a lot of examples of how to respond to conflict in Chapters 8 and 9. This is where the art of dialogue facilitation takes place. You will find your own alchemy of how to respond to conflict in the heat of the moment.

CHAPTER 10

Managing Resistance Among Different Stakeholders

Our Story: A Case Study

In doing race dialogue work with a variety of constituencies over the past decade, we have encountered pushback not only from participants as discussed above, but also from other stakeholders who, for a variety of reasons, feel as though their interests are being compromised. We have made a lot of mistakes managing these stakeholders along the way and have learned some valuable lessons that we hope will be useful to others who want to initiate dialogue programs.

In the section below, we share with you the evolution of our near-peer dialogue program involving college students facilitating race dialogues in high school classrooms as a case study. We use our experience to shed light on how different stakeholders responded to our work and how we learned to improve our practice.

PROGRAM DEVELOPMENT

In Chapter 2, we shared how our current near-peer model of intergroup dialogue is integrated into all freshmen English classes and how it evolved from parent requests to incorporate the curriculum, formerly in an extra-curricular diversity and leadership program, into the school day. We discussed how we train college student facilitators and how they co-facilitate 11-week, once-per-week dialogues.

Because the race dialogue program, known as ICD (Intercultural Dialogue), is run in the high school's freshman and sophomore English classes, Sheri, the English department chair first engaged with the English teachers as well as with the high school curriculum council to share the dialogue curriculum and near-peer facilitation format to ascertain if the teachers were interested in including the program in their classrooms. Teacher buy-in was a mandatory precondition for us to move forward with the dialogue program. The teachers supported the program adoption despite the fact that ICD imposed some additional responsibilities on them. Participating teachers must:

- Make room in their annual syllabus for about 11 days of dialogue curriculum
- Be present when the near-peer, college students are facilitating the program or facilitate it themselves
- Be on the front lines when parents (occasionally) express concerns about the program
- Attend several meetings during the school year related to the program

Despite these additional responsibilities, the participating teachers have been and remain overwhelmingly supportive. Moreover, not only have teachers repeatedly endorsed the program, they have also shared with us that in hosting near-peer facilitators and participating in the facilitation of the dialogue curriculum, they have developed new skills to successfully manage race relations in their classrooms (Kaplowitz, Lee, & Seyka, 2018). For example, teachers have reported using skills like PALS to interrupt racially biased comments in their classes; using dignity and respect to welcome differing opinions into their classrooms; and building on the curriculum to cover other areas of diversity like gender. When new teachers are assigned to English 1 and 2 classes, we offer a workshop to help them learn the basics of the program. And though teachers are not required to participate, all of them have opted in.

RESISTANCE

In this section, we reveal the bumpy ride we took to get to where we are today in the hopes of helping others avoid some of the pitfalls we encountered

Parent Resistance

The strongest resistance to the high school race dialogue curriculum has come from parents. The parents who are resistant are concerned that the race dialogue curriculum is clandestinely "trying to push an agenda" that is at odds with their family values. They have articulated this repeatedly in their Freedom of Information Act [FOIA] requests, Institutional Review Board [IRB] requests, emails to administrators and state officials, private meetings with us, and in their public comments at the school board podium.

Though our high school dialogues focus primarily on race, when we talk about racial identity, because of the intersectionality of this work, other identities invariably rise to the surface including social class, gender, sexual orientation, and religion. A small, vocal group of parents repeatedly expressed their fear that we will include discussion of sexual orientation in our dialogues, and this group has presented the biggest obstacle to our work. While the group who has objected to the curriculum is a small minority of parents in the district (less than 1% of the total population of parents in the district), they have been very powerful in their resistance. In fact, over time since the inauguration of the first extracurricular diversity and leadership club, at least one high school administrator and one university administrator has bowed to accommodate parental pressure from a small minority of parents.

Response to Parent Resistance

Through trial and error, we have developed a successful approach for addressing parental concerns that seems to have satisfied even the most vocal resisters. We do the following:

1. School board adoption of curriculum. We asked the school board to review and officially adopt the race dialogue curriculum as part of the English curriculum. The school board did this after several public meetings in which some of the parents resistant to dialogues used their public comment time to voice opposition. There were also parents voicing their support of the curriculum. Our dialogue curriculum is now a board-approved part of the high school freshman and sophomore English curriculum and is treated as such by the school district. Though our school board was not particularly progressive, the data was compelling enough to convince the board skeptics to incorporate race dialogues into the curriculum. Not all school districts need to go to the board for approval, and many teachers may choose to implement dialogue as a stand-alone program in their classroom, but having support from the top—board, superintendent, principal, or other leader—is helpful.

2. Pre-Launch parent meeting. We hold a well-publicized evening meeting for parents of participating students prior to the launch of the race dialogues in the classrooms, similar to what is done prior to sex education units in some schools.

Members of the school board, high school administration, participating teachers, collaborating professors, and the undergraduate near-peer facilitators all attend the meeting which is run by the English Department chairperson. After a brief PowerPoint explaining the curriculum and sharing data from previous years, parents are invited to ask questions. Some of their common questions and teacher/administrator responses include:

- *"We teach our children to be colorblind. Doesn't your program promote differences between races?"* The teachers respond to this concern by sharing that they, too, once thought being colorblind was the best way to deal with racism, but that they have learned that it is important to talk about race because it impacts peoples' lives and because our students are talking about it. Sharing their own growth around issues of race helps dignify this question. It may also be helpful to share a clip from the Anderson Cooper investigative series, *Kids on Race* (see Chapter 11 and Appendix I).

- *"Why are we talking about race when there are other issues like ability that are more important and overlooked?"* Teachers validate this question by indicating that there *are* a lot of important issues that are not covered in this curriculum, thereby honoring the parent concern. They share that the curriculum does tangentially touch on things like ability, gender, social class, and sexual orientation, but only in a very limited way, and that those are important topics that are not covered in this curriculum. In our case, the race dialogue curriculum aligns well with the literature in 9th and 10th grade. It is also helpful to point out the discord happening across the nation when it comes to issues of race, as well as the ways in which race is prevalent in disparities in discipline and academic achievement in schools.

- *"I am a Person of Color. How are my kids going to feel in your program?"* Teachers and administrators respond to this question by honoring the concern and sharing that they, too, worry deeply about this, since so many of our near-peer facilitators identify as White and virtually the entire high school faculty is White, while the Students of Color in our collaborating high school is about 50%. We discuss how we have incorporated People of Color into the development of all aspects of the program, and how the facilitators are trained in multipartiality and honoring everyone's perspective. We also have years of data that show that our Students of Color and our White students feel positively about the race dialogues.

We have found that parents' questions lead to stimulating and valuable conversation. We have also found that by the end of the evening even previously skeptical parents often thank us for this work. While the parent meeting is human resource-intensive, it has provided the necessary background to address much of the concern that existed in years prior.

Finally, it should be noted that parents can opt their students out of the program, which several of them did early on. Students are assigned different readings during the time that the dialogues take place, and they are offered alternative venues (like the library) to do their reading. However, with the passage of time, most parents, despite some of their concerns, have opted to keep their students in the classrooms.

3. Monthly newsletter. In response to parent requests, we have developed a monthly newsletter which we write and share with parents. It reflects what students have done since the last newsletter and what we are planning over the next few weeks. The newsletter is sent to parents of current participants.

4. Family Education Nights. As a result of parent questions, conversations, as well as reflective feedback from classroom teachers, students, and school administrators, we have begun to offer educational evening events specifically for parents. These Parent Education Nights address themes like implicit bias so that parents can begin to do their own work. We think this particular aspect of our work is an area of growth, and we would like to develop additional programming to engage families in deeper work around race.

We encourage others who are considering introducing similar dialogue programs in their communities to be mindful of our hard-earned experience. Undoubtedly, every program and every school, university, or organization will have different needs. However, putting in the work to establish a strong foundation that communicates with parents and other stakeholders and is supported by educational professionals, administrators, and leadership will save significant time, resources, and headaches in the long run. Take it from us, dealing with numerous FOIA requests, repeated emails demanding information, unwarranted (in our opinion) public rebuke at the school board microphone, public outcry in the press, and threatened lawsuits is no fun at all. Worst of all, our experience has shown us that unwarranted pushback by a small handful of naysayers is all that it takes for some leaders to back down and withdraw their support for this important work.

School District and University Administration Resistance

Over time we have found that administrators, while generally supportive of our goals, have different ways of responding to parental resistance. Some of the initial administrators we worked with at both the school district and the university level were less willing to stand with the program and its faculty, teachers, and students against the handful of parents who complained. We learned valuable (and painful) lessons about how to approach and work with controversy-shy administrators that have proved fruitful for our program in the long run.

In our nascent years as we were developing the program as an after-school voluntary extracurricular opportunity (before it was integrated into the school-day curriculum), one specific White, Christian, conservative parent who carried a lot of social power in some parts of the community by virtue of her father's leadership as a local employer decided that the program was a threat to her family values. She relentlessly attacked the program and threatened to sue the school district over unfounded alleged violations of the state's sex education laws. She brought her allegations to the state-level agency charged with sex education administration and the agency's administrators denied the validity of her complaint. Nevertheless, the White, male district superintendent at the time decided that the publicity and threat of a lawsuit was uncomfortable enough to "postpone" the continuation of the extracurricular program for the following several years. After that superintendent left the district, subsequent superintendents (one was a Black woman, another was a White woman) overrode their predecessor's decision and enthusiastically endorsed the program, despite their recognition that doing so could (and did) bring out parental challenges. We have now weathered three changes of superintendent, and, with the passing of time and the development of data showing beneficial outcomes (see Chapter 2), there is strong administrative support for the program.

Unfortunately, we faced a similar situation at the university with a White male administrator who was uncomfortable with negative publicity that came from a handful of school district parents' efforts to discredit the program. In that situation, despite the fact that the local school district administration and the upper-level university administration supported the program, the university dean who housed the program chose to discontinue the dialogue course through which the high school collaboration originally existed. Fortunately, another White, female university administrator with more commitment to the topic and less fear of public response eagerly adopted the curriculum into the college of education where it has flourished.

Response to Administrative Resistance

As with our response to parent opposition outlined above, we have learned from our experiences and can offer some recommendations for working with administrators at the school district and college level.

1. Transparency. When we were invited to move our program to a new college on campus, we were entirely forthcoming and transparent about the likelihood of possible opposition from parents. Our new department chair was aware of the history and told us that she believed deeply in our mission and that she would support us facing any potential parent resistance—and she has.

We have shared every aspect of the program with the high school and district level administrators and the school board so that they have always had all the program information at their fingertips. We do not want there to be any surprises or missing information.

2. Involve all aspects of governance/curricular review. We have taken all required and many unrequired steps to have our program's curriculum reviewed by our department and university and by the school district. At the university, this included having the IRB review our evaluation protocol and instrument and discussing our program at departmental and college-level meetings. In the local school district, we spoke with the superintendent and curriculum director, and the academic committee of the school board. We presented the proposed curriculum to the high school principal, members of the English Department, the school-level curriculum review team, and the school board.

3. Collect data. From the very beginning of this work, we have had to justify its existence, and we adopted a rigorous quantitative evaluation program to assess the ICD program using quantitative methods: pre-surveys, formative surveys, and retrospective pre–post surveys. Additionally, we have collected qualitative data using one-on-one interviews. Our research (see Chapter 2) has shown the power of participating in the program and the life-transforming results for many of participants. Having the hard data to back up our work has proven effective at addressing pushback.

THE BIG LESSON LEARNED

We have learned that this work can be difficult at every level. We still get resistance from time to time, but now we have supportive administrators who understand our program, its goals and objectives. In new districts where we work, we share our experiences working with resistance, and we encourage principals interested in bringing the program to their district to make sure they have support from administration. Fortunately, we have been able to collaborate with thoughtful and committed groups of teachers who have embraced the collaborative program in their classrooms. Moreover, we have been transparent about all aspects of the curriculum (including potential and ongoing parent opposition) with our school district administrators and school board. As a result, school district administrators and school board members have been willing to take a stand for what they believe is the right thing (not the easy thing) to do. And we have found a permanent home for the collaboration in the university's college of education where informed and engaged administrators and faculty colleagues have embraced the work despite the occasional parent pushback.

We are satisfied and feel rewarded that our dialogue program is now both part of one college of education's teacher education curriculum and fully established as part of the local high school curriculum. There were certainly bumps in the road and years when we had to retrench and redevelop the program, but we now directly engage almost 400 public high school students in racial dialogues each year. We hope that with the publication of this book, our approach to fostering dialogues across differences can be repeated (without our growing pains!) in schools, communities, and institutions across the country.

CHAPTER 11

Race Dialogues Curriculum

Over the past decade, we have written race dialogue curricula for elementary, middle, and high school students, low-income youth in a federally funded housing community, undergraduate and graduate students, nonprofit leaders, teachers, school administrators, parents, college faculty, university administrators, and university staff. We have learned through these experiences that, while many people are eager to intentionally talk about race and would like to facilitate such conversations in their own settings, they often struggle with the question: "What *exactly* do we do?" This chapter answers that question.

What follows is a 14-lesson curriculum that can be used for high school, college, and graduate students, P–12 educators, university faculty, and others. The curriculum is designed to help dialogue participants

1. Increase personal awareness about privilege and oppression, especially as it relates to race
2. Improve intergroup understanding and build relationships across difference, especially racial difference
3. Strengthen their capacity to work together in order to create social change

Each lesson plan includes goals, relevant social justice concepts, experiential activities to choose from, and suggested modifications and extensions for various audiences. A number of the lessons utilize, build on, and adapt activities and videos developed by the University of Michigan's Program on Intergroup Relations, Allies for Change, Adams and Bell's *Teaching for Diversity and Social Justice* (2016), and MTV News' *Decoded* with Franchesca Ramsey series. Other lessons and activities have been originally developed by the authors.

Every lesson opens with an introductory narrative that is meant to help facilitators understand the purpose of the lesson and is written in such a way that it can be shared immediately to introduce the lesson to participants. While it is possible to use our lesson plans nearly verbatim, we encourage you to adapt the lessons to your specific audience, available time, resources, facilitators, and community needs. Similarly, although we have developed the curriculum to follow a logical progression of conceptual ideas, you may choose to rearrange the order of concepts, add or eliminate content, or assign films or reading to accompany lessons based on the needs of your particular group.

Readers should note that although this curriculum is focused on race dialogues, a number of the lessons are relevant to dialogues about other social identities as well, such as gender, class, or sexual orientation, and could be adapted for this purpose.

DIALOGUE STRUCTURE

Each of the lessons as currently designed take about 60 minutes but can be modified for various session lengths and numbers of meetings (see Figure 11.1). For example, you could decide to use the curriculum as is in 12 to 14 hour-long weekly meetings, which best accommodates high school classes. You could do eight 90-minute sessions, six 3-hour sessions, or you could hold 3 or 4 full-day sessions, taking place biweekly or monthly, which allows participants time to reflect and incorporate their learning into their practice, as we have done with educators in professional development settings. You could even assign supplemental readings during the intervening weeks.

HOW TO STRUCTURE A DIALOGUE SESSION

Regardless of the model you are using or the specific order of lessons, every dialogue session should be structured similarly. Each session should begin with an *icebreaker or community builder.* We have found that icebreakers are an essential step in the dialogic process. They help build relationships, commonality, and trust among participants. When participants know one another, they are more likely to vulnerably share their experiences, a fundamental element of dialogue.

For shorter dialogue sessions such as those that are 60–90 minutes, consider using longer community builders for a few of the sessions and doing a quick check-in, such as a go-around in which each participant shares one word about how they are feeling, for the rest of the sessions. (See Appendix B for a list of community builders to use in your dialogue sessions.)

The majority of each dialogue session should focus on introducing participants to new *social justice concepts,* often clarified through a visual aid such as a chart or video, and engaging them in one or more *activities* meant to elucidate those concepts. Introducing social justice concepts ensures that participants are building a common language to use while in the dialogue space, as well as in their broader lives as they become more engaged in social

Figure 11.1. Dialogue Curricular Models

Option A 12–14 60-Minute Sessions	Option B 8 90-Minute Sessions	Option C 6 3-Hour Sessions	Option D 3 Full-Day Sessions	Option E 4 Full-Day Sessions [*for Advanced Groups]
SESSION 1 Lesson 1: Why Are We Talking About Race? **SESSION 2** Lesson 2: How Do We Engage in Dialogues About Race? **SESSION 3** Lesson 3: Developing Group Norms **SESSION 4** Lesson 4: The History of Racism **SESSION 5** Lesson 5: Understanding Social Identities **SESSION 6** Lesson 6: Interpersonal Racism & Microaggressions PALS **SESSION 7** Lesson 7: Individual Racism: Implicit Bias & Cycle of Socialization **SESSION 8** Lesson 8: Exploring Group Privilege & Oppression	**SESSION 1** Lesson 1: Why Are We Talking About Race? Lesson 2: How Do We Engage in Dialogues About Race? Lesson 3: Developing Group Norms **SESSION 2** Lesson 5: Understanding Social Identities PALS **SESSION 3** Lesson 4: The History of Racism **SESSION 4** Lesson 6: Interpersonal Racism & Microaggressions PALS Lesson 9: Institutional Racism 4 Corners	**SESSION 1** Lesson 1: Why Are We Talking About Race? Lesson 2: How Do We Engage in Dialogues About Race? Lesson 3: Developing Group Norms **SESSION 2** Lesson 5: Understanding Social Identities PALS 4 Corners **SESSION 3** Lesson 4: The History of Racism	**SESSION 1** Lesson 1: Why Are We Talking About Race? Lesson 2: How Do We Engage in Dialogues About Race? Lesson 3: Developing Group Norms Lesson 4: The History of Racism **SESSION 2** Lesson 5: Understanding Social Identities Lesson 6: Interpersonal Racism & Microaggressions	**SESSION 1** Lesson 1: Why Are We Talking About Race? Lesson 2: How Do We Engage in Dialogues About Race? Lesson 3: Developing Group Norms Lesson 4: The History of Racism **SESSION 2** Lesson 5: Understanding Social Identities Lesson 6: Interpersonal Racism & Microaggressions PALS Lesson 7: Individual Racism: Implicit Bias & Cycle of Socialization Lesson 8: Exploring Group Privilege & Oppression

Figure 11.1. Dialogue Curricular Models, continued

Option A 12–14 60-Minute Sessions	Option B 8 90-Minute Sessions	Option C 6 3-Hour Sessions	Option D 3 Full-Day Sessions	Option E 4 Full-Day Sessions [*for Advanced Groups]
SESSION 9 Lesson 9: Institutional Racism **SESSION 10*** Lesson 10: Caucus Groups & Fishbowls [*for advanced participants/optional] **SESSION 11*** Lesson 11: Hot Topics [*for advanced participants] **SESSION 10 or 12** Lesson 12: Allyhood I—Interrupting Individual Racism **SESSION 11 or 13** Lesson 13: Allyhood II—How to be an Aspiring Ally **SESSION 12 or 14** Lesson 14: Adjourning the Dialogue	**SESSION 5** Lesson 7: Individual Racism: Implicit Bias & Cycle of Socialization Lesson 8: Exploring Group Privilege & Oppression **SESSION 6** Lesson 10: Caucus Groups & Fishbowls [*for advanced participants] **SESSION 7** Lesson 11: Hot Topics [*for advanced participants] **SESSION 8** Lesson 12: Allyhood I—Interrupting Individual Racism Lesson 13: Allyhood II—How to be an Aspiring Ally Lesson 14: Adjourning the Dialogue	**SESSION 4:** Lesson 6: Interpersonal Racism & Microaggressions Lesson 7: Individual Racism: Implicit Bias & Cycle of Socialization **SESSION 5:** Lesson 8: Exploring Group Privilege & Oppression Lesson 9: Institutional Racism **SESSION 6:** Lesson 12: Allyhood I—Interrupting Individual Racism Lesson 13: Allyhood II—How to be an Aspiring Ally Lesson 14: Adjourning the Dialogue	PALS Lesson 7: Individual Racism: Implicit Bias & Cycle of Socialization Lesson 8: Exploring Group Privilege & Oppression **SESSION 3:** Lesson 9: Institutional Racism Lesson 12: Allyhood I—Interrupting Individual Racism Lesson 13: Allyhood II—How to be an Aspiring Ally Lesson 14: Adjourning the Dialogue	**SESSION 3** Lesson 9: Institutional Racism Lesson 10: Caucus Groups & Fishbowls [*for advanced participants] Lesson 11: Hot Topics [*for advanced participants] **SESSION 4** Lesson 12: Allyhood I—Interrupting Individual Racism Lesson 13: Allyhood II—How to be an Aspiring Ally Lesson 14: Adjourning the Dialogue

Figure 11.2. Facilitation Planner

Session Number and Title:		
Goals & Social Justice Concepts:		
Session Content	**Activities & Debrief Prompts**	**Length of Time**
Community Builder		
Main Activity(ies)		
Closing		

justice work. (See Appendix A for definitions of all of the social justice concepts covered in the curriculum.) After each activity, facilitators should give participants the opportunity to debrief their new learning through individual reflection, paired or small group dialogue, and/or large group dialogue.

Every dialogue session should end with a *closing* exercise. Dialogue, by design, impacts peoples' affective ways of knowing. An intentional closing allows participants to reflect on their experience and prepare to move beyond the dialogue. Closings might take the form of a journal entry, a written prompt handed in anonymously, or a verbal go-around in which each person shares something they are taking away from the session, either in small groups or in the large one. Like community builders, for shorter dialogue sessions you may choose to do something that takes a relatively short amount of time, such as a simple one-word go-around, and save the longer closing exercises for only the most emotionally weighty sessions. We have included a number of suggestions for closure in Appendix C. (See Figure 11.2 to help you plan your dialogue sessions.)

DEBRIEFING

Debriefing is the predominant mechanism for engaging participants in dialogue. It should take place after community builders, after new social justice concepts are introduced, after activities, and even as a way of closing sessions. Part of the art of facilitation is to decide how to invite participants to reflect on what they are experiencing and share those reflections and thoughts with others in the group. Debriefing can take the form of silent, individual reflection, such as inviting participants to write in a journal or think quietly to themselves; in pairs or small groups; or as an entire large group. It is often a good idea to go through all three of these stages, first letting individuals reflect alone, then inviting them to share with a partner, and finally, opening up the space for learning to be shared aloud with everyone.

Facilitators should consider the dynamics of the group when deciding how to debrief. If a group is talkative and seems very comfortable processing verbally, it may not be as necessary to provide journal time after every activity. In contrast, if the group seems to have a lot of internal processors with perhaps a few participants who dominate, facilitators should make special effort to provide journaling time and opportunities for dialoguing in pairs and small groups.

Each lesson in the Race Dialogues Curriculum offers suggested debrief prompts. You will notice that the prompts always ask participants to reflect on both the process—how participants are *feeling*—and the content—what participants are *learning*. It can also be a good idea to include a debrief prompt that asks participants to consider what action they could take or change they could make as a result of what they have learned.

PARTICIPANT JOURNAL

We have found it very useful for participants to be given structured time to reflect on their dialogue experiences in writing and to do so in a central location. We highly recommend that participants keep journals throughout the dialogue. There are a number of ways you could facilitate journaling:

1. Provide a blank journal to participants during the first session
2. Ask participants to bring their own paper or electronic journal
3. Provide a premade journal for participants that includes social justice concepts from each session, reflection prompts for each activity, and blank space for additional reflection

Journals are private spaces for participants to record and explore their affective and content learning. Be clear to inform participants that you will not be reading or collecting their journals.

GROUPING

Deciding how to group participants for activities, dialoguing, and debriefing is another very important part of facilitation. Throughout the lessons, there will be many opportunities to divide participants into smaller groups for dialogue. Grouping should be done intentionally with the following considerations:

1. *Do you want participants to talk to the people they are most comfortable with or build new relationships across difference?*

For some activities you may want participants to be as comfortable as possible in order to facilitate deep reflection, in which case it is a good idea to let them pick their own pairs or groups. If your intention is to stretch participants beyond their comfort zones, it is a good idea to assign groups in advance or randomly during the session by counting off or using another randomized method.

2. How will various social identities be reflected in the groups?

It is likely that your group will not be completely balanced when it comes to race, gender, and other social identities. Facilitators should consider how the larger group makeup will translate into smaller group assignments and ensure that they are not putting marginalized members in the problematic position of acting as representatives of their group. For example, if there are only four People of Color in a 20-person dialogue group, it is a better idea to divide the groups in such a way that there are two People of Color in two of the small groups, rather than making four groups that each have only one Person of Color. This is also something to consider when using more randomized methods of grouping. It is a good idea for facilitators to "pre-count" before asking the group to count off to be aware of what the final groupings will look like. Sometimes starting one person to the left or right, or dividing into groups of four rather than five, can drastically alter the makeup of the final groups.

3. What size should the groups be?

Facilitators should keep in mind what their goals are and how much time they plan to allot to small group dialoguing. If the goal of a group is to give each person a chance to share vulnerably, it may require pairs or a smaller group to get through everyone in a reasonable amount of time. If the goal is for participants to hear multiple perspectives, facilitators should consider slightly larger groups. Facilitators may also decide to use the "groups within a group" method. For example, if the facilitator would like participants to discuss three different things, they might first divide the overall group into thirds: group 1, group 2, and group 3. However, if there are 30 participants, each group will have 10 members—a relatively large number of people. One way to handle this is to divide the groups again by asking each of the three groups to break into pairs or triads. Facilitators could then invite a person from group 1 to find a person from groups 2 and 3 and form a new triad in order to share learning across the three groups as an alternative or addition to a large group share out.

TIME CONSTRAINTS

Finally, facilitators must also consider how much time they have to dialogue. In our experience, it never feels like there is enough time. Given the long, pervasive history of racism in our country, this should be no surprise.

Even doubling the number of sessions for this work would not be enough time to deeply engage in all we need to in order to truly dismantle systems of White supremacy. Knowing this limitation, facilitators should be prepared to make difficult decisions about what it is possible to fit in a session. Remember that activities are often just a tool to spark conversation. When a dialogue is going well, facilitators do not need tons of activities to fill the time. Participants may even request more time for reflection and debriefing. One way to respond to this request is to be flexible. Consider in advance what is essential content and what you can let go of in the event that the dialogue is rich enough to sustain itself.

A NOTE FOR HIGH SCHOOL EDUCATORS

Given the rigorous demands of the Common Core State Standards (CCSS), it can be difficult to find the time to incorporate race dialogues into the curriculum. However, it is possible to align the Race Dialogues Curriculum with CCSS. For example, after intense deliberation, the school district where Sheri works decided to incorporate the race dialogue curriculum in *all* 9th grade English classes and offer an advanced dialogue curriculum in all 10th grade honors English classes, with school board approval. This decision was made for several reasons.

First, some of the goals of dialogue can be found in the National English Common Core State Standards (CCSS):

CCSS.ELA-Literacy.SL.9-10.1. Initiate and participate effectively in a range of collaborative discussions (one-on-one, in groups, and teacher-led) with diverse partners on grades 9–10 topics, texts, and issues, building on others' ideas and expressing their own clearly and persuasively.

CCSS.ELA-Literacy.SL.9-10.1.c. Propel conversations by posing and responding to questions that relate the current discussion to broader themes or larger ideas; actively incorporate others into the discussion; and clarify, verify, or challenge ideas and conclusions.

CCSS.ELA-Literacy.SL.9-10.1.d. Respond thoughtfully to diverse perspectives, summarize points of agreement and disagreement, and, when warranted, qualify or justify their own views and understanding and make new connections in light of the evidence and reasoning presented.

Second, almost all high school English teachers are tasked with teaching literature that addresses racism, segregation, discrimination, privilege, and oppression. Unfortunately, while English teachers are responsible for discussing these themes, very few have been properly trained to facilitate these discussions. As a result, some teachers try to avoid addressing racially sensitive issues, or worse, attempt discussions that have gone very poorly and lead to anger and frustration on the part of students, teachers, and families. This curriculum provides an opportunity for teachers to better lead the discussions they have already been having. For example, in *A Raisin in the Sun*—a book commonly taught in high school English courses—the Younger family is dissuaded from moving into a White neighborhood because of institutional racism in the housing market. The lesson on institutional racism and housing acts as an important supplement to this material.

In addition to required courses, high school educators could also consider offering a Race Dialogues course as an elective, or engaging students in these conversations in an afterschool or co-curricular program.

LESSON 1: WHY ARE WE TALKING ABOUT RACE?

Goals

Participants will:

- Build community
- Understand why it is important to talk about race

Introductory Narrative

Talking about race in classrooms, workplaces, and other structured settings is a rare experience for most, especially in intergroup settings in which people from diverse racial backgrounds are talking together. As a result, it can feel uncomfortable and even difficult to do so. You are likely to be challenged in new and unexpected ways during these sessions. This is normal and to be expected. We invite you to view discomfort not as a bad thing, but instead as an opportunity for transformation and growth.

Our hope is that over the course of these sessions we will build a brave learning community in which we are able to be vulnerable and tell our stories so that we can

1. Increase our personal awareness about privilege and oppression, especially as it relates to race
2. Improve intergroup understanding and build relationships across difference, especially racial difference
3. Strengthen our capacity to work together in order to create much needed social change

It is very likely that many of you have been socialized to believe that simply talking about race is racist. This can be especially true for those of you who are White and have been raised not to "see color." You may have come here believing that "colorblindness" is the desirable end goal in race relations. In turn, the first step in having dialogues about race is to move beyond the desire to ignore race. "Colorblindness" is not the goal.

Not only is it impossible to be "colorblind"—after all, unless we are blind, we can see physical differences that lead to racial assumptions—"colorblindness" is not an answer for ending racial inequality. Instead of treating race as an important and pressing social issue to be tackled, "colorblindness" treats race as irrelevant.

The current practice in our country of not talking about race, especially across race, has led to misunderstandings, mistrust, and more importantly, the continuation of racial inequality. For example, the United States has huge racial wealth gaps, with People of Color much more likely to live in poverty than White people (Annie E. Casey Foundation, 2018); African Americans are more likely to be incarcerated than White Americans, even when they commit the same crimes (U.S. Department of Justice, 2011); People of Color have historically been the targets of race-based hate crimes, and continue to make up the overwhelming majority of victims of such crimes (Levin, 2018); Black women are 3.5 times more likely to die in childbirth than White women (Tucker et al., 2007); Native Americans and Latinx people are more than twice as likely to be uninsured than White Americans (Moonesinghe et al., 2013); in the entire history of the United States only 1.5% (30 out of 1,974) of Senators have been People of Color (U.S. Senate); 80% of K–12 teachers and principals in the United States are White (NCES, 2016); and Children of Color are significantly more likely to be suspended and expelled from school than their White counterparts, for the same infractions, starting as early as preschool (NAACP Legal Defense Fund, 2016; U.S. Department of Education, 2016). In virtually every sector of our society, there are stark racial inequities caused by generations of racism. This incessant reality is why it is essential that we openly discuss race so that we can better work together to end racism.

Ice Breaker/Community Builder

Choose an icebreaker from Appendix B.

Social Justice Concepts: Racism, Prejudice, and Discrimination

Introduce the following terms from Appendix A.

- Individual Racism
- Interpersonal Racism
- Institutional Racism
- Prejudice
- Discrimination

Modifications and Extensions

A. **Developing Definitions.** Instead of giving participants the book definition, ask them to work in small groups to define each term for themselves. Invite each group to share what they came up with. At the end, compare their definitions to those from the book. Rewrite definitions collectively. Note that this activity will take more time.

B. **Rewriting Definitions.** Present the definitions from the book to participants. Ask them to rewrite the definitions in a way that would resonate with their community or peers.

ACTIVITY 1.1: OVERCOMING "COLORBLINDNESS"

Share one of the following videos with participants and debrief.

1. Why Colorblindness will NOT End Racism. *Decoded,* MTV News. Franchesca Ramsey: www.youtube.com/watch?v=H4LpT9TF_ew
2. Should We Be Colorblind? UrbanEntryVideo: www.youtube.com/watch?v=wEZJ5rDX9-E
3. The Costs of Racial Color Blindness. *Harvard Business Review,* Michael I. Norton: www.youtube.com/watch?v=RG6cVIDneis

Debrief Prompts

1. How did this video make you feel?
2. What information was new to you? Why do you think that is?
3. What beliefs do you have that this video challenged or confirmed?

ACTIVITY 1.2: THE ART OF APOLOGIZING

Note: You may decide to use this activity in the final session when talking about allyhood as well. It is useful, however, to present methods of apologizing at the start of dialogues so participants have the tools to use throughout the dialogue sessions.

Talking about race is hard, but it is important to do it anyway. The one thing we know for sure is that we will make mistakes when we do this work. Learning how to apologize is an important method of addressing mistakes and learning to view mistakes as learning opportunities.

Share with participants the following video which presents steps to a good apology: (1) do not get defensive, listen; (2) do not focus on your intent, attend to the impact; (3) take responsibility for your actions; and (4) make a commitment to change.

Getting Called Out: How to Apologize. Franchesca Ramsey: www. youtube.com/watch?v=C8xJXKYL8pU

Introduce participants to the acronym Re-AACT to help them remember how to apologize well:

1. **Reflect** and listen if you have made a mistake
2. **Acknowledge** and take responsibility for your mistake
3. **Apologize**
   a. AVOID "BUT or IF"
   b. Do not talk about intent
4. Commit to changing your behavior
5. Say **THANK YOU** for bringing this to my attention

Debrief Prompts:

1. How did the video make you feel?
2. How do these suggestions differ from the way you have previously made apologies?

ACTIVITY 1.3: PRACTICE APOLOGIZING

Divide participants into pairs. Invite each person to think of a scenario in which they did something wrong and failed to apologize adequately or in which someone harmed them and failed to apologize. Ask participants to role play this scenario using the Re-AACT steps to practice a good apology.

Debrief Prompts:

1. What did it feel like to apologize in this way?
2. Could you imagine using this method outside of the dialogue group?

Closing

Select a closing from Appendix C.

LESSON 2: HOW DO WE ENGAGE IN DIALOGUE ABOUT RACE?

Goals

Participants will:

- Build community
- Understand the practice of dialogue and how it is different from debate
- Understand the difference between comfort zone and brave space
- Learn how to identify and respond to triggers
- Learn how to be a generous listener

Introductory Narrative

Some of you may be wondering, what exactly IS dialogue? Dialogue is a very different form of conversation than most of us are used to. In our culture, debate is the most common form of communication between people who disagree. Most of us have learned to deal with conflict by competing to prove that someone else is wrong and that we are right. In debate, the goal is to win the argument. However, dialogue is not about winning. Instead, the goal of dialogue is to add to a common pool of knowledge. In this lesson, we will learn how to dismantle combative communication patterns in order to reach deeper understanding across difference and create opportunities for learning and growth.

Refer back to the elephant drawing in Figure 2.1. Dialogue is like the blindfolded people in the picture. Each person thinks they know the whole story about the elephant by experiencing only their part of the elephant. The person who feels the elephant's ear thinks it is a fan, the person who feels the tail thinks the elephant is a rope. Each individual person thinks they understand the whole truth, but in fact, they only know part of the truth. It is only when they share their part of the picture with others that they can understand reality more completely. That is what dialogue is all about, sharing everyone's story so that we can better understand the whole picture.

Social Justice Concepts: Dialogue vs. Debate

Introduce the following terms by handing out Figure 11.3 and reading through the definitions as a group.

- Dialogue
- Debate

ACTIVITY 2.1: PRACTICING DIALOGUE AND DEBATE

Divide participants into pairs. Give each pair 1 minute to practice *debating* the following prompts. When they are finished, ask them to try engaging in a *dialogue* about the same prompts. You can use different prompts for

Figure 11.3. Dialogue vs. Debate

Dialogue	Debate
Goal: Grow together; add to the common pool of knowledge to discover our shared truth	Goal: Win an argument; prove the other person is wrong
A form of communication between two or more people that is directed toward common understanding	A form of communication between two or more people where an issue is discussed and opposing arguments are put forward
Assumes many people have the answer and that only together can people find the solution	Assumes there is one right answer and that you have it
Is collaborative; participants work together toward a common understanding	Is about proving someone else is wrong and winning an argument
Is about learning through listening to other people and discovering new ideas	Is about listening to find flaws and weaknesses in other people's ideas.

Source: Adapted from University of Michigan, Program on Intergroup Dialogue, 2013.

this exercise if you wish. Make sure when choosing a prompt that it is low-stakes so that participants can focus on the mechanics of dialogue and debate rather than on a hot topic. Keep in mind that participants are not yet ready to discuss race or racism.

A. Oldest children are more responsible than younger children
B. Dogs are better than cats
C. Chocolate ice cream is better than vanilla

Debrief Prompts

1. What did you notice in each situation?
2. Where in your body did you feel tension?
3. Which situation, dialogue or debate, is more common for you to find yourself in?
4. Which situation, dialogue or debate, did you prefer?

ACTIVITY 2.2: VISUALIZING DIALOGUE AND DEBATE

We will now engage in two different visualization exercises designed to help you deepen your understanding of dialogue. Invite participants to close their eyes if they are comfortable. Read the following statements out loud to participants:

First visualization. "Imagine you are having a conversation with a group of friends, classmates or family members about a controversial topic and the conversation is getting heated and intense. A lot of opinions and perspectives are coming out, and people disagree. You want to say something, but it is hard to get a word in. When you finally share your opinion, you are quickly interrupted and told that your position is wrong. You begin to dig your heels in and find flaws in others' arguments. You start interrupting people to make sure your opinion is heard. The room is getting more and more tense. It seems like everyone thinks they have the right answer and others are wrong. You disengage because you realize nobody is really listening to each another and you are feeling insulted."

Invite participants to reflect privately in their journals or to keep their eyes closed and think to themselves about their initial reactions to this scenario.

Second visualization. "Now imagine another conversation. Like the last scenario, you're talking with a group of people about a controversial topic. You nervously share your opinion because not many people agree with you. Everyone is really curious. Different people ask you questions to better understand what you are saying. As the conversation continues, people say that what you are sharing is adding to their own thoughts about the topic. You also get curious and start asking questions of others. During this process you realize that there are lots of good points being made by different people. The group begins to share more openly and considers everyone's point of view. You all begin thinking about the topic in new ways you had not previously considered."

Invite participants to slowly open their eyes (University of Michigan, Intergroup Dialogue National Institute, 2013).

Debrief Prompts

1. Which situation are you in more often?
2. When people talk about race and racism, which scenario is more common?
3. Where in your body did you feel each scenario?
4. What would it take to help us stay in the 2nd scenario?

During dialogue sessions we are striving to create a space aligned with the second visualization.

Social Justice Concepts: Three Levels of Listening

One of the most important components of dialogue is generous listening. Dialogue is about listening deeply enough to one another to be open to changing our own ideas. This is a hard concept for many of us to imagine because we live in a society where it is normative to interrupt one another, and to listen only long enough to form our own response. We are going to learn more about how we can begin listening more deeply.

Introduce the following terms by handing out Figure 11.4 and reading through the definitions as a group.

- Internal Listening
- Generous Listening
- Global Listening

It is very normal to primarily listen in an internal way in which you are most focused on preparing your own response, opinions, stories, or judgements. However, in dialogue, we should be working to understand what the speaker is trying to communicate, and to be in a place of curiosity in which we are trying to learn more from the speaker.

ACTIVITY 2.3: EVERYONE TALKS ABOUT THEMSELVES

Share the following video with participants and debrief.

Everyone is Waiting to Talk About Themselves. *CollegeHumor:* www.youtube.com/watch?v=BjXq22kkLAg

Debrief Prompts

1. What did this video remind you of?
2. Who is someone you feel really listens to you? What do they do to make you feel they are listening deeply to you?

ACTIVITY 2.4: PARTNERED LISTENING

Facilitator(s) roleplay an example of *internal listening* and then an example of *generous listening* using one of the prompts below. Remember to model asking questions rooted in curiosity.

After modeling, divide participants into pairs. Give each pair 1 minute to practice *generous listening* about one of the following prompts. You can use different prompts for this exercise if you wish. Make sure when choosing a prompt that it is low-stakes and does not privilege some groups over others.

    A. What is your favorite place?

    B. What is your favorite food or recipe?

Debrief Prompts

1. What did it feel like to be generously listened to?
2. What did it feel like to listen generously?
3. How is this different from normal/internal listening?

Modifications and Extensions

Practice generous listening. Invite participants to try generous listening with their friends and family before the next session. During the next session, ask participants what they discovered when trying to listen generously in their everyday lives.

Social Justice Concepts: Brave Space & Learning Edge

Introduce the following terms from Appendix A.

- Brave Space
- Learning Edge

Figure 11.4. Three Levels of Listening

Internal	Generous	Global
Attention is on your own inner voice	*Attention is directed entirely at the speaker*	*Attention is on everything in the room*
• Thinking about your own response (What can I say next?) • Interjecting your experiences, stories, and opinions (How can I add my story to what this person is saying?)	• Internal voice is off • Led by curiosity • Asking questions rather than adding information • Not focused on your own opinion	• Noticing who is responding and how • Paying attention to energy in the room • Noticing body language of participants
• "I had an experience just like that. . . " • "That reminds me of when I did X."	• "Tell me more about that." • "I'm curious about what you said about X. Can you say more?" • "What is important to you?"	• "I'd like to hear from some people who haven't shared yet." • Observe when the conversation has faded and transition to the next piece of the agenda.

ACTIVITY 2.5: BRAVE SPACE

Divide participants into pairs or small groups. Share Figure 11.5 and note that we do not learn when we are comfortable. Instruct participants to share with their partners a time they knew they were on a learning edge. We often give the example of learning to ride a bike. It is not comfortable, we make mistakes and fall, but when we get it, it is life changing.

Debrief Prompts

1. *How* do you know when you are learning something new?
2. What does it *feel* like?
3. Where do you feel it in your body?

Remind participants that this is the experience we aspire to have in dialogues.

Social Justice Concept: Triggers

Introduce the following term from Appendix A.

- Trigger

ACTIVITY 2.6: RECOGNIZING TRIGGERS

Share the list of typical trigger responses (see Figure 11.6). Ask participants to work individually and circle the responses they are most likely to enact when they experience a provocation. When they have finished, ask them to look at the list again and star the responses they think are best for engaging in dialogue: "Which are most likely to de-escalate tension and allow people to remain in dialogue with each other?" Some examples may include: pausing, breathing, naming the trigger, discussing the trigger, and getting curious.

Debrief Prompts:

1. Is there overlap between how you generally respond and the best responses for dialogue?
2. What responses conducive to dialogue would you like to try?
3. What topics or specific situations are most likely to trigger you?

As facilitators, it is helpful to ask participants to be brave enough to let you know when they are uncomfortable. Invite participants to use the statement "I am triggered" if they are triggered during the dialogue process.

Figure 11.5. Learning Edges

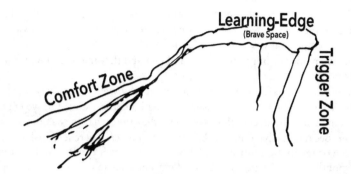

ACTIVITY 2.7: GROUP DYNAMICS

Narrative

Before we close today, we want to familiarize you with Bruce Tuckman's stages of group dynamics. As we embark on our dialogues together, it is likely that we will go through the typical stages that groups go through. We want you to be aware of this because although we are in the "norming" stage now, it is likely that we will hit a "storming" stage at some point. This is normal and expected. We just want you to be aware ahead of time so when we remind you of typical group dynamics, you will have seen it before. (See Chapter 3, Table 3.1, for Tuckman's stages of group dynamics.)

Closing

Select a closing from Appendix C.

LESSON 3: DEVELOPING GROUP NORMS

Goals

Participants will:

- Build community
- Develop a set of group norms agreed upon by all participants

Introductory Narrative

One of the goals of dialogue is to surface differences—a process that is guaranteed to produce conflict. Developing a set of group norms will give us a

Figure 11.6. Typical Trigger Responses

Anthropology Hat: We intellectualize the experience and try to evaluate why the person would say such a thing.

Attack: We respond with an intention to hurt or offend whoever has offended us.

Avoidance/Withdrawal: We avoid future encounters with the individual and withdraw emotionally. We may leave the room.

Confront: We name the hot button issue and demand that the offending behavior or policy be changed.

Confusion: We feel upset but are not clear about why we feel that way.

Curiosity: We view the hot button issue as something interesting and we engage the person in genuine conversation about why they said what they said.

Discretion: Because of dynamics in the situation (power differences, risk of physical violence or retribution, for example), we decide that it is not in our best interest to respond to the hot button at that time but choose to address the trigger at another time.

Discuss: We name the hot button issue and invite discussion about it with the triggering person or organization.

Freeze: We do not respond because we cannot think about how to respond at the moment

Humor: We respond with humor to make people laugh.

Internalization: We internalize the hot button issue. We believe it to be true. "I must be stupid."

Misinterpretation: We are feeling on guard and expect to be provoked so we misinterpret something someone says and are offended by our misinterpretation rather than by what was actually said.

Name: We identify what is upsetting us to the person or organization that said or did the offending thing.

Pause: We pause the conversation, identify the concern we have with what was said, and ask them to share more about why they said it.

Rationalization: We convince ourselves that we misinterpreted the hot button issue, that the intention was not to hurt us, or we tell ourselves we are overreacting so that we can avoid saying anything about the issue.

Release: We notice the hot button issue, but we do not take it in. We choose to let it go. We do not say anything about the hot button issue.

Shock: We are caught off guard, unprepared to be triggered by this person or situation, and have a difficult time responding.

Silence: We do not respond to the hot button situation even though we feel upset by it. We endure without saying or doing anything.

Strategize: We work with others to develop a programmatic or political intervention to address the issue in a larger context.

Surprise: We respond to the hot button issue in an unexpected way.

Source: Adapted from Hardiman, Jackson, & Griffin (2007).

framework for respecting each other's opinions and deeply understanding each other's lived experiences, especially in times of conflict. More than once, when one of our dialogues has erupted into conflict, revisiting the agreed-upon norms has helped de-escalate the interaction and return the group to a learning space. We should note that, like dialogue itself, we view group norms as a living document. This means there may be times when as a group we recognize we need to adjust them.

ACTIVITY 3.1: DEVELOPING GROUP NORMS

In our experience, having between 7 and 15 guidelines is a good rule of thumb. Too many guidelines can be difficult for the group to remember. Similarly, we have found that it is difficult to address all the issues that might arise in fewer than 7 or 8. Facilitators should make sure the agreed upon norms are visible every time the group meets. This may be by writing them on a board, printing them as a handout, or putting them in an electronic presentation. There are two ways to develop group norms.

Method A. The first method is to allow each dialogue group to organically develop their own set of group norms by prompting them with the following question: "What rules/norms/agreements do you need to feel you can be brave while participating in this dialogue?" Remind participants that surfacing differences is the goal of dialogue, and that some conflict is to be expected and viewed as an opportunity for learning. After everyone has shared their suggestions, craft a list that is agreed upon by all by combining those that overlap.

Method B. The second way to develop group norms is for the facilitators to present a predetermined list and then ask the group for input, additions, or deletions. This method works especially well if time is limited. It can also be a good method if you are planning to hold multiple dialogue cohorts within the same school or organization and want there to be a shared list that everyone can reference. For example, Shayla currently offers a regular dialogue series to educators from one county. In order to make sure she is helping them cultivate shared language and tools they can use when they return to their specific schools and buildings, she presents the same guidelines to each group.

Regardless of the method chosen, as facilitators we also have certain non-negotiable norms that we insist upon in our dialogue spaces. The following are the norms we regularly use and that we have found most helpful.

Sample Group Norms

1. Take the learning, leave the stories. It is our hope that participants take what they learn in dialogue and apply it to the rest of their lives. At the same time, in order for dialogue to be a brave space, participants need to be able to trust that they can be vulnerable and that the stories they share about their personal lives and experiences will not be repeated outside of the group. While facilitators cannot absolutely guarantee that every participant will honor confidences, they should set this as the expectation. One good rule of thumb for sharing learning with those outside of the group is for participants to focus on what they have personally learned and how they have individually grown, rather than on someone else's experience. For example, rather than saying, "Today someone in our group shared their experiences with racism, let me tell you about it!" they might say, "I'm now thinking about racism differently and realize that there are so many experiences I've just never had because I'm White."

2. Be present and engaged; avoid technology distractions. In order for people to share vulnerably and bravely, they must feel that the other participants are also invested in the dialogue. It is important that all participants commit to being present, staying engaged, and avoiding using electronic devices or checking out of the dialogue in other visible ways.

3. Share airtime. In dialogue it can be easy for those participants who feel most comfortable speaking up in large groups to dominate the conversation and for those who are more introverted to stay quiet. However, in order for everyone to grow and learn most, it is important to balance who is sharing. Challenge participants to be reflective about how often they are speaking up and to participate in ways that are outside of their comfort zone.

4. Speak from your own experience. In dialogue, participants sometimes assume that everyone in the room shares similar perspectives and experiences. Participants may be tempted to begin comments with statements like "We all know . . . " or "Everyone here feels . . . " or "We're preaching to the choir; it's other people who really need to be here." These sorts of sweeping generalizations can be a hindrance to honesty and deep personal reflection.

Similarly, participants may assume that their experience and worldview is universal in ways that silence those who are different, or even those who share racial identities but experience things differently. When someone shares their experience in dialogue, others should not challenge whether the individual interpreted the experience appropriately. We are each experts in our own lives and experiences. This is especially important when thinking about stories involving microaggressions. For example, if a person of color shares that they noticed nobody sat next to them on a crowded bus and believed it was because of racism, it would violate this group norm if a participant suggested that it may not have had anything to do with their racial identity, but that perhaps people wanted to stand. One helpful method is to encourage participants to use "I" statements when sharing.

5. Be aware of intent and impact. We often refer to the difference between intent and impact when facilitating dialogue. We remind people that no matter how good their intentions might be, if the impact of what they said was hurtful, then they probably need to apologize. Often, when misunderstandings arise around the topic of race, people from the privileged group especially focus on what they intended. For example, they may say things like, "I didn't mean it that way." However, an important part of social justice work is to center the feelings of those who experience oppression, microaggressions, and victimization. In turn, participants should focus primarily on the impact of their words and actions and apologize if someone points out that they have said or done something hurtful. If you break someone's leg, not intending to do so does not erase the need to apologize, take the person to the hospital, and even help cover the cost of their medical treatment.

6. Listen to learn, not to respond; listen harder when you disagree. In typical conversations and debates, people focus primarily on what they are planning to say next. This might look like trying to tear down someone else's argument or it could be as innocent as adding a story to a conversation in which the participant has had a similar experience. In both of these instances, people are thinking about themselves rather than truly attending to what their dialogue partner is trying to communicate. In dialogue, it is important to generously listen to one another. Participants should listen even harder when someone is saying something about which they vehemently disagree to try to understand their perspective.

7. Do not freeze people in time. The primary goal of dialogue is personal growth. In the most successful dialogues, participants have gone through transformative growth between the first and last session. Dialogue requires that participants take risks, be brave and vulnerable. This inevitably means participants will make mistakes. It is from encountering mistakes that we often learn and grow the most. Hence, when we ask one another "not to freeze people in time," we are recognizing that we all want the opportunity to grow without being judged or remembered in perpetuity for a mistake we might make along the way.

Participants should also work not to freeze *themselves* in time. Just because they thought or did something in the past, does not mean it defines who they are in the present or who they will be in the future. This can be a particularly important guideline for educators engaged in dialogue because they may have made mistakes in the past in their efforts to teach students about racial injustice.

8. Expect and accept discomfort (and joy); we are on our learning edge. As we have highlighted, learning happens when you are in your brave space on your learning edge, not when you are feeling comfortable. In this work, you are guaranteed to encounter challenging material that you might find uncomfortable. We invite you to view discomfort as an indicator that learning is happening to and to recognize that new learning can also lead to feelings of pride, understanding, and growth.

9. Anticipate unfinished business. Racism touches every facet of our society. It is widespread and deeply entrenched. It will not be possible to solve racism in this dialogue. While it is our hope that participants will leave with greater knowledge about racism, more skills for combating injustice, and a deep commitment to doing so, a part of dialogue is accepting that the work is ongoing and that racism will not be solved in our lifetimes.

Debrief Prompts:

1. What is one of these norms that you are confident you will be able to do well in our dialogue sessions? Why?
2. What is one that will be a challenge for you? Why?
3. What is one norm that you want to focus on practicing today?

Closing

Select a closing from Appendix C.

LESSON 4: THE HISTORY OF RACISM

Goal

Participants will:

- Deepen understanding of the history of racism in the United States

Introductory Narrative

One reason why talking about race can be a challenge is because most of us do not know much about race and racism in our country. This lesson is designed to begin rectifying these gaps in knowledge by helping participants understand the long history of racism on U.S. soil.

Facilitation Consideration

Participants are often shocked by how little of the history reviewed in this lesson they actually learned in school. The weight of this new information can lead to a lot of emotion in the room and even tears. Facilitators should inform participants that this level of emotion is to be expected.

ACTIVITY 4.1: HISTORY OF RACISM READ AROUND

The Racism Read Around is based on an activity originally developed by Melanie Morrison (2014), director of Allies for Change, and adapted for our dialogues. Participants will read aloud a selection of historical events that span 500 years of racism in the United States (see the list below). While it is impossible to include every racist event in history, facilitators should select 50–75 particularly poignant moments that reflect the experiences of diverse groups of People of Color. Print the historical facts in readable type, with the date clearly indicated. Cut out each event separately into small strips of paper and pass them out to participants sitting in a circle or horseshoe in chronological order. Participants may get multiple facts to read. Instruct the person with the earliest date to start. Each person should read their fact slowly, clearly, and loudly. In order to allow the information to resonate with the participants, ask them to remain quiet (except for their respective speaking parts) during the activity and to allow for a 4-second pause in between each fact. In best practice, have readers read each slip twice with a moment in between in order to better retain the information. This adds significant time to the activity.

History of Racism Read Around—Sample Events

1662: Virginia enacted a law of hereditary slavery, meaning that children born to an enslaved mother are also enslaved. The law was intended to enslave the increasing number of children fathered by White men through rape.

1763: Items taken from a smallpox infirmary were distributed among Native American populations as "gifts" during a peace conference with Pontiac's Confederacy. About 100,000 Native Americans died of smallpox in the epidemic that followed.

1882–1943: The Federal Government passed a law prohibiting the immigration of all Chinese laborers to the United States. The Chinese Exclusion Act of 1882 was the first law implemented to prevent a specific ethnic group from immigrating to the United States.

1930: The Great Depression shut down Mexican immigration. The first deportation programs forced Mexican workers to return to Mexico.

Between 300,000 to 500,000 Mexicans, many of whom were U.S. citizens, were returned to Mexico over the next 5 years.

2011: Black people accounted for only 12% of the U.S. population, but 44% of all prisoners in the United States were Black and the average prison term for Black people was 69% longer than the term for White people convicted of the same offense.

Debrief Prompts

Note for this exercise: It is a good idea to give participants time to journal individually, then share with a partner or small group, before sharing with the larger group.

1. How did this activity make you feel?
2. Which events were new to you or stood out? Which would you like to know more about?

Modifications and Extensions

A. **Local and relevant events.** Facilitators can change the historical events to make them more relevant to their specific participants. For example, high school teachers may want to include facts related to their specific curriculum. When working with adult educators or preservice teachers, it can be helpful to include examples particularly relevant to the history and current reality of schooling and education in our country. It is also a good idea to incorporate local historical events relevant to the city or community where you are engaging in dialogue. We have found that the exercise is even more profound when participants see how it relates directly to their lives, work, and communities.

B. **Slides.** Facilitators may also decide to include slides with the read around that feature the historical events or facts along with an image that powerfully elucidates them. This approach can be especially helpful for visual learners.

C. **Timeline.** If time permits, you can add an additional activity to this exercise in which participants first attempt to create their own timeline of "Racism" and "Resistance to Racism." On butcher block paper, a chalkboard, a dry-erase board, or a series of large sticky notes, draw a long timeline divided into centuries (1500 through today). At the top of the paper write, "Racism in the United States." At the very bottom write, "Resistance to Racism in the United States." Give each participant a marker or sticky notes and ask them to brainstorm racist events and events in which activists resisted racism without using their phones or computers to help. Ask participants to write or place their examples of racism in the appropriate chronological space *above* the timeline, and moments of resistance to racism *below* the timeline. Participants can work together on this activity. After 10 minutes, invite participants to do a "gallery walk" of the timeline and read through what the group came up with silently.

Debrief Prompts

1. What did it feel like to do this activity?
2. What do you notice about how much you knew and did not know?
3. How did you come to know what you know?

Resistance to Racism Read Around

A. **Timeline with research.** An alternative way to do the timeline exercise is to ask participants to research examples of racism and resistance to racism in advance of the session. They can then write those facts on the timeline based not on memory or guessing but based on their own research, which can deepen their knowledge base and may lead to more trust of the information they are learning.

B. **Voices of resistance.** After the History of Racism Read Around, engage participants in a second read around with examples of people who have fought back against racism. Unlike the racism read around, you should do fewer of these that are more in depth. Make sure the resistors you pick come from racially diverse backgrounds and include not only people from marginalized racial groups who have worked for liberation and justice, but also White antiracists who have as well. This exercise is a good way of giving participants hope and helping them see ways in which they too might work to resist racism.

Debrief Prompts

1. What did it feel like to do this activity?
2. How can you act to resist racism?

Resistance to Racism Read Around—Sample Prompt

2016: Colin Kaepernick, NFL quarterback for the 49ers, and his teammate, Eric Reid, begin taking a knee during the national anthem in order to bring attention to the numbers of unarmed Black people being killed by the police. Kaepernick is especially vilified for this decision.

Closing

This can be an emotional activity for many participants. Make sure you leave time at the end of the lesson for a closing round. Choose a closing from Appendix C.

LESSON 5: UNDERSTANDING SOCIAL IDENTITIES

Goal

Participants will:

- Understand the concept of social group identities
- Understand that different social group identities carry different social power

Introductory Narrative

In this session, you will begin thinking about your own social identities. All of us have various identities that make us a part of different social groups. Some of the groups we are a part of have social power, and others do not.

Facillitation Note: This lesson can be challenging for participants, as it might be the first time they recognize their own privilege or oppression.

Social Justice Concept: Social Group Identity and Intersectionality

Introduce the following terms from Appendix A. Present participants with Figure 11.7 and review the various examples of social group identities. The bolded identities are those that have unearned privilege in the United States

- Social identity groups.
- Intersectionality

ACTIVITY 5.1: UNDERSTANDING INTERSECTIONALITY

Share the following video with participants and debrief.

1. The Urgency of Intersectionality. TED Talk, Kimberlé Crenshaw
2. Long Version (18:50min): www.ted.com/talks/kimberle_crenshaw_the_urgency_of_intersectionality?language=en

Figure 11.7. Social Identity Groups

Category	Social Identity Groups (Examples) (privileged groups are in bold)
Race	Asian, Black, Latinx, MENA, Multiracial/Biracial, Native American/Indigenous/First Peoples, Pacific Islander, **White**
Ethnicity	Chinese, Nigerian, Italian, Jewish, Palestinian, Polish, Puerto Rican, Salvadoran
Sex Assigned at Birth	Female, Intersex, **Male**
Gender Identity	**Cisgender**, Genderqueer, **Man**, Nonbinary, Transgender, Woman
Religion	Agnostic, Atheist, Buddhist, **Christian**, Hindu, Jewish, Muslim
Sexual Orientation	Lesbian, Gay, Bisexual, **Heterosexual**
Socioeconomic Class	Poor, Working Class, **Middle Class, Upper Middle Class, Wealthy**
Ability	**Able-bodied**, Disabled, **Non-Disabled, Neurotypical**, Person Living with a Disability, Temporarily Disabled
Age	**Adult**, Child, Elder, Infant, Pre-teen, Teen
Native Language	Chinese, **English**, French, Igbo, Lakota, Spanish, Vietnamese, Yoruba
Nationality/ Citizenship Status	**U.S. citizen from birth**, Naturalized Citizen, Lawful Permanent Resident, Undocumented Immigrant, Unauthorized Immigrant
Body Type	**Athletic**, Average, Fat, Heavyset, Large, Petite, Short, Skinny, **Tall**, Thick

3. Short Version with Animation (6min): www.youtube.com/watch?v=DtOL33_TbDQ

See Appendix I for more videos on intersectionality.

Debrief Prompts

1. How did you feel watching this video?
2. What did you learn?
3. What questions do you still have?
4. How has intersectionality been significant in your life?

ACTIVITY 5.2: SOCIAL IDENTITY CHART

Pass out the social identity chart to participants (Figure 11.8). Invite participants to complete the first column of the chart by writing the social identity
groups they belong to. Under each subsequent column, participants should
check the identities for which the statement is true.

Facilitators should use their own identities to model for participants
how to complete the chart.

Debrief Prompts

1. How did it feel to complete this chart?
2. What was the easiest part of filling out the identity chart? What were
   the hardest parts?
3. What identity do you think most about? Least? Why do you think
   that is?
4. What identity do you think has the greatest influence on how other
   people see you? Least?
5. For the categories in which you belong to a group with less social
   power, would you want to change those identities? Why or why not?
6. What is something you would want others to know about you?
7. How do privilege and power matter in the identities we think about
   the most and the least?

Modifications and Extensions

A. **Different social identities.** The social identity chart can be modified
   to include fewer social identity categories. This can be a useful
   approach if you want to focus the conversation on specific identities.
B. **Different prompts.** You can also modify the prompts at the top of the
   chart depending on the needs, make-up and goals of your particular
   group. Other possible prompts include:
   » You have the earliest memories of
   » Has the greatest influence on how students & families see you
   » Has the greatest influence on how teachers see you
   » Has the greatest influence on how colleagues see you
   » You have received positive messages about (from your family/
     media/school)
   » You have received negative messages about (from your family/
     media/school)
   » What message(s) have you received about this identity from
     parents/media/school (note: this prompt would be one in which
     participants could reflect more deeply, rather than simply check
     a box)

Figure 11.8. Social Identity Chart

	Group(s) you belong to (write below)	Group(s) you belong to with *more* social power (√ if true)	Group(s) you belong to with *less* social power (√ if true)	You think about this identity *a lot* (√ if true)	You *don't* think about this identity much (√ if true)	You have experienced discrimination or bullying (√ if true)	Has the greatest influence on how others see you (√ if true)
Race(s)							
Ethnicity(ies)							
Sex assigned at birth							
Gender Identity							
Religion							
Sexual Orientation							
Socio-Economic Class							
Ability							
Age							
Native Language							
Citizenship Nationality							
Body Type							

Social Justice Concepts: Privilege and Oppression

Introduce the following terms from Appendix A.

- Privilege
- Oppression (Marginalization)

Narrative

People often think the least about the identities where they have the most power and privilege, and the most about the identities where they experience the most marginalization and oppression. The areas where we have privilege and power are usually those where we are seen as "normal" or where we are in the majority. For example, because White people, the racially privileged group, do not experience racial discrimination, it is easy for them to go through life without having to think much about their race. In contrast, most People of Color spend their lives not seeing themselves reflected in the media, experiencing microaggressions and blatant racism, going to stores where they cannot easily find products for their hair or make-up that matches their skin color, and so forth. It is not surprising that these experiences lead many People of Color to think a lot about their racial identities.

Having privilege does not make a person good or bad. Privilege is almost always outside of your direct control. In most instances privilege is given or denied based on social group identities you were born with or that are immutable. This also means that privilege is not something you can give up or get rid of. While you cannot eliminate your privilege, you can choose how to use your privilege to help create a more socially just world. Becoming aware of the privilege you hold is an important first step in this process.

Facilitation Considerations

It is often taboo to discuss privilege in our culture. This part of the session often triggers some participants, especially those who have more unearned advantages than others. Some people feel guilty when they begin to think about their privilege. Facilitators should share with participants that it is okay to recognize feelings of guilt, but in the long run, guilt is not helpful. Invite participants instead to recognize systemic injustices and develop ways to confront inequity.

Modifications and Extensions

A. Identity pie. Invite participants to draw a circle (or use one you provide) and to divide the "pie" into identity slices according to how much they think about each of their identities. For example, if they think about their race a lot, that slice of the pie would be bigger than another identity. Ask them to label the slices with the social identity group it represents and then shade in the slices that give them unearned advantage. This activity visually represents the relative weight of different aspects of our identity.

Debrief Prompts

1. What did it feel like to do this activity?
2. Which of your identities occupied the largest slices of the pie? Why do you think that is?
3. How do privilege and power matter in the identities we think about the most and the least?

B. **Identity toss.** Provide five 3 x 5 cards to each participant and ask them to write their race on one card, and three other identities of the facilitator's choice on a second, third, and fourth card. (*Note:* Facilitators should avoid choosing sexual orientation, sex, or gender identity unless they are working with a group in which this is a part of the ongoing dialogue and they are sure everyone feels safe enough to be out.) On the last card, invite participants to write an aspect of their identity that is important to them but not already covered. Divide participants into pairs, trios, or foursomes. In the first round, ask each participant to remove the card that is least important to their identity and discuss why with their partner(s). In each subsequent round ask them to toss the next least important card until they have only two cards left. In the final round, ask the partner or one of the group members (not the card holder) to select between the final two identities based on which they think is most important to the holder.

Debrief Prompts

1. What did it feel like to do this activity?
2. Which identity did you toss first? Why?
3. How did it feel to have your final identity taken from you?
4. How did power and privilege relate to the identities you tossed and kept?

Remind participants that everyone has different identities that are most salient to them. These identities may be the ones that are most visible to others or may not be. In fact, people often interact with others who ignore or erase some of our identities. A final debrief prompt could include asking participants:

1. How can you respond when it feels like people are erasing your identities?
2. What can you do to make sure you do not make inaccurate assumptions about the identities of others?

C. **Identity walk.** Post four or five social identities around the room in large print. (Note: facilitators should avoid choosing sexual orientation unless they are working with a group in which this is a part of the ongoing dialogue and they are sure everyone feels safe enough to be out). After participants have completed the Social Identity Chart, ask them to stand or sit next to the social identity posted that they think about the *most*. When everyone is at their identity ask them to silently look around the room and see where people are. Ask them to find a partner in their group and share why they chose this identity. Next, ask participants to walk to the identity they think about the *least*. Again, they should take note of where other participants are in the room. Ask participants to find a partner in their group and share why they chose this identity.

Debrief Prompts

1. How did it feel to do this activity?
2. Why do you think about some identities more than others?
3. How did power and privilege relate to the identities you chose?

Closing

Choose a closing from Appendix C.

LESSON 6: INTERPERSONAL RACISM AND MICROAGGRESSIONS

Goals

Participants will:

- Understand the difference between institutional and individual racism
- Explore individual experiences with racism
- Learn to identify and respond to microaggressions

Introductory Narrative

When the term "racism" is used in casual conversation, people are often referring to how an individual treats another individual. However, as we have been learning, in the United States, racism is not just about how people treat each other. It is also about how various systems and institutions give White people more access to privilege and power. This lesson will reintroduce the concept that racism can manifest at multiple levels: individually, interpersonally, and institutionally. We will then focus on how interpersonal racism has impacted our lives through several activities. (We discuss individual racism in Lesson 7 and institutional racism in Lesson 9.)

Social Justice Concepts: Racism

Introduce the following terms from Appendix A.

- Individual Racism
- Interpersonal Racism
- Institutional Racism

ACTIVITY 6.1: FOUR CORNERS

The Four Corners Activity (adapted from University of Michigan's Program on Intergroup Relations) is designed to help participants think deeply about times they have been the victims of interpersonal racism, or other forms of oppression, as well as times they have been perpetrators.

Post each of the four prompts below in a different area of the room. Note that you may shift the language used in the prompts to describe experiences of discrimination depending upon the age of the group and their understanding of social justice concepts.

Prompt 1. Share a time when you were targeted (bullied, oppressed, discriminated against) because of one of your social identities. How did it make you feel then? How do you feel about it now? If you have not experienced being targeted, why do you think that is?

Prompt 2. Share a time when you targeted (bullied, oppressed, discriminated against) someone else because of one of their social identities. You could have done this intentionally or accidently, and it could have been through social media. How did it make you feel then? How do you feel about it now?

Prompt 3. Share a time when you interrupted or stopped someone who was targeting (bullying, oppressing, discriminating against) another person because of one of their social identities. How did it make you feel then? How do you feel about it now?

Prompt 4. Share a time when you witnessed someone targeting (bullying, oppressing, discriminating against) another person for one of their social identities and you did not intervene. How did it make you feel then? How do you feel about it now?

Divide participants into groups of 3–7 people. Each group should start at one of the four prompts. Give each person in the group 2–5 minutes to share their story in relation to the prompt posted.

Remind participants to engage in generous listening. Participants should not interrupt their group members' stories and should ask only questions that deepen the stories and dialogue. Facilitators may need to assist in this process. Groups should rotate through each corner, giving each group member an opportunity to answer the prompt, until all of the prompts have been answered by all participants.

Keep in mind that group size and sharing time can drastically alter the length of this activity. If possible, it is helpful to keep groups equally sized so that each person in the room has the same amount of time to share their stories. If the group is large, we actually divide it in half and run two four-corner activities simultaneously.

Debrief Prompts

1. What was it like talking about the four situations?
2. Which corner was easiest for you to think about? Hardest? Why?
3. Were there things others said that you did not want to hear? Why?
4. Were you reluctant to talk in any corner? Why?
5. What do you want to do as a result of participating in this exercise?

Social Justice Concept: Microaggressions

Introduce the following term from Appendix A.

• Microaggressions

ACTIVITY 6.2: UNDERSTANDING MICROAGGRESSIONS

Share one (or more) of the following videos and debrief.

1. What Kind of Asian Are You? Ken Tanaka: www.youtube.com/watch?v=DWynJkN5HbQ
2. #HatchKids Discuss Microaggressions. SheKnows, Media KidsSpeak: www.youtube.com/watch?v=8RfwnibEd3A
3. How Microaggressions are Like Mosquito Bites. Fusion Comedy, Same Difference: www.youtube.com/watch?v=hDd3bzA7450
4. If Microaggressions Happened to White People. MTV News, *Decoded,* Franchesca Ramsey: www.youtube.com/watch?v=KPRA4g-3yEk
5. Where are You Really From??? MTV News, *Decoded,* Franchesca Ramsey: www.youtube.com/watch?v=igWYMo4z2OQ

Debrief Prompts

1. How did you feel watching the video(s)?
2. How were the interactions depicted examples of racism?
3. How did the video resonate with your own experiences?

Facilitation Considerations

A number of these videos illuminate the many ways in which individual racism can manifest through microaggressions. Some things you might want to point out include:

- Focusing on foods and festivals—assuming that the most significant thing about a racial or ethnic group different than yours is what they eat or the holidays they celebrate and using your limited knowledge about those differences as your primary point of connection.
- Lumping groups together—assuming that, for example, Asian people from different countries are basically all the same.
- Entitlement—the feeling on the part of privileged people that they are owed an explanation from oppressed people about their identities, histories, or bodies, even if they do not have any relationship of significance.
- Curiosity as a cover for racism—the belief that finding something "curious" or "interesting" justifies questioning oppressed people, even when you have not put forth any individual effort to do basic research or learn more about the topic.
- Assuming privileged group is "normal" and everyone else is "different" or "other."

After watching the video(s), ask participants to reflect on racial micro-aggressions they have heard and jot them down individually on sticky notes. Instruct participants to post their examples on the wall. Invite participants to silently move around the room in a "gallery walk" and read the microaggressions shared by their co-participants.

Debrief Prompts

1. How did reading one another's microaggressions make you feel?
2. What did you notice when reading through the microaggressions?
3. What is one thing you could do differently as a result of this activity?

Modifications and Extensions

Recognizing microaggressions and the messages they send. Pass out the handout "Tool: Recognizing Microaggressions and the Messages They Send" (adapted from Sue, 2010; see also academicaffairs.ucsc. edu/events/documents/Microaggressions_Examples_Arial_2014_11_12. pdf). Ask participants to read through the list of microaggressions and circle the ones they have personally experienced, put a star next to the ones they have perpetrated, and check the ones they have witnessed. You can also invite them to add any additional microaggressions they have experienced, perpetrated or witnessed. Use the same debrief prompts as above.

ACTIVITY 6.3: SKILL PRACTICE: PALS

After discussing microaggressions, it is important to introduce PALS: Pause, Acknowledge, Ask, Listen, Share Your Story, which gives participants a concrete skill to address microaggressions that they can begin practicing immediately. (See Chapter 9 and Appendix H for PALS handout.)

After introducing PALS and talking about each step, divide the group into pairs. Ask each pair to imagine a scenario in which one partner has just said the punchline of a racist joke. Facilitators can provide an example or ask each pair to come up with one they have heard before, such as one they noted when doing the microaggressions activity. One partner should pretend to be the perpetrator while the other practices interrupting. Then instruct them to switch roles. Remind participants that interrupting racism takes practice, courage, and hard work, and the only way to get better at it is to try. While it will likely be uncomfortable to do so at first, making the effort is what counts.

Facilitation Considerations

In introducing this activity, caution participants against actually saying racial slurs in their role play or pretending to be someone of a different racial background by using fake accents or gestures.

Debrief Prompts

1. How did you feel during this activity?
2. What was the hardest part for you?
3. Is this something you can imagine doing outside of this session?
4. What will be the hardest part of taking a stand outside of this group?
5. What if other people laugh at you? Or get angry at you?

6. How would it feel to notice an oppressive comment and NOT say something?

Note: You should include practicing PALS in subsequent sessions if time permits.

Closing

Select a closing from Appendix C.

LESSON 7: INDIVIDUAL RACISM: IMPLICIT BIAS AND THE CYCLE OF SOCIALIZATION

Goals

Participants will:

- Understand the concept of socialization and reflect on their own socialization
- Understand the concept of implicit bias and reflect on their own biases
- Practice PALS

Introductory Narrative

This lesson will focus on individual racism—what we think, feel, and believe about different racial groups because of the ways we have been socialized. This session is designed to help you reflect on how you were socialized when it comes to race and racism and how this socialization has resulted in implicit biases that we are likely not even aware we have.

Social Justice Concept: Socialization

Introduce the following term from Appendix A. Share Figure 11.9 and talk through each stage (See Chapter 8 for more information.)

- Socialization

We were all born into a society with formal and informal rules that we have to learn in order to function successfully. Some of these rules we learn and teach consciously, like what to do when driving if the street light turns red; but we pick up many rules subconsciously through our day-to-day interactions with others. Learning how the world works, and how we are expected to behave in it, is called "socialization."

Figure 11.9. Cycle of Socialization

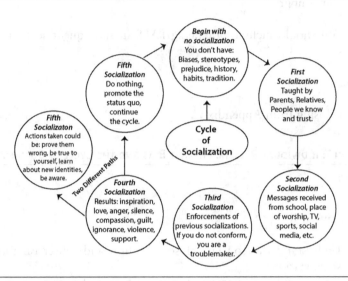

Note. Adapted from Adams & Bell, 2016.

We experience socialization not only with regard to traffic rules, but also when it comes to race and racism. We were all born without awareness of race or racism, but we acquire attitudes, values, and beliefs about race through socialization. Most of our socialization is subtle rather than overt. We may not even be aware of how we were socialized.

ACTIVITY 7.1: CYCLE OF SOCIALIZATION

Post five large poster-size sticky notes around the room with the titles: 1st Socialization, 2nd Socialization, through 5th Socialization. Give each participant five sticky notes. Ask them to label sticky notes 1–5. Invite them to write a personal example of each stage of the cycle of socialization on each note. For example, they might write, "1st Socialization: I learned from my parents that all of our friends are the same race as me because all of the people who came to our house looked like us racially;" "2nd Socialization: On TV I learned that most People of Color were portrayed as criminals." After participants have finished recording something for each part of the cycle, instruct them to post their sticky notes on the appropriate posters around the room. Invite them to move around the room "gallery-walk" style and read through one another's experiences.

Debrief Prompts

1. How did you feel doing this exercise?
2. What was difficult about this exercise?
3. What did you learn about yourself through this exercise?
4. What keeps us in this cycle?
5. Are there things we might do differently now after thinking about the cycle of socialization?

Modifications and Extensions

A. **Socialization in small groups.** Divide the group into five smaller groups and assign each group one part of the cycle. Each group should brainstorm as many examples as possible of the socialization stage they were assigned. They should then share their examples with the larger group.

B. **Personal narrative.** Ask participants to write a personal narrative of their own race socialization at each of the five stages. After they have finished writing, divide them into pairs and ask them to share, to the extent they feel comfortable, with a partner.

Social Justice Concept: Implicit Bias

Introduce the following term from Appendix A.

* Implicit Bias

ACTIVITY 7.2: UNDERSTANDING IMPLICIT BIAS

Share one (or more) of the following videos or podcasts describing the concept of implicit bias.

1. American Denial: Implicit Bias Test. PBS *Independent Lens,* Mahzarin Banaji: www.youtube.com/watch?v=ZWa09tUzqf4
2. How the Concept of Implicit Bias Came Into Being. NPR, Mahzarin Banaji: www.npr.org/2016/10/17/498219482/how-the-concept-of-implicit-bias-came-into-being
3. Who, Me? Biased? Series. *The New York Times,* Saleem Reshamwala www.nytimes.com/video/who-me-biased
4. How to Overcome Our Biases? Walk Boldly Toward Them. TED Talk, Verna Myers: www.youtube.com/watch?v=uYyvbgINZkQ
5. A Look at Race Relations Through a Child's Eyes. CNN, Anderson Cooper: www.youtube.com/watch?v=GPVNJgfDwpw-

Debrief Prompts

1. What did it feel like to watch this video?
2. What new information did you learn?
3. How can you become more aware of your own implicit biases?

Narrative

Unlike overt racism, because of the common ways in which we have been socialized, implicit bias is something we all have. Unfortunately, we are also likely unaware of the implicit biases we hold because they are activated involuntarily and without our control. Even deep reflection does not necessarily lead to awareness of our implicit biases. However, implicit biases are not immutable. We can change our biases. Some ways we can work to change our biases are:

1. Audit your behaviors and interactions. Take note of who you respond to, whose opinion you value, who you hang out with, who you feel most connected to. These things are likely influenced by your implicit bias.
2. Notice when you feel, act, or think in a way that may be prejudiced or biased.
3. Be conscious of those feelings and try to interrupt them by talking to yourself internally about why your thought was biased or inaccurate. For example, you might tell yourself, "I know this is just a bias I have that is not based in fact."
4. Avoid social media and other forms of media that perpetuate negative stereotypes about marginalized racial groups.
5. Read new things, engage in new activities, and surround yourself with images that challenge stereotypes and expose you to attitudes and people from backgrounds different than your own.

Invite participants to continue brainstorming ways they can notice and address their implicit biases.

Modifications and Extensions

A. **Project Implicit bias test** (implicit.harvard.edu/implicit/). Ask participants to take the Implicit bias test, either during the session or prior to the session. After finishing the test, many participants, including Participants of Color, are surprised to discover they have implicit preferences for White people.

Debrief Prompts

1. How did it feel to take the test?
2. What are some things you learned about yourself?
3. What do you think you would like to do with this information?

B. **Image Review.** Select 12 pictures of people from different backgrounds that might evoke some implicit bias in the viewers. (For example, people of different ethnicities and races, people who are heavy, athletic, goth, tattooed, wearing a hijab, etc.). Flash each picture for 10 seconds and invite participants to write one or two words that come to their mind for each image. Suggest they avoid thinking too hard about the images, just record the first thing that comes to their minds.

Debrief Prompts

1. How did it feel to do this activity?
2. What did you notice about your responses?
3. Where do you think your ideas came from?
4. How did you learn to make those assumptions and associations?
5. How might your assumptions impact your interactions with the individual in the picture if you were meeting them in real life?
6. What can you do to change those reactions?

C. **Word Association.** Read the following list of race terms, pausing for 10 seconds after each: Indigenous, Asian, Black, Caucasian, Middle Eastern, Latinx, White, Multiracial, Hispanic, Native American, Arab, Latina, African American, Pacific Islander, Mixed.

Ask participants to write three words or draw a picture of the first thing that comes to their mind when they hear each term. After all prompts have been read, debrief using the questions above and below.

Debrief Prompts

1. How did it feel do to this activity?
2. What did you notice about your responses? What did you find surprising?
3. How did different terms for similar groups elicit different responses from you? For example: White and Caucasian; Black and African American; Latina, Latinx, and Hispanic?

D. **Extended Anderson Cooper Video:** CNN's Anderson Cooper did a longer investigative series that includes interviews with children of different ages as well as interviews with parents. Consider showing other clips or the entire series. A Look at Race Relations Through a Child's Eyes.: www. youtube.com/watch?v=GPVNJgfDwpw

Debrief Prompts

1. Why do you think the children in the video responded in this way?
2. How did it make you feel to watch the children respond?
3. How are the children's responses connected to the concept of socialization?
4. What specific things could parents and teachers do differently to change young people's attitudes, beliefs, and biases about race?

Closing

Select a closing from Appendix C.

LESSON 8: EXPLORING GROUP PRIVILEGE AND OPPRESSION

Goals

Participants will:

- Understand privilege and oppression
- Explore their own levels of privilege and oppression

Introductory Narrative

In Lesson 5, we introduced the concepts of "privilege" and "oppression"—unearned advantage and unearned disadvantage based on social identities. In this lesson, we will deepen our understanding of privilege through an activity that helps us visually represent these concepts.

It is important to remember that having privilege does not mean that a person has not had struggles or challenges. It simply means that they have not experienced challenges *because of* the particular identity where they hold privilege. Similarly, experiencing oppression does not mean that an individual has done anything wrong. Instead, it means that they live in an unjust society in which they are treated unfairly. Privilege is not about individual choices or decisions. Instead, privilege is related to how systems have been set up in our country.

This activity can be emotionally difficult. Our goal in doing this activity is not to blame or shame anyone, but to help you become more aware of your privilege so that you can take action to make our society more equitable.

Social Justice Concepts: Privilege and Oppression

Reintroduce the following terms from Appendix A.

- Privilege
- Oppression (Marginalization)

ACTIVITY 8.1: UNDERSTANDING PRIVILEGE

Share the video below and debrief.

- Why Does Privilege Make So Many People Angry? MTV News, *Decoded,* Franchesca Ramsey: www.youtube.com/watch?v=qeYpvV3eRhY

Debrief Prompts

1. How did this video make you feel?
2. What did you learn from watching this video?

ACTIVITY 8.2: PRIVILEGE WALK

Prior to beginning the exercise, facilitators need to find a large, open space suitable for this activity. We often conduct the exercise in a hallway, gym, or outside.

Ask participants to stand in a horizontal line facing forward. If the room is not wide enough for all participants to stand in one line, you can ask that they make two parallel lines, close together. Inform participants that this is a reflective exercise that can bring up a lot of emotion and ask that they complete the entire exercise in silence. Share that standing together represents a level playing field where everyone has the chance to be successful.

Next, facilitators read a series of statements that are examples of privilege or marginalization (see Appendix F). Participants should step forward, backward, or stay in place in response to each statement as instructed. Facilitators should choose prompts relevant to what they already know to be true about the group. Sometimes participants have questions about a particular prompt. Let them know that rather than asking for clarification, they should stay silent and interpret the questions as they see fit. Finally, facilitators should mention the value of everyone taking the same size step throughout the activity. Usually, about 30 prompts make for a good exercise.

After the final statement is read, invite participants to look around and notice where everyone is standing. Then divide participants into three groups: those roughly in the front, those in the middle, and those at the back. Groups should sit or stand where they are to debrief the activity. Depending on the size of the group, you may invite the entire group to talk or ask them to divide into pairs or triads within their front, middle, and back grouping. It is usually a good idea to begin the debrief with a journal reflection.

Debrief Prompts

1. How did it feel to participate in this exercise?
2. What stood out? What surprised you? What troubled you?
3. What were you proud about? What embarrassed you?
4. What question(s) really impacted you?
5. What does this activity say about you?
6. If you could change your position, would you?
7. How are you going to talk about this activity when you leave this space?

Modifications and Extensions

A. **Journal prompt.** Before doing the privilege walk, invite participants to journal about what they think privilege means in relation to racism and to reflect on their own privilege related to their various social identities.
B. **Hold hands.** Ask participants to start the privilege walk holding hands. As they move in response to the prompts, they will likely be forced to let go of the hands next to them. Adding this piece can increase the emotional impact of the exercise. This version should not be used in groups in which it could be inappropriate to a participant's culture or religion to hold hands.
C. **Privilege Prompts only.** Write all prompts as a statement of privilege. For example, instead of, "If English is not your first language, take one step backward," facilitators would say "If English is your first language, take one step forward." Ask all participants to start in a horizontal line at the back of the room. They should take a step forward if the privilege applies to them and stay where they are if it does not. Taking this approach to the exercise emphasizes the focus on privilege and power.
D. **Walk as a Student or Colleague.** In this version rather than answering the statements for themselves, participants think of a peer, student, or colleague they struggle with or are challenged by in some way. Use only privileged statements. When the statements are read participants should move forward if the privilege applies to the person they are imagining, stay still if they do not know, and take a step back if the privilege does not apply. This activity not only illuminates privilege, it also reveals how much participants know about the people who challenge them most, and provides an opportunity to emphasize the importance of building relationships across difference.

Remind participants of the importance of confidentiality for this exercise. They should not share with anyone else who they were thinking of. It can be a good idea to hand out a list of prompts first and let participants individually answer for themselves on paper before walking as someone else. This allows them to compare their answers with those of the person they are challenged by.

Debrief Prompts

1. How much do you know about the person you were thinking of who you find challenging? How might this be impacting your relationship?
2. How did your answers for the person you are challenged by differ from your own?
3. How do social group identities matter when it comes to the people you are and are not challenged by?

E. **Watch a Privilege Walk Video.** Instead of engaging participants in a privilege walk (especially if you do not have a diverse group of students), show participants one of the videos below of a diverse group of participants doing a privilege walk and debrief:

1. www.youtube.com/watch?v=EIJqtWUiUCs
2. www.youtube.com/watch?v=hD5f8GuNuGQ

Debrief Prompts

1. How did it feel to watch this video?
2. What did you notice?
3. Where do you think you would have ended up if you were a member of that group?

F. **Blue Eyes/Brown Eyes.** Share the following 6-minute video about the famous 1968 Jane Elliot experiment with 3rd graders based upon eye color and debrief.

- A Class Divided (edited). Jane Elliot: www.youtube.com/watch?v=dzXw75bOeXs

Debrief Prompts

1. What was going on in the video?
2. How did it make you feel?
3. Why do you think Jane Elliott decided to do this experiment?
4. Do you think you would have responded the same way in 3rd grade?
5. How does this video relate to privilege and oppression?

Facilitation Considerations

    A. **Deciding to engage.** This exercise can be very challenging not only for the people with a lot of privilege but also for those who end up in the back of the room. In turn, there are a number of things facilitators should consider before deciding to engage participants in a privilege walk:

        (1) Is there a balance of White participants and Participants of Color? If there is not racial balance in the group, this activity may be too risky because it can further isolate the People of Color and put them in the unfair position of having to speak for their entire group.

        (2) What are the roles and power dynamics of the participants in the group? If there are significant differences in power among group members, this exercise may be too risky. For example, if school secretaries are doing this exercise with school administrators from the same district, this exercise may negatively impact work relationships. One way to address the risk of asking participants to walk as themselves in situations in which there are racial and/or other power imbalances is to use one of the above modifications.

    B. **Timing.** If you decide to reorder the lessons, keep in mind that in order for the privilege walk to be effective it requires a significant level of trust among participants, and it is helpful to have a shared understanding of some core social justice concepts. In turn, it is best practice to avoid doing this exercise early in a dialogue series.

    C. **Single vs. multiple identities.** If you have a racially balanced group, you can do the privilege walk using prompts that exclusively focus on race. However, if the group is predominantly one race, you should only do this activity using prompts that address multiple identities such as race, class, and gender.

Social Justice Concepts: Equality, Equity, Inclusion, Diversity, & Social Justice

Introduce the following terms from Appendix A.

- Equality
- Equity
- Inclusion
- Diversity
- Social Justice

Show the image in Figure 11.10, "Equality, Equity, Social Justice."

Figure 11.10. "Equality, Equity, Social Justice"

EQUALITY   EQUITY   SOCIAL JUSTICE

Illustration by Andrew Kaplowitz.

Debrief Prompts

1. What is the problem with the "Equality" image?
2. How does the "Equity" image solve the equality issues, and what still remains at issue?
3. What are the remaining limitations, even if the fence is removed? (Example: Implicit bias still remains).
4. How does this illustration relate to privilege and oppression?

Closing

Select a closing from Appendix C.

LESSON 9: INSTITUTIONAL RACISM

Goals

Participants will:

- Understand the difference between individual and institutional racism
- Learn data about institutional racism

Introductory Narrative

When most people think of racism they think of individual racism: someone being treated badly because of their race. However, racism is more complicated than that. In today's world when scholars talk about racism, they think in terms of systems—how organizations and institutions treat people differently because of their racial identity. This lesson is designed to explore and dialogue about present-day examples of institutional racism.

Social Justice Concept: Institutional Racism

Reintroduce the following term from Appendix A.

- Institutional Racism

ACTIVITY 9.1: UNDERSTANDING INSTITUTIONAL RACISM

Share one or more of the videos below and debrief.

1. Structural Discrimination: The Unequal Opportunity Race. African American Policy Forum: www.youtube.com/watch?v=eBb5TgOXgNY
2. How Race Settled the Suburbs. Upworthy, *Adam Ruins Everything*: www.facebook.com/Upworthy/videos/796326533903423/
3. Race the House We Live In. California New Reel, *Race: The Power of an Illusion:* www.youtube.com/watch?v=mW764dXEI_8
4. *Selma* Movie Clip: www.youtube.com/watch?v=1YRUUFYeOPI

Debrief Prompts

1. How did watching this make you feel?
2. How has institutional racism impacted your life? If you do not think institutional racism has affected your life, what might that mean?
3. What other examples of institutional racism can you think of? Consider what you have seen in the news and current events.

ACTIVITY 9.2: RESEARCHING INSTITUTIONAL RACISM

Divide the participants into five groups. Assign each group one of the following institutions: criminal justice, employment, housing, health, and education. Ask each group to do their own research on how institutional racism manifests in their assigned system in the present day. They may do this as homework before the session or during the session on an electronic device. Ask each team to present 3–5 findings to the larger group either verbally or by making a poster that lists or visually represents their findings.

Debrief Prompts

1. How did this exercise make you feel?
2. What did you notice while doing the activity? What was surprising?
3. How is institutional racism different from individual racism?

4. What are some of the things we can do to combat institutional racism?

Modifications and Extensions

A. **Examples of institutional racism.** Facilitators create a list of well-researched facts that illustrate institutional racism in five institutions: criminal justice, employment, housing, health, and education. Divide participants into five groups and assign each an institution. Ask them to read their section of facts and pick out and discuss with their group any information they find surprising, concerning, or enlightening. Encourage them to do supplemental research on their electronic devices related to the facts provided. Ask each group to share out their learnings and findings.

B. **Sort the data.** Facilitators create a list of well-researched facts that illustrate institutional racism in five institutions: criminal justice, employment, housing, health, and education. Cut all of the data points into individual pieces of paper, mix them up, and pass them out to the group so that every person has a similar number of facts. Put large sheets of paper on the floor or wall with a different institution clearly marked on each poster. Ask participants to sort the facts into different institutions.

C. **Film screening.** Screen one of the following and debrief.

1. We Need to Talk About an Injustice. TED Talk, Bryan Stevenson: www.ted.com/talks/bryan_stevenson_we_need_to_talk_about_an_injustice

2. Episode 3: The House We Live In. California New Reel, *Race: The Power of an Illusion*: www.newsreel.org/nav/title.asp?tc=CN0149

Debrief Prompts:

1. How did you feel watching this?
2. What new information did you learn?
3. How does this information connect to your own life?
4. What is something you want to do after watching this film?

Closing

Select a closing from Appendix C.

LESSON 10: CAUCUS GROUPS AND FISHBOWLS

Goals

- Learn about the dynamics of intra-group relationships—relationships between people from the same racial identity group
- Explore questions related to race and racism within own racial group

Introductory Narrative

In this lesson, you will have a unique opportunity to grapple with questions of race and racism with people from your own racial group. Some of you may think that dividing into race-based caucus groups is contradictory to the larger purpose of learning across difference and may be feeling uncomfortable with the idea of breaking up. However, we have found that providing time for People of Color to talk to each other without White people in the room, and for White people to talk to other White people without People of Color in the room, is important for social justice work for a few reasons.

First, because of the ways that privilege and oppression work, White people and People of Color are impacted differently by race and racism. As a result, these two groups actually have somewhat different needs when it comes to learning how best to work toward equity and justice. Dividing into caucus groups allows space for each group to focus on what they need.

Second, although we have been working to build a brave space, we are often more cautious when talking about race in mixed settings. Breaking into caucus groups allows us to let our guard down a bit more and focus on our own learning and growth without having to worry so much about saying something offensive or triggering to the other group.

Finally, while we have worked hard to avoid dynamics in which the People of Color in the group are seen as the "teachers" when it comes to race, it is likely that we at times failed to achieve this goal. Breaking into caucus groups allows White people to take responsibility for their own racial learning without emotionally burdening People of Color.

Facilitation Consideration

This exercise is riskier than others in the curriculum. Facilitators working with high school students especially may want to weigh the pros and cons of such an activity before moving forward.

ACTIVITY 10.1: CAUCUS GROUPS

Before the lesson begins, facilitators should identify an appropriate space for this activity. Facilitators should also decide in advance what the caucus groups will be based on the racial makeup of their group. For example, you may decide to host three groups: White, People of Color, and multi- or biracial. If there are at least three people from a specific racial group, facilitators could divide the group even further. For example, White, Asian, Black, biracial (Black and White), biracial (Asian and White). If there are multiple participants who identify as multi- or biracial, it important to form a group for them rather than asking those individuals to choose between their racial identities.

Invite participants to select the group they feel they most belong to. While facilitators should generally allow participants to organize themselves as they see fit within the options available, they should not allow White participants to join the groups of People of Color or vice versa.

Groups should meet in separate rooms. If one group needs to stay in the original room, it is best practice to let People of Color stay and ask White participants to move as a way of interrupting racial hierarchies.

Facilitators should also go to the group they identify with racially. If there are enough facilitators from the appropriate racial backgrounds for each group, they can help focus the dialogue. Otherwise, facilitators can give group members a list of prompt questions and let them discuss independently or float back and forth between groups. Be clear in telling groups how much time they will have in their caucus groups so that they can be mindful during their discussion, especially if there will not be a facilitator with them. We suggest a *minimum* of 30 minutes.

Caucus Prompts

1. How does it feel to be identified as a member of this group?
2. How do you feel about dividing up into caucus groups?
3. What messages did you receive about being a member of this group at home/school/worship centers/media?
4. What has the impact of that socialization been on your life? Consider costs and benefits.
5. What do you like about being a member of this group? If that is a difficult question, share why.
6. Are there questions you would like to ask people in this group about what it is like to be a member of this group?
7. When have you felt good or proud about being a member of this group?
8. What is easy or difficult about being a member of this group?

9. How can we use our common and different experiences and awareness to resist or challenge systems of oppression?
10. What do you wish members of the other group(s) knew about your group?
11. How has this caucus group experience influenced the way you think about your own identity and the other identity groups?

Five minutes before the end of the caucus group, invite participants to free-write their reactions to the discussion.

ACTIVITY 10.2: FISHBOWL

After the caucus groups, all group members return to the common space, and enter into a "fishbowl." Arrange the chairs in the room in two concentric circles, one inside the other, with enough chairs in the middle section for all of the members of the first group to sit and enough chairs in the outside circle for the rest of the participants. Using the prompts below, engage the group in the center circle to speak with one another while the outside group(s) listen to them talk. After the inside circle has finished sharing, ask members of the outer circle to verbally acknowledge one thing they heard from the inner circle. They should not ask questions or make further comments.

After the first group has gone, the other caucus group(s) should repeat the same exercise. It is a good idea to select the group with more power to go first in the fishbowl, allowing the group with less power to have the "final word." In other words, the White group should go first, and the People of Color group should go second.

If you plan to do the fishbowl activity following the caucus groups, you should ask that each caucus group decide in advance what they would like to share with the full group. Discuss the guidelines "take the learning, leave the stories" and "speak from your own experience" to remind the groups of the importance of confidentiality and that while they may share their own learning and their own personal stories and reflections, they should not share someone else's story or experience. You should also make a point to let the groups of People of Color especially know that they should not feel compelled to share. It is not the responsibility of People of Color to teach White people about race. If they would prefer not to share what they took away from their caucus discussions, that is acceptable.

Debrief Prompts

1. What was easy/hard about meeting in caucus groups?
2. What are some of the highlights of your caucus group conversation that you would like to share with the other group(s)?

3. Is there anything additional you would also want to share with your group or the other group?

Overall Debrief Prompts

1. How did it feel to participate in this activity?
2. What was it like to be in the inner circle? Outer circle?
3. What did you learn from this activity?

Closing

Select a closing from Appendix C.

LESSON 11: HOT TOPICS

Goals

Participants will:

- Examine how socializations impact feelings, beliefs, thoughts, and actions
- Discuss current topics and events related to issues of race and racism
- Learn how to stay in dialogue even when perspectives differ, and conflicts emerge
- Learn how to use conflict to deepen learning

Introductory Narrative

In this lesson, we are inviting you to engage in dialogue about pressing issues of race and racism that are being hotly debated in our society. Unlike the other dialogue sessions, this lesson is not structured around predetermined activities, videos, or handouts. Instead, it is an opportunity to practice the kind of dialogue you are most likely to have in your life outside of this group. These are also the kinds of conversations that we tend to avoid out of concern that they will lead to conflict. However, as we've learned in our time together, conflict can be productive and can lead to growth and greater understanding. During this lesson it will be especially important to remember the group norms.

Facilitation Considerations

This lesson is often a more difficult facilitation experience because of its unpredictable nature. Facilitators should remember to use all of the tips and suggestions provided in this book related to asking strong questions, affirming people's perspectives, and remembering the larger goals of dialogue, especially adding to the common pool of knowledge and exploring how to build bridges across difference. Like the Caucus Group and Fishbowl lessons, we advise high school teachers to do this lesson with caution.

ACTIVITY 11.1: HOT TOPIC DIALOGUE

Prior to engaging in this lesson, facilitators should invite participants to contribute ideas for the "hot topics" session related to issues of race and racism. Facilitators should provide examples of hot topics such as: interracial relationships, affirmative action, the N-word, #BlackLivesMatter, the crack cocaine vs. opioid crisis, free speech on campus, the Indigenous water protectors, or immigration. Facilitators should review suggestions from participants in advance of the session and consider themes that emerge from the participant ideas. We encourage facilitators to select topics that deal with both interpersonal and institutional racism. They should be topics that lend themselves to learning across different racial groups within the context we have established in dialogue. Facilitators should plan to do some background research so they can provide accurate data and information if necessary.

Consider the amount of time you will have to engage in this dialogue when choosing how many topics to address. It is generally a good idea to have at least two topics prepared for discussion. On the day of the session, introduce the chosen topic(s) and invite participants to freely dialogue while being mindful of the guidelines.

Debrief Prompts

1. How are we doing as a group?
2. Were you forthcoming today?
3. What are some ways we have used dialogic skills?
4. What are some ways we have failed to use those skills?
5. What are some challenges you are experiencing?
6. How did your differing social identities impact your participation today?
7. Were there particular tensions present today that have not been present in the past?
8. Do you have ideas about moving forward either individually or as a group?

Closing

Make sure you offer participants an opportunity to share their feelings either within the group or anonymously in a written response. Choose a closing from Appendix C.

LESSON 12: ALLYHOOD I—INTERRUPTING INDIVIDUAL RACISM

Goals

Participants will:

- Understand what it means to be an aspiring ally
- Practice strategies to interrupt racist jokes, biased comments, and microaggressions

Introductory Narrative

This lesson is designed to help you think about concrete actions you can take to act as an ally by interrupting racist comments and microaggressions.

Social Justice Concept: Ally

Ask participants to brainstorm what they think being an "ally" means in relation to racism. After hearing their responses, introduce the term *ally* from Appendix A.

"Ally" is a verb, as well as a noun. The test of whether or not one is an ally is whether or not you are standing up to injustice in any given moment in a way that the group you are acting as an ally to feels is productive. Having an intellectual commitment to justice is not enough. Allies are people who lend their support and resources, interrupt oppression when they see it, and speak up, even when it is difficult. While you might act as an ally in one moment or on one day, you could easily fail to do so at another. Moreover, while you may think of yourself as an ally, it is the right of the oppressed group to determine who is and is not acting as an ally to them. For these reasons, we often recommend that people use the term "aspiring ally" which implies that they are striving toward allyhood, rather than claiming they have arrived. "Aspiring ally" recognizes that the work of being an ally is lifelong.

Facilitator Consideration

Although the term "ally" is commonly used to describe the work of privileged groups, People of Color can also be allies to other racial and ethnic groups. For example, there are many opportunities in which a Black person can be an ally to someone who is Latinx, or an Asian person can be an ally to someone who is Black.

ACTIVITY 12.1: ALLY BRAINSTORMING

Divide participants into pairs or small groups and ask them to share a time when they experienced someone acting as an ally to them. Their example might not be related to issues of race. Instead, it can be any time someone stood up for them. Use the following prompts to guide the conversations:

1. What did the other person do that made them a good ally?
2. How did other people respond to your ally's actions?
3. What do you think you can learn from their example?

Ask groups to share out their reflections and, as a large group, create a list of characteristics of being a good ally.

Debrief Prompts

1. How did it feel to do this activity?
2. What obstacles might you face in trying to be an ally? How can you overcome these obstacles?

Modification and Extension

Five tips for being an ally. As a supplement to the list the group developed, share with participants the following video which offers five tips for being a good ally: understand your privilege; listen and do your homework; speak up, not over; apologize when you make a mistake; remember, ally is a verb.

- 5 Tips for Being an Ally. Franchesca Ramsey: www.youtube.com/watch?v=_dg86g-QlM0

Debrief Prompts

1. What additional ideas did Franchesca offer?
2. What will be hard for you to do? What do you think will be easy to do?

ACTIVITY 12.2: INTERRUPTING RACIST JOKES

Narrative

We tend to think about humor as innocuous. However, over the years of doing this work, we have found that humor is one of the most pervasive ways that people couch racist (sexist, classist, homophobic, etc.) ideas in acceptable discourse. Humor often reinforces oppression and discrimination. Learning how to interrupt problematic jokes is one important step in being an ally. Share the following video with participants:

- How Do You Handle a Racist Joke? MTV News, *Decoded*, Franchesca Ramsey: www.youtube.com/watch?v=Bg1aTLsS69Y

At the conclusion of the video, ask participants to reflect on how they have responded to offensive jokes in the past. Dialogue about strategies to use when hearing racist jokes. Some concrete suggestions for responses to racist jokes include: sarcasm, silence, play dumb, use PALS (see Lesson 7 above), and, our favorite, be honest and direct about the offense.

Divide participants into pairs and give them time to practice various strategies with their partner. Invite each pair to share out a specific strategy they would like to employ the next time they hear a racist or discriminatory sentiment masquerading as a joke.

Debrief Prompts

1. How did it feel to do this activity?
2. Where do you most witness racist humor in your life?
3. What would it take for you to interrupt these comments when you hear them?

ACTIVITY 12.3: THE HISTORY OF THE N-WORD

Like racist jokes, the N-word is ubiquitous and rarely discussed in racially mixed company. To begin this dialogue, tell participants that they should use the term "N-word" rather than using the slur to make sure that the space is as safe as possible for all participants. Note that although the word is often used in hip-hop and is perhaps even casually used by many in the group or larger community, the word is inextricably linked with violence and brutality against Black people.

Share one of the following videos which explore the historical roots of the N-word with participants:

1. The N-Word Through History. *The Washington Post:* www.youtube.com/watch?v=9Yv2BnfbUFs
2. Where Did the N-Word Come From? CNN: www.youtube.com/watch?v=OFnF1c2Tbfw

Debrief Prompts

1. What did it feel like to watch this video?
2. What new information did you learn?

Facilitator Considerations

The above videos use the full version of the N-word and may be triggering to participants. Facilitators should warn participants in advance about the content. If facilitators or participants feel the videos will be too triggering for participants, you can simply discuss some of the history of the word. If you take this approach, be cautious not to say the word.

ACTIVITY 12.4: WHO CAN SAY THE N-WORD?

Share with participants that as a rule it is never okay for White people to use the N-word, even when singing or rapping along to a song. However, there still remains debate among Black scholars and community members about whether or not it should be used within the Black community. Some argue that because of the word's history even Black people should never use it. Others feel that like many words that have been used as slurs against marginalized groups, the N-word has been reclaimed by Black people in ways that are empowering. Share the following video with participants and debrief:

- When Every Word Doesn't Belong to Everyone. Ta-Nehisi Coates: www.youtube.com/watch?v=QO15S3WC9pg

Debrief Prompts

1. Can you think of words that you can use within your group but that would be inappropriate for another group to use?
2. When have you wondered about whether using the N-word was appropriate?
3. What is something you can do if you hear someone using the N-word? How do the social identities of the person saying the word matter? How do your social identities matter?

Modifications and Extensions

A. **"What the N-Word Feels Like."** Share the following additional video with participants which explores how some Black people feel when they are called the N-word by White perpetrators and debrief.

- "What the N-Word Feels Like." BuzzFeedYellow: www.youtube. com/watch?v=qaqBLZZd6Ns

Debrief Prompts

1. What did it feel like to watch this video?
2. What reflections do you have about what was shared?
3. What could you do differently as a result of what you have learned?

B. **Are other slurs racist?** Share the following additional video with participants and debrief.

- Are Cracker, White Trash, & Redneck Racist? MTV News, *Decoded*, Franchesca Ramsey: www.youtube.com/watch?v=wIIt-gTHWOY

Debrief Prompts

1. What did it feel like to watch this video?
2. What new information did you learn?
3. What could you do differently as a result of what you have learned?

Skill Practice: PALS

After a very intense series of activities around allyhood, it is useful to reintroduce PALS and have participants practice it again (see Lesson 7).

Modifications and Extensions

A. **Speed dating.** This exercise helps participants reflect on what they have learned over the course of the dialogue series. In advance of this activity select discussion prompts and write them on individual cards (see examples below). The number of discussion prompts needed will depend on the size of your group.

Instruct participants to stand in two lines facing each other. Give each pair one of the prompts. Give each pair 2 minutes to respond to their prompt—1 minute for each person to share while their partner listens. In this activity, participants should refrain from interrupting or asking questions when their partner is sharing. After they have finished sharing, instruct everyone to leave their prompt where it is, and have each line move to the right. Every person should now be matched with a new partner and a new prompt. Repeat the exercise until everyone has answered all of the prompts.

Sample Prompts

- How does racism hurt you?
- What is one privilege you have?
- What is one disadvantage you have?
- What is something you wish people knew about you?
- If there was one thing you could to improve our society, what would it be?
- When you think back on your own relatives, who gives you the greatest sense of hope?
- Who inspires you to be a better person?
- Share a time when you witnessed racism.
- Share a time when you were hyperaware of you own race.
- Share a time when someone defended you when another person said something disparaging about one of your identities.
- Share a time when you interrupted racism.
- What is the most significant thing you have learned so far in our dialogue sessions?

B. Trade Cards. Alternatively, facilitators could hand out blank 3x5 cards and let each participant write their own question related to the content of the dialogue series. Facilitators then collect all of the cards, quickly check to make sure the questions are appropriate, shuffle them, and pass them back out. It is a good idea for the facilitator to have a few cards they made in case some of the questions submitted are inappropriate. Instruct every person to find a partner, read their question, and let their partner answer. The pairs should then trade cards and go find another partner. Repeat for as much time as you have.

Closing

Select a closing from Appendix C.

LESSON 13: ALLYHOOD II—HOW TO BE AN ASPIRING ALLY

Goals

Participants will:

- Continue to develop their identity as an ally with the skills to respond to injustice
- Learn about their spheres of influence
- Develop a toolbox for responding to injustice

Introductory Narrative

This lesson is designed to help you develop concrete skills for acting as an ally in a variety of different areas.

ACTIVITY 13.1: ASPIRING ALLY

Remind participants to think of the term "ally" as an action verb. Ask participants to brainstorm attributes of an aspiring ally in pairs, small groups, or the large group. Share the following list as a supplement to what participants brainstorm.

An Aspiring Ally:

- Is aware of own social identities
- Learns about other groups' experiences
- Listens to and respects the perspectives of others
- Acknowledges and works to eliminate privilege and ensures others are also treated justly
- Is aware of own implicit biases and knows it is a lifelong process to unlearn them
- Is willing to take risks, try new behaviors, and act in spite of fear
- Engages in self-care
- Acts against social injustice out of understanding that it is in all of our interest to do so, including those of us who are privileged
- Is willing to make mistakes and learn from them
- Is willing to be confronted about own problematic behaviors and change
- Is committed to taking action against social injustice in spheres of influence
- Understands the importance of being on a learning edge
- Believes they can make a difference by acting and speaking out
- Supports other allies and does not compete to be the best

Figure 11.11. Spheres of Influence

Illustration by Tori Griffin.

Social Justice Concept: Spheres of Influence

Introduce the following term from Appendix A and introduce Figure 11.11. Talk though each sphere of influence.

• Spheres of Influence

ACTIVITY 13.2: SPHERES OF INFLUENCE

This activity is designed to assist participants in thinking more deeply about how they can be change agents in different arenas in their lives. Prior to the session, post four large poster-sized sticky notes around the room with the following labels: "1st Sphere—Self," "2nd Sphere—Friends and family," "3rd Sphere—Local community," "4th Sphere—Larger community/world." Invite participants to talk about each sphere of influence and give examples from their own lives.

Give each participant 4–8 small sticky notes and invite them to write 1, 2, 3, 4 on the top of four different sticky notes. Ask participants to write at least one action that they could take for each of the four spheres of influence on the appropriate sticky note. Participants then post the appropriate small sticky notes on the posters.

Once everyone has posted their notes, invite the group to do a gallery walk in which they silently walk around and read everyone's ideas, or divide them into four groups and ask them to organize the ideas presented in their particular sphere into categories. Have each group share out their findings to the larger group.

Debrief Prompts

1. Which of these actions are the easiest to do? Which are the hardest?
2. Which do you think is most important to do?

3. What will be the hardest part about taking a stand?
4. What if other people laugh at you or get angry at you?
5. How will it feel to notice an oppressive comment but not do anything?
6. Which action will you try today?

Facilitators should remind participants that interrupting racism is really hard and that it takes a lot of courage and practice. The actions they have brainstormed are their "Allyhood Tool Box." They should plan to reference this toolbox and draw on the ideas they came up with when confronting oppression in their lives. Remind participants that each small action they take is important in dismantling systems that have been in place long before any of us were born.

After this session, facilitators should type up the sticky notes into one cohesive document labeled "Allyhood Tool Box" and print it to share with the group in the final session.

Closing

Select a closing from Appendix C.

LESSON 14: ADJOURNING THE DIALOGUE

Goal

Participants will:

- Bring closure to the dialogue experience

Introductory Narrative

We are now in the "adjourning" phase of group development. The focus of this session is to share our learning and appreciation with each other. You all have done a lot of hard work together! Although this is our final session, this is only the beginning of work that we hope will last for the rest of your life. We expect you to continue thinking deeply about and engaging in dialogue and action around racism.

Moreover, as a group, there are a number of ways you can continue to support one another. Many past groups have found the work together so intense and valuable that they do not want to adjourn (what a great problem to have!) and seek other ways to remain in touch. We have had dialogue groups that develop social media platforms to stay connected after the group work has ended, attend movies together, or continue to meet informally after the dialogue work is over.

Facilitation Considerations

We encourage you to spend a significant amount of time on closing the dialogues. We offer several activities below to consider in your closing session, but we know the choice of closing is specific to every group and should be designed by the facilitators who are most familiar with the group. We suggest that facilitators share their own experience with the group and let the participants know how meaningful the work has been for them.

Some facilitators and groups may also want to engage in sharing their learning with their larger community by way of adjourning. When we run multiple dialogues in the same school, district, or organization simultaneously, we have found it rewarding to bring the various facilitators and participants together in a final celebration. It allows different dialogue groups to see that they are not alone in doing this hard work, and it continues to stimulate learning. Other options involve sharing the learning that took place in dialogue with a broader audience beyond dialogue participants. Some possibilities for this are listed below.

As a final note, in our experience, facilitators often wonder if they have really gotten through to participants and sometimes doubt the effectiveness of their work. Remember, as facilitators "we are planting seeds." We may not see the blossoms from our seeds because for some participants it may take years for the dialogue material to germinate, but we have faith that this work is vital, and we know it changes lives.

ACTIVITY 14.1: DIALOGUE GROUP CLOSING

Engage the group in one or more of the following adjourning activities.

A. **Closing round.** Invite participants to go around the circle and share their most memorable moment in dialogue or the most important lesson they think they will take away from the dialogue experience.

B. **Affirming notes.** Pass out stacks of 3 x 5 cards and an envelope to each group member. Ask each person to write something affirming about every other participant in the group. Give the group quiet time to reflect on how each group member impacted them. When participants are finished writing, each person should deliver their notes to the envelope of the participants for whom they are written. Participants all leave with an envelope full of affirmations. Many participants have reported back that they save those notes for years to come and find inspiration and encouragement to continue the work as they move beyond the group. It is a nice touch to play music and serve snacks during this exercise.

C. **Affirming posters.** Bring one large, colorful poster board for each member of the group. Invite group members to pick a poster and write their name at the top. Tape all of the posters to the walls or lay them on the floor. Give each participant a marker and invite them to walk around the room and write affirmations on each of their dialogue partners' posters. At the end of the session, each participant has a poster they can hang with affirmations about their contributions to the group. Some participants have let us know that they hang their posters in places that continue to inspire them. Again, it is a nice touch to play music and serve snacks during this exercise.

ACTIVITY 14.2: COMMUNITY SHARING

Engage the group in one or more of the following adjourning activities.

A. **Culminating project gallery.** At the high school level, we incorporate the production of a final project into many of our lesson plans throughout the dialogue sessions. Each class collaborates on identifying an important theme from the dialogue sessions and creates something that can be used to educate others about their new learning. Some of the projects have included: video productions of examples of microaggressions and responses to microaggressions; games designed to teach others about institutional racism; rap songs; models of the privilege walk in various forms; and a class quilt with individual squares representing different lessons from the series.

Each of the dialogue groups' final prompts are displayed in a common area in the high school, and everyone in the school community (including parents, school board members, administrators, students, teachers) is invited to come to a lunchtime or evening opening of the gallery. Participants are asked to share their projects with invited guests and to view one another's projects.

B. **Public celebration.** At the closing of our dialogue series at the university level, we hold a final reception for all participants and facilitators and invite specific university administrators and supporters of the the dialogue program to come. We keep it short (no more than 90 minutes) and we invite each dialogue group to select one or two participants to speak publicly about their learning experience during the dialogue. We also present each participant and facilitator with a certificate of completion and a small token (a lapel pin for example) to carry forward as a gift from the dialogue team. We have found that this closing exercise allows separate dialogue groups that have been meeting simultaneously over the course of the semester to witness the larger community they belong to, and to share their learning outcomes with one another. It is invariably a very moving ceremony.

Conclusion

As we type the final words and edit this book for what feels like the thousandth time, our country has been rocked by an unprecedented time of hate and terror. Our country is in crisis. In Kentucky, two Black people were shot by a White man spewing racist vitriol, yet another extrajudicial shooting of Black people that has stained our country across centuries. Across the country 14 people and organizations who opposed President Trump's policies were sent pipe bombs. In Pittsburgh, 11 Jewish people who were praying during Shabbat services were gunned down by a White man shouting anti-Semitic sentiments. On our southern border, tear gas was lobbed by government officials at children and families seeking asylum in the United States. Across the globe, New Zealand was rocked by a horrific hate crime against its Muslim community. Any semblance of civil discourse seems absent from the public domain. And so, this book and our work training people about how to dialogue with civility across difference, feel all the more urgent. We firmly believe that it is hard to hate someone whose story you know.

We attempted to share the myriad of facilitation tools we have developed over decades of trial and error while building upon the vital work of those who have come before us. Writing this book gave us an opportunity to think together deeply about some things we have erroneously assumed, or incorrectly analyzed. We hope that within these pages our readers find the courage and the love—as well as the tools—to begin a conversation about race. Here are some of our final thoughts about race dialogues.

If you wait until you think you know everything about facilitation, or about race, you will never start. That does not mean that you should dive in haphazardly, but we believe that with the information contained in these pages, our readers will have a pretty good launching pad. We presented PALS—a way to de-escalate conflict, whether it occurs at the Thanksgiving table or in classrooms or international conflict. We also gave you some useful advice about how to apologize, which we find is helpful in nearly everything we do, whether it has to do with race dialogues or something altogether different. A good apology is life-giving. It is always good to say "I am sorry" when you mean it.

We believe that the only way to get out of this mess we are in—growing hate crimes, incivility, and mounting distrust—is to start vital conversations with people who think differently than we do, and to listen deeply, generously, and curiously. Whether you are sitting at the dinner table with people you love, or you are trying to build understanding across racial differences in your places of work, or in your city, there are tools contained in these pages that will help. Believe that people are doing their best. Listen wholeheartedly to their stories. Be open to changing your own mind. Be vulnerable and share your truth with people with whom you disagree. Add to the common pool of knowledge. This is the way we create real change, one conversation at a time.

Do not be discouraged if you do not see immediate change. We tell our participants that this work takes lifetimes. We are planting seeds. Sometimes we are lucky enough to see our seeds germinate and blossom. Mostly, we do not. But it is still important to have these conversations. We cannot tell you the number of times we have worried that we have not gotten through to one of our students or dialogue participants, and how, weeks, months, or years later they come back to us and share their transformation. Each of us, Sheri, Donna, and Shayla, is building on the work of previous generations, and we do this work for future generations. We likely will not live to see the day of racial justice in our country, but we believe that we are doing our small part in making that day a possibility.

And here are our final words of wisdom: Once you start doing this hard work of listening deeply enough to be changed by what you hear, and guiding others in dialogues about race, you will find joy in the process. Even when there are unthinkable acts of injustice happening outside your door, as there have been since our country was founded, this work brings deep meaning to our lives. It brings a sense of community and belonging. It aligns with our values. Through this work, we have found friendship, compassion, awareness, and we have become more fully human. No matter how painful dialoguing about race with folks who see the world in radically different ways can be, ultimately, it fills us with fierce hope. And hope is in short supply these days. So, expect joy as you forge your own path leaning in to dialogue across difference. There are boundless dialogic opportunities waiting for you to make them happen. Build human connection. Dig in.

Social Justice Concepts

Though this is not a complete list of social justice concepts or terminology, these are some useful terms that you might provide participants so everyone has a common understanding of the language you are using.

Ally: A member of one or more privileged social identity groups (groups with unearned advantage) who uses social power to take a stand against social injustice directed at marginalized groups (e.g., White people who speak out against racism, men who are anti-sexist). Some people prefer the terms "Accomplice" or "Aspiring Ally."

Brave Space: A space where we challenge ourselves to get out of our comfort zone, make mistakes, be vulnerable, and learn new things. Brave space occurs when we are on our learning edge. In this space, conflict may emerge but is viewed as a learning opportunity.

Dialogue: A form of face-to-face communication between two or more people that is directed toward common understanding and adding to the common pool of knowledge.

Discrimination: The unequal treatment of people of various social identity groups, often on the basis of prejudice.

Diversity: A variety of people, voices, attributes, identities, and ideas. Diversity is often used as code language for talking about People of Color. For example, people often describe an all-Black school as a "diverse" school—a factually inaccurate statement. When true diversity is present there is representation of people from an array of different backgrounds. While diversity can be a laudable goal, it alone does not lead to more equity or justice. The presence of diversity does not guarantee that everyone is included, safe, or empowered.

Equality: When everyone is given exactly the same thing or treated in exactly the same way. While there are times when it may be useful to treat people equally, equality often falsely assumes that everyone is the same and has the same needs. Equality of inputs does not lead to equality of outcomes.

Equity: When everyone gets what they need. Equity strives to attain more equal outcomes which will often require differences in inputs. For example, Deaf students will likely need an interpreter and/or an FM system to do as well as hearing students in the same classroom.

Facilitator: A trained or experienced individual who provides structure, guides conversation, maintains group norms, and leads reflection opportunities for dialogue groups. Can be alone or in pairs or triads.

Generous Listening: A form of listening when all of our attention is focused on the speaker. We do not interject our own stories or concern ourselves with what we will say next. Instead, we are authentically curious and ask lots of questions such as, "Can you say more about that?" or "I'm curious about what you said. Keep talking" or "What is important to you?" or "Could you tell me more about why you think that way?"

Global Listening: When the listener is aware of everything in the room, including the energy and the emotions of the participants. This level of listening is a useful skill for teachers, group leaders, and facilitators.

Hot Button Issue: Something that an individual says or does that makes us feel offended, threatened, stereotyped, discounted, or attacked. In social justice work, we often use "Trigger" synonymously with "Hot Button."

Implicit Bias: Attitudes or stereotypes that affect our understanding, actions, and decisions in an unconscious manner. Implicit biases are activated involuntarily and without our awareness or control. They are not always accessible through introspection. They are often talked about in relations to social identities such as race, class, gender, or sexual orientation. Also commonly referred to as "Unconscious Bias." Implicit bias is one facet of racism at the individual level.

Inclusion: When all people, from a range of diverse backgrounds, feel respected, heard, valued, and understood—especially those from marginalized groups.

Individual Racism: Beliefs, attitudes, feelings, and values of individuals that support or perpetuate racism. For example, the belief that White people are naturally better at math than Latinos or the belief that Black men are inherently more dangerous than White men. Individual racism can occur at both an unconscious and conscious level, Unconscious bias is also known as "Implicit Bias."

Institutional Racism: Policies, rules, laws, procedures, practices and systems enacted by organizations and social institutions that disadvantage People of Color and advantage White people. Examples include school rules that are designed in line with White cultural norms and the differences in sentencing for Black and White drug offenders.

Internal Listening: Listening in a way that is focused on your own inner voice. During this form of listening, you are primarily preparing for a response, opinions, stories, or judgements. Some examples of internal listening: "I had an experience just like that"or "That reminds me of when I did X."

Interpersonal Racism: Actions, behaviors, and language that support or perpetuate racism. When people typically talk about racism, they are referring to the interpersonal level—how an individual treats other people across race. Examples include using racial slurs, crossing the street if a person of color is walking toward you, or punishing more harshly a student of color who misbehaves in class than a White student.

Intersectionality: A term used in reference to experiences of oppression. It is the idea that every individual has multiple social group identities which intersect and can lead to unique experiences of oppression. For example, the experience of being a Black woman is different than that of being a Black man or a woman of a different racial background. Moreover, Black women can experience specific forms of discrimination that Black men and women of other racial backgrounds do not. Intersectionality holds that there is no universal experience of members of any one social identity group.

Learning Edge: See "Brave Space."

Marginalized Groups: Groups denied access to power or privilege. Also known as "Oppressed Groups."

Microaggressions: Everyday encounters of subtle discrimination that people of various marginalized identities experience throughout their lives. These may be perpetrated intentionally or unintentionally. In both cases they communicate hostile, derogatory, or negative ideas about the social identity group of the person targeted.

Oppression: Unearned disadvantage. The denial of access to power or privilege. See "Marginalized Groups."

Prejudice: A judgment or opinion that is formed on insufficient grounds before facts are known or in disregard of facts. Prejudice is a preconceived opinion that is not based on reason.

Privilege: A special right or advantage available only to a specific group of people. Privilege grants advantages, favors, opportunities, resources, and benefits to members of groups with more power at the expense of groups with less power. These advantages are unearned, often invisible, and they are not available to groups with less power.

Race: A social construct that artificially divides people into distinct groups based on historical geography and perceived differences in physical appearance. Scientists agree that there is no biological or genetic basis for racial categories.

Racism: A system of advantages based on race that benefits White people and disadvantages People of Color.

Social Group Identity: Identities that indicate that you belong to a broader social group that grants or denies you access to power and privilege. Often, though not always, these group identities are things you are born with or that are immutable. Social group identities affect the opportunities you have access to, the ways you are expected to behave, the official and unofficial rules you must follow, the resources available to you, and the way you are treated in our society. In this way, they are different than personal identities (such as being a person who really loves pie). Common social identities include race, gender, sexual orientation, social class, and ability. Also known as "Social Identities" or "Social Identity Groups."

Social Justice: The dismantling of systems of privilege and oppression at the individual, interpersonal, and institutional levels to create a society that is diverse, equitable, and inclusive.

Socialization: The formal and informal rules about how the world works that shape what we believe and how we behave, passed down through our interactions with family, friends, school, places of worship, and other people and institutions.

Stereotype: An exaggerated or distorted belief about a group of people that systematically lumps people together and refuses to acknowledge differences among group members.

Trigger: See "Hot Button Issue."

Icebreakers/Community Builders

1. Culture box: Facilitators can describe the activity in the following manner: Please prepare a culture box and bring it with you. A culture box contains at least three physical objects that represent important parts of your life story, especially as related to your social identities. Social identities include, for example, race, gender, ethnicity, age, ability status, religion, sexual orientation, socioeconomic class, job status, nationality, and so forth. Please focus on whatever social identities you feel are most important to your personal story, but make sure *at least one* of your objects reflects your experiences with your racial identity. The goal of the box is to help others gain a *deep* understanding of some of the experiences that have made you who you are, including joyous experiences and/or difficult struggles that you have related to your identities. Please let the culture box become a way for your friends and colleagues to get to know you even more fully and richly. Be creative, take prudent risks to tell your story deeply, but please do not feel any pressure to reveal anything you do not wish.

Have each person share one thing from their culture box and explain why they chose it and what meaning it has for them.

2. History of your name: Explain the origins and story of your name. Everyone go around the circle and share. Give each person a specific amount of time. If using in later sessions, consider asking participants to reflect on how their racial identity matters when it comes to their name, and how their name has given them advantage or disadvantage in a racist system.

3. Roses and thorns:

- Something good that happened to me this week is . . .
- Something bad that happened to me this week is . . .

4. Speed dating: Arrange participants at long tables with one group facing the other. They may stand and face one another as well. Give them one minute each to answer the question written on an index card in front of them. Each participant gets 1 minute, then everyone moves clockwise one seat to talk to a different person about the next question.

The following questions are some ideas for the index cards:

1. Where are you from? (not in the sense of a single place, but more broadly)
2. What is the difference in this world that you want to make?
3. What are you really good at?
4. What are your passions and how do use them in your everyday life?
5. What is the theme song for your life?
6. What do you hope to get out of the dialogue experience/class?
7. What are your worries/fears/concerns about the dialogue experience/ class?
9. Complete this idea: "This I Believe. . . ."
10. What is the most meaningful book you have read? Why?

5. Basket: Provide students with a basket and have each student write on a slip of paper or index card something that would surprise others about them. The students should not include their names. Have each participant choose a card. Then, during the course of the dialogue, give them time to ask questions of one another to try to identify whose card they have.

6. Hopes and fears: Hand out an index card to each participant and have them write their hopes for the dialogue on one side and the fears on the other side. Do not have them sign their names. Have facilitators collect everyone's cards and shuffle them and then pass them out again. Go around the circle reading everyone's fears first, and then hopes. Debrief this activity by asking students about what they noticed about shared fears and hopes? How did this activity make them feel?

7. Written testimonial: Using your own voice, compose a 2–3 page "testimonial" telling your social identity story. (One of your social identities should be related to the dialogue topic: race, gender, sexual orientation, etc.) Think of your testimonial as a mini-autobiography in which you reflect on your own identity and the ways in which that identity informed your development of self (i.e., how you think about yourself in the world). If you wish, you may also choose to write about a second identity (e.g., gender, sexual orientation, religion, ability, social class, etc.) because we are keenly aware of how all of our identities intersect. You will have 3 minutes to share your testimonial with the group. Please address the following questions:

1. When were you first aware of this identity?
2. What was the environment like in your family regarding this identity?
3. What was the environment like in other larger institutions you belong to regarding this identity (i.e., school, religious affiliation, community, work)?

4. How did this identity (and the other identity, if you have chosen to look at two) shape your experiences in larger institutions to which you belong (schools, religious, civic, social groups, clubs, etc.)? For example, how did being Black/White/Latinx/Asian/Native American impact your relationships in different institutions? How did being straight/queer/bi/gay impact your experience in different institutions?

5. How have the institutions to which you belong shaped the development of your racial identity? (i.e., what have your experiences at school/church/clubs/etc., taught you about your identity?)

6. Please consider how you have gained privilege or been disadvantaged by society based on your racial identity.

8. *Slide show testimonial:* Slide show. Invite participants to create a 10-slide testimonial in which they have 30 seconds to share 10 slides about themselves (or set a number based upon your available time). Ask them to bring in slides that relate to their racial identity, as well as other identities like gender, age, sexual orientation, ability, nationality, social class, religion, and any other identity they wish to share. This allows participants to see one another through an intersectional lens and helps build context and empathy as participants work through the dialogue together.

Closing Activities

1. **Closing word:** Go around the room and invite each participant to use one word to describe how they feel about today's lesson.
2. **Closing written or verbal prompt:** Have everyone take out paper and respond to a prompt. You may make this anonymous or not. You may prefer to have people do this verbally. Some possible prompts could include:
   - Write one new thing you have learned today.
   - Write one thing that would make you more comfortable in this space.
   - Name one thing that someone said that made you think about something in a new way.
   - Name one thing you would like to share with close family or friends from today's session.
   - How did dialogue cause you to reconsider any of your beliefs or actions?
   - Are there topics you would like to explore further as a result?
   - How could your facilitators do better next time?
   - How well did we as a group follow the group norms?
   - How did the activity help the dialogue?
   - Who is someone who helped you feel included in the dialogue?
   - Have you felt heard and understood?
   - Which perspectives were not represented today?
   - What can we talk about next time to further the dialogue?
   - Moving forward, what could/would you do differently as a result of what you are learning here?
   - What can we do as a group to share what we are learning?
   - What can we do before the next meeting to make sure we are prepared?
   - What is one thing you can do to interrupt racism as a result of today's lesson?
3. **Poster prompts:** Give each participant a sheet of paper or a poster and invite them to write 3–5 of their values in the center, along with their name. Then have other participants write down a time when they witnessed the participant living their values.

Modifications

A. Have participants reflect on one of the following prompts for each member of the dialogue: Something I learned from you; Something I admire about you; Something I will remember about you.
B. Rather than using a poster, you may hand out 3 x 5 cards and invite participants to write affirmations on the 3 x 5 cards for each participant in the dialogue.

Values List

Accomplishment	Expression	Peace
Accuracy	Family	Performance
Acknowledgement	Focus	Personal power
Adventure	Freedom	Privacy
Aesthetics	Friendship	Productivity
Ally	Fun	Prosperity
Altruism	Growth	Protection
Authenticity	Harmony	Purity
Authority	Health	Quiet
Beauty	Helping	Reason
Being	Hierarchy	Recognition
Belonging	Honesty	Religion
Body	Humor	Respect
Caring	Humility	Risk-taking
Choices	Inclusion	Romance
Collaboration	Independence	Safety
Community	Individuality	Self
Competition	Integrity	Selflessness
Connection	Intelligence	Service
Curiosity	Intimacy	Skepticism
Dignity	Joy	Solitude
Directness	Justice	Spirituality
Discipline	Leadership	Study
Difference	Learning	Success
Efficiency	Love	Tradition
Elegance	Nurturing	Trust
Emotion	Opportunity	Uniqueness
Empowerment	Orderliness	Vitality
Equality	Originality	Vulnerability
Equity	Partnership	Wealth
Excellence	Passion	Wholeheartedness
Exercise	Patriotism	

Facilitator Feedback Form

Session Date:

Co-facilitator(s):

Lesson Name/Week#:

1. Curriculum/session plan
   (a) What about the design/plan worked well and why? What did you leave out, if anything, and why?
   (b) What about the design/plan did not work well and why? What would you do differently to strengthen this session and why?
2. Dialogue group dynamics
   (a) Briefly describe the quality of interaction and engagement during this session:
   (b) What group dynamics need attention and why? What might help the group go where it needs to go?
   (c) How was it for you to co-facilitate this session? How well did you work together? What are some things you will need to address as you get ready for your upcoming session?
3. Your learning
   (a) Describe any issues that came up in dialogues, how they were dealt with, and what you would have done differently that could help in the future.
   (b) What is something new you have learned this week either about dialogue content or process?
   (c) What do you need from your co-facilitator to enhance the outcome next time?

Privilege Walk Statements

If, growing up, you could easily find dolls or action figures with skin color and hair like yours, take one step forward.

If English is not your first language, take one step backward.

If you grew up with parents of two (or more) different races, take one step backward.

If your ancestors were forced against their will to come to the American continent, step back.

If you have ever been called hurtful names because of your identity, step back.

If your family employed people in your house as cleaning ladies, gardeners, snow removal, step forward. If they were People of Color, take another step forward.

If you have been embarrassed or ashamed by your lack of material possessions, step back.

If most of your family work in careers requiring a college education, step forward.

If you ever tried to change your appearance, behavior, or speech to avoid being judged on the basis of your racial identity, step back.

If you have ever been confused with or mislabeled as a race other than your own, take one step backward.

If you frequently see members of your race depicted in healthy and positive ways in mass media, please take one step forward.

If you have ever been forced to check a single box (and not one labeled "Multiracial"), take one step backward.

If you are guaranteed to have your religious holidays off from school/work without request, please take one step forward.

If the history of your race was taught as a special month or special chapter in U.S. History classes, step back.

If you have never had to worry about accessibility for a disability, visible or invisible, step forward.

If people question why you segregate yourself with people of your identity in the cafeteria or other places, please take one step back.

If people consider your race to be exotic, please take one step back.

If you have ever thought you have been pulled over by the police because of your race, take one step back.

If there were more than 50 books in your house when you grew up, step forward.

If you or someone in your family never had to skip a meal or were hungry because there was not enough money to buy food when you were growing up, step forward.

If one of your parents stayed home by choice, step forward.

If you have ever had difficulty finding hair or body products in a supermarket, take one step backwards.

If your parents encouraged you to attend college, step forward.

If you can buy "flesh-toned" bandages and/or nude stockings that match your skin tone, take one step forward.

If you rarely think about your race, take a step forward.

If you attended a summer camp or traveled overseas, step forward.

If you are a "hyphenated American," take a step back.

If because of your race or ethnicity, people assume you do not speak English, take a step back.

If you have ever been told you cannot do something because of your gender or sexuality, step back.

If you do not know anyone in jail or prison, please step forward.

If people have asked you or family members to see your legal documents, step back.

If you feel you do not have a lot of experience with race, take a step forward.

If anyone has ever asked if they could touch your hair because it was "different," take a step back.

If you or someone you love suffers from invisible disabilities (mental health issues or physical health issues), step back.

If one of your parents did not complete high school, step back.

If you have felt clerks watch you more than others in a store, step back.

If you have been offered a job or other opportunities because of your association or connection with a friend, family member, or mentor, step forward.

If you are more likely to be stopped by security guards in public places (schools, government offices, office buildings) because of your race, step back.

If you or people you care about worry about holding hands with someone they like in public, step back

If you could not go somewhere because you worried about the price of gas, step back.

If you have ever felt uncomfortable about a joke related to your identity, but not felt able to confront the situation, step back.

PASK: Facilitator Personal Assessment Chart

What are some personal resources that you bring to the Social Justice framework and some that you still need to develop in order to be an effective facilitator?

Directions: Under each PASK resource below, think about where you stand at this point in time and check the box on the right that best relates.	I feel comfortable with this and can be a resource to others	I have some resources but need more	I do not have this resource
(P) PASSION			
Energy for this work			
Can lead with my heart			
Deep personal reason for doing this work			
Commitment on personal/professional levels			
Can demonstrate compassion			
Ability to share feelings with others			
(A) PERSONAL AWARENESS			
Clarity about my identity(ies)			
Clarity about my values			
Internal emotional balance			
Secure about my status and privileges			
Recognize my blinders			
Awareness of the impact of my personal style on others			

	I feel comfortable with this and can be a resource to others	I have some resources but need more	I do not have this resource
Awareness of the impact of my social identity group memberships on myself			
Awareness of the impact of my social identity group memberships on others			
Awareness of my triggers			
(S) SKILLS			
Ability to work with people from different groups			
Ability to challenge others			
Ability to take risks			
Ability to discuss issues			
Ability to accept others' leadership			
Ability to utilize others' support			
Ability to give and receive feedback			
(K) KNOWLEDGE			
Knowledge of difference between prejudice, discrimination, and institutional isms			
Knowledge of my own groups(s) culture/history			
Knowledge of other group(s) culture/history			
Can recognize isms			
Knowledge of group process issues			
Knowledge of intergroup issues			
Knowledge of theories and terminology which inform and guide multicultural work			

Source: Adapted from Beale, R., Thompson, M., & Chesler, M. (2000). Training peer facilitators for intergroup dialogue leadership. In D. Schoem & S. Hurtado (Eds.), *Intergroup dialogue: Deliberative democracy in school, college, community and workplace* (pp. 227–246). Ann Arbor, MI: The University of Michigan Press.

The PALS Approach

The PALS approach is a methodology to use when you hear someone say something that may be hurtful or problematic to a specific group of people or yourself. The major objective of this approach is to stay connected with the person and speak your truth clearly.

PAUSE

- Pause/Halt/Stop/ Slow the conversation
- Things you can say: "Wait a second," "Excuse me," "Um, hold on a second . . . ."
- The goal here is to interrupt the flow of the conversation to let the speaker know that you are interested in learning more about something they just said. Use your own instinct and language, but the most important first step is pausing the conversation when you hear something that you think might need to be addressed further.

ACKNOWLEDGE/ASK

- Acknowledge what the person saying. This sends the message that you are trying to understand what they said, even if it is at odds with your own ideas. It shows respect/dignity/interest in collaboration/dialogue.
- Things you can say: "What I hear you saying is . . ." or "I appreciate your thinking on this."
- Ask for clarification, get curious, make sure you understand what the person said. Maybe you misunderstood the person. Keep your voice calm. Sometimes that is all you need to do.
- Things you can say: "I think you just referred to your friend as a Jewish American Princess." "Did you just say Black people are lazy?" "I think you said that gender defines who makes a good leader."

LISTEN

- Listen to what the person said. Reflect back to them what you think you heard them say. Connect. What really matters to the person? Treat the person with dignity.
- Though listening may sound simple, it is probably the most important thing you can do to continue to engage the person. There is a difference between simply hearing a person in order to think of a response and the more generous listening that takes place when you are truly trying to understand the meaning of what is being said. It is important to get curious and authentically listen.
- Things you can say: "Tell me more," "I'm curious about what you just said." (And then listen!)

SPEAK YOUR TRUTH/SHARE STORIES

- Speak your truth. Tell stories to illustrate your point. Be clear. Describe your objection. Speak calmly.
- Share your learning through stories. There is something powerful in storytelling. While sharing factual data may be helpful to some, we know that people are often moved to open up and understand other perspectives when they hear personal stories. You may share your own story or share a story about someone you know (with permission).
- Things you can say: "I have a Black friend who works two jobs to make ends meet, and goes to school. He works harder than anyone I know. Calling Black people lazy is a hurtful stereotype about People of Color. There are lazy people of all races. That expression perpetuates racism."

Videos

Allyhood

5 Tips for Being an Ally. Franchesca Ramsey: www.youtube.com/watch?v=_dg86g-QlM0

Apologize

Getting Called Out: How to Apologize. Franchesca Ramsey: www.youtube.com/watch?v=C8xJXKYL8pU

Colorblindness

Should We Be Colorblind? UrbanEntryVideo: www.youtube.com/watch?v=wEZJ5rDX9-E

The Costs of Racial Color Blindness. *Harvard Business Review,* Michael I. Norton: www.youtube.com/watch?v=RG6cVIDneis

Why Colorblindness will NOT End Racism. *Decoded,* MTV News, Franchesca Ramsey: www.youtube.com/watch?v=H4LpT9TF_ew

Implicit Bias

American Denial: Implicit Bias Test. PBS *Independent Lens,* Mahzarin Banaji: www.youtube.com/watch?v=ZWa09tUzqf4

How the Concept of Implicit Bias Came Into Being. NPR, Mahzarin Banaji: www.npr.org/2016/10/17/498219482/how-the-concept-of-implicit-bias-came-into-being

How to Overcome Our Biases? Walk Boldly Toward Them. TED Talk, Verna Myers: www.youtube.com/watch?v=uYyvbgINZkQ

Kids on Race: The Hidden Picture. Anderson Cooper: www.youtube.com/watch?v=GPVNJgfDwpw-

Peanut Butter, Jelly and Racism. Who, Me? Biased? *The New York Times,* Saleem Reshamwala: www.nytimes.com/video/us/100000004818663/peanut-butter-jelly-and-racism.html

Institutional Racism

How Race Settled the Suburbs. Upworthy, *Adam Ruins Everything:*
www.facebook.com/Upworthy/videos/796326533903423/
Race: The House We Live In. California New Reel, *Race: The Power of
an Illusion:* www.youtube.com/watch?v=mW764dXEI_8
Selma Movie Clip: www.youtube.com/watch?v=1YRUUFYeOPI
Structural   Discrimination: The   Unequal   Opportunity   Race.
African American Policy Forum: www.youtube.com/watch?v=
eBb5TgOXgNY
We Need to Talk About an Injustice. TED Talk, Bryan Stevenson:
www.ted.com/talks/bryan_stevenson_we_need_to_talk_about_an_
injustice

Intersectionality

A Letter to White Queers, A Letter to Myself. Andrea Gibson: www.
youtube.com/watch?v=gpBUenMIe8U
Aint I A Woman. Kai Davis www.youtube.com/watch?v=Z0F_
6GMOa-8
Being Queer and Muslim is Possible. Wazina Zondon: www.facebook.
com/HuffPost/videos/1764803620253928/
I'm a Black Gentrifier in Harlem. Morgan Jerkins: www.theguardian.
com/us-news/2015/aug/25/black-gentrification-harlem-not-a-good-
feeling
Intersectionality & Collaboration. Tony Parker: www.youtube.com/
watch?v=x5Fnz0rfuj4
On   Intersectionality.   Kimberlé   Crenshaw: www.youtube.com/
watch?v=JRci2V8PxW4
#RaceAnd. Jamia Wilson www.youtube.com/watch?v=4o-qnznd10Y
#RaceAnd.   Kay   Ulanday   Barrett: www.youtube.com/watch?
v=CSHcKFn7zZw

Listening Skills

Everyone is Waiting to Talk About Themselves. CollegeHumor: www.
youtube.com/watch?v=BjXq22kkLAg
Ten Ways to Have a Better Conversation. TED Talk, Celeste Headlee:
www.ted.com/talks/celeste_headlee_10_ways_to_have_a_better_
conversation#t-692065

Microaggressions

HatchKids Discuss Microaggressions. SheKnows, Media KidsSpeak:

www.youtube.com/watch?v=8RfwnibEd3A

How Microaggressions are Like Mosquito Bites. Fusion Comedy, Same Difference: www.youtube.com/watch?v=hDd3bzA7450

If Microaggressions Happened to White People. MTV News, *Decoded*, Franchesca Ramsey: www.youtube.com/watch?v=KPRA4g-3yEk

What Kind of Asian Are You? Ken Tanaka: www.youtube.com/watch?v=DWynJkN5HbQ

Where are You Really From??? MTV News, *Decoded*, Franchesca Ramsey: www.youtube.com/watch?v=igWYMo4z2OQ

The N-Word

Are Cracker, White Trash, and Redneck Racist? MTV News, *Decoded*, Franchesca Ramsey: www.youtube.com/watch?v=wIIt-gTHWOY

What the N-Word Feels Like. BuzzFeedYellow: www.youtube.com/watch?v=qaqBLZZd6Ns

When Words Don't Belong to Everyone. Ta-Nehisi Coates: www.youtube.com/watch?v=QO15S3WC9pg

Where Did the N-Word Come From? CNN: www.youtube.com/watch?v=OFnF1c2Tbfw

The N-Word Through History. *Washington Post:* www.youtube.com/watch?v=9Yv2BnfbUFs

Privilege

A Class Divided. Jane Elliot: www.youtube.com/watch?v=dzXw75bOeXs

Aamer Rahman Fear of a Brown Planet—Reverse Racism. www.youtube.com/watch?v=dw_mRaIHb-M

Privilege Walks: www.youtube.com/watch?v=EIJqtWUiUCs, www.youtube.com/watch?v=hD5f8GuNuGQ

Why Does Privilege Make So Many People Angry? MTV News, *Decoded*, Franchesca Ramsey: www.youtube.com/watch?v=qeYpvV3eRhY

Racist Jokes

How Do You Handle a Racist Joke? MTV News, *Decoded*, Franchesca Ramsey: www.youtube.com/watch?v=Bg1aTLsS69Y

References

Aaker, J. (2013). Harnessing the power of stories. Stanford Graduate School of Business [video]. Retrieved from vimeo.com/80117083

Accapadi, M. M. (2007). When White women cry: How White women's tears oppress women of color. *The College Student Affairs Journal*, 26(2), 208–215.

Adams, M. (2007). Pedagogical frameworks for social justice education. In M. Adams, L.A. Bell, & P. Griffin (Eds.), *Teaching for diversity and social justice* (2nd ed.) New York, NY: Routledge.

Adams, M., & Bell, L. A. (Eds.). (2016). *Teaching for diversity and social justice* (3rd ed.). New York, NY: Routledge.

Alexander, M. (2012). *The new Jim Crow: Mass incarceration in the age of colorblindness.* New York, NY: New Press.

Allport, G. W. (1979). *The nature of prejudice.* (25th Anniversary Ed.). New York, NY: Basic Books.

Annie E. Casey Foundation. (2018). Kids Count Data Center. Retrieved October 26, 2018 from datacenter.kidscount.org/data/tables/44-children-in-poverty-by-race-and-ethnicity

Arao, B., & Clemens, K. (2013). From safe spaces to brave spaces. *The art of effective facilitation: Reflections from social justice educators* (pp. 135–150). Sterling, VA: Stylus.

Banks, J. (June, 2017). *Global migration, failed citizenship and civic education.* Presentation at Michigan State University Equity and Mobility Conference, East Lansing, MI.

Banks, J., Cookson, P., Gay, G., Hawley, W., Irvine, J. J., Nieto, S., Schofield, J. W., & Stephan, W. G. (2001). Diversity within unity: Essential principles for teaching and learning in a multicultural society. *Phi Delta Kappan*, 83(3), 196–203.

Banks, W. (1996). *Black intellectuals: Race and responsibility in American life.* New York: W.W. Norton.

Bauman, D. (2018). After 2016 election, campus hate crimes seemed to jump. Here is what the data tell us. *The Chronicle of Higher Education*, 64(25). Retrieved September 26, 2018 from www.chronicle.com/article/After-2016-Election-Campus/242577

Beale, R., Thompson, M., & Chesler, M. (2001). Training peer facilitators for intergroup dialogue leadership. In D. Schoem & S. Hurtado (Eds.), *Intergroup dialogue: Deliberative democracy in school, college, community and workplace* (pp. 227–246). Ann Arbor, MI: The University of Michigan Press.

Bonilla-Silva, E. (2005). "Racism" and "new racism": The contours of racial dynamics in contemporary America. In Z. Leonardo (Ed.), *Critical pedagogy and race* (pp. 1–36). Malden, MA: Blackwell.

Bonilla-Silva, E. (2018). *Racism without racists: Color-blind racism and the persistence of racial inequality in America.* (5th Ed.). New York, NY: Rowman & Littlefield.

Broockman, D., & Kalla, J. (2016). Durably reducing transphobia: A field experiment on door-to-door canvassing. *Science, 352*(6282), 220–224.

Brown, B. (2010). The power of vulnerability. TED Talk. Retrieved July 7, 2018 from www.ted.com/talks/brene_brown_on_vulnerability#t-82594

Brown, B. (2012). *Daring greatly: How the courage to be vulnerable transforms the way we live, love, parent and lead.* New York, NY: Gotham.

Brown, B., (2018). *Dare to lead: Brave work. Tough conversations. Whole hearts.* New York, NY: Random House.

Brown v. Board of Education, 347 U.S. 483 (1954).

Carter, D. J. (2008). On spotlighting and ignoring racial group members in the classroom. *Everyday antiracism: Getting real about race in school,* 230–234.

Checkoway, B. (2009). Youth civic engagement for dialogue and diversity at the metropolitan level. *The Foundation Review, 1*(2), 41–50.

Chesler, M. (n.d.). The role of facilitators. The Program on Intergroup Relations, The University of Michigan, Ann Arbor, MI. [Distributed at the National Intergroup Dialogue Institute].

Crenshaw, K.W. (2003). Traffic at the crossroads: Multiple oppressions. In R. Morgan (Ed.), *Sisterhood is forever: The women's anthology for a new millennium* (pp. 43–47). New York, NY: Washington Square Press.

Delpit, L. (1988). The silenced dialogue: Power and pedagogy in educating other people's children. *Harvard Educational Review, 58*(3), 280–299.

Delpit, L. (2006). *Other people's children.* New York, NY: The New Press.

Delgado, R., & Stefancic, J. (2012). *Critical race theory: An introduction.* New York, NY: New York University Press.

DiAngelo, R. (2011). White fragility. *International Journal of Critical Pedagogy, 3*(3), 54–70.

Dunbar-Ortiz, R. (2014). *An Indigenous peoples' history of the United States.* Boston, MA: Beacon Press.

Dweck, C. (2016). *Mindset: The new psychology of success.* New York, NY: Ballantine Books.

Dymski, G., Hernandez, J., Mohanty, L. (May 2013). Race, gender, power, and the U.S. subprime mortgage and foreclosure crisis: A meso analysis. *Feminist Economics.* Critical and Feminist Perspectives on Financial and Economic Crises, *19*(3), 124–151.

East Lansing High School (ELHS). (2016). *School improvement plan.* East Lansing, MI: Advance Education.

Fisher, R., & Petryk, T. (2017). *Balancing asymmetrical social power dynamics.* IGR Working Paper #3.

Freire, P. (2007). *Pedagogy of the oppressed.* New York, NY: Continuum Press. (Original published 1970)

Gershenson, S., Hart, C. M. D., Lindsay, C., & Papageorge, M. (2017). *The long-run impacts of same race teachers.* Bonn, Germany: IZA Institute of Labor Economics. IZA DP No. 10630.

Gerzon, M. (2006). Moving beyond debate: Start a dialogue. Retrieved from www.scribd.com/document/370675616/Moving-Beyond-Debate-Start-a-Dialogue

Goleman, D. (1995). *Emotional intelligence.* New York, NY: Bantam Books.

Goodman, D. (2011). *Promoting diversity and social justice: Educating people from privileged groups*. New York, NY: Routledge Press.

Greenblatt, J. (2017). ADL CEO Jonathan Greenblatt delivers keynote speech at National Council of La Raza annual conference. Retrieved from www.adl.org/news/adl-ceo-jonathan-greenblatt-delivers-keynote-speech-at-national-council-of-la-raza-annual

Griffin, S. R. (2015). *Those kids, our schools: Race and reform in an American high school*. Cambridge, MA: Harvard Education Press.

Griffin, S. R., Brown, M., & warren, n. m. (2012). Critical education in high schools: The promise and challenges of intergroup dialogue. *Equity & Excellence in Education, 45*(1), 159–180.

Gurin, P. (2011). Intergroup dialogue: Education for broad conception of civic engagement. *Liberal Education, 97*(2), 46–51.

Gurin, P., Nagda, B. A., & Zúñiga, X. (2013). *Dialogue across difference: Practice, theory and research on intergroup dialogue*. New York, NY: Russell Sage Foundation.

Hamad, R. (May 7, 2018). How White women use strategic tears to silence women of color. *The Guardian*. Retrieved from www.theguardian.com/commentisfree/2018/may/08/how-white-women-use-strategic-tears-to-avoid-accountability

Hannah-Jones, N. (June 9, 2016). Choosing a school for my daughter in a segregated city. *The New York Times*. Retrieved from www.nytimes.com/2016/06/12/magazine/choosing-a-school-for-my-daughter-in-a-segregated-city.html

Hardiman, R., & Jackson, B. W. (1992). Racial identity development: Understanding racial dynamics in college classrooms and on campus. *New Directions for Teaching and Learning*, (52), 21–37.

Hardiman, R., Jackson, B., & Griffin, P. (2007). Conceptual foundations for social justice education. In M. Adams, L. A. Bell, & P. Griffin (Eds.), *Teaching for diversity and social justice* (2nd ed., pp. 35–66). New York, NY: Routledge.

Headlee, C., (2016). Ten ways to have a better conversation. TED Talk. Retrieved from www.ted.com/talks/celeste_headlee_10_ways_to_have_a_better_conversation#t-692065

Helms, J. (1990). *Black and White racial identity: Theory, research, practice*. New York, NY: Greenwood Press.

Hicks, D. (2011). *Dignity: Its essential role in resolving conflict*. New Haven, CT: Yale University Press.

Hicks, D. (2018). *Leading with dignity*. New Haven, CT: Yale University Press.

hooks, b. (1994). *Teaching to transgress: Education as the practice of freedom*. New York, NY: Routledge.

Hopkins, L. E., & Dominguez, A. D. (2015). From awareness to action: College students' skill development in intergroup dialogue. *Equity and Excellence in Education, 48*(3), 392–402.

Howard, G. R. (2006). *We can't teach what we don't know: White teachers, multiracial schools* (revised ed.). New York, NY: Teachers College Press.

Hu-DeHart, E. (1993). The history, development, and future of ethnic studies. *The Phi Delta Kappan, 75*(1), 50–54.

Ignatiev, N. (1995, 2009). *How the Irish became White*. New York, NY: Routledge.

Ipsos. (2017). *Reuters/Ipsos/UVA Center for Politics Race Poll*. Reuters/Ipsos poll conducted in conjunction with the University of Virginia Center for Politics. Retrieved from www.centerforpolitics.org/crystalball/wp-content/uploads/2017/09/2017-Reuters-UVA-Ipsos-Race-Poll-9-11-2017.pdf

Ireland, J. (Trans.) (2007). *"Udana" and "Itivuttaka": Two classics from the Pali canon* (Vol. 214). Sri Lanka: Buddhist Publication Society.

Jarvis, B. (2017). Who decides who counts as Native American? *The New York Times Magazine.* Retrieved from www.nytimes.com/2017/01/18/magazine/who-decides-who-counts-as-native-american.html

Joseph, P. E. (2013). Black studies, student activism, and the Black Power movement. In P. E. Joseph (Ed.), *The Black Power movement: Rethinking the civil rights-Black Power era.* New York, NY: Routledge.

Kaplowitz, D. R. (2017). *MSU dialogues: Facilitator's guide.* Michigan State University Office for Inclusion and Intercultural Initiatives.

Kaplowitz, D. R. (2018a). *ELPS survey: Preliminary results.* Report for East Lansing Public Schools, presented May 14, 2018.

Kaplowitz, D. R. (2018b). *MSU dialogues: A brief review of program data.* Report for Office for Inclusion and Intercultural Initiatives, Michigan State University, presented June 21, 2018.

Kaplowitz, D. R., Lee, J. A., & Seyka, S. L. (2018). Looking to near peers to guide student discussions about race. *Phi Delta Kappan, 99*(5), 51–55. doi.org/10.1177/0031721718754814

Killermann, S., & Bolger, M. (2016). *Unlocking the magic of facilitation: 11 key concepts you didn't know you didn't know.* Austin, TX: Impetus Books.

Knauer, J. T. (2011). Democracy lab. In K. Maxwell (Ed.), *Facilitating intergroup dialogues: Bridging differences, catalyzing change.* Sterling, VA: Stylus Publishing.

Kristof, N. (2014). When Whites just don't get it, part 2. *The New York Times.* Retrieved from www.nytimes.com/2014/09/07/opinion/sunday/nicholas-kristof-when-whites-just-dont-get-it-part-2.html?_r=0

Kruger, J., & Dunning, D. (1999). Unskilled and unaware of it: How difficulties in recognizing one's own incompetence lead to inflated self-assessments. *Journal of Personality and Social Psychology, 77*(6), 1121–1134.

Ladson-Billings, G., & Tate W. (1995). Toward a critical race theory of education. *Teachers College Record, 97*(1), 47–68.

Lakoff, G. (2014). *Don't think of an elephant.* White River Junction, VT: Chelsea Green Publishing.

Landreman, L. M. (2013). *The art of effective facilitation.* Sterling, VA: Stylus Press.

Learner, H. (2013). *Marriage rules.* New York, NY: Gotham Books.

Lee, H. (1960.) *To kill a mockingbird.* New York, NY: HarperCollins.

Leonardo, Z. (2013). *Race frameworks: A multidimensional theory of racism and education.* New York, NY: Teachers College Press.

Levin, B. (2018). *Hate crimes rise in the U.S.* Center for the Study of Hate & Extremism, California State University, San Bernadino. Retrieved from csbs.csusb.edu/sites/csusb_csbs/files/2018%20Hate%20Report%205-141PM.pdf

Livesey, A. (2017). Conceived in violence: Enslaved mother and children born of rape in nineteenth-century Louisiana. *Slavery and Abolition, 38*(2), 373–391.

Lo Wang, H. (2018). No Middle Eastern or North African category on 2020 census, bureau says. *National Public Radio National News (NPR National)*. Retrieved from www.npr.org/2018/01/29/581541111/no-middle-eastern-or-north-african-category-on-2020-census-bureau-says

Loewen, J. W. (2007). *Lies my teacher told me*. New York, NY: Touchstone.

Lutz, Mallory (2017). The hidden cost of *Brown v. Board*: African American educators' resistance to desegregating schools. *Online Journal of Rural Research & Policy, 12*(4).

Lynch, I., Swartz, S., & Isaacs, D. (2017). Anti-racism oral education: A review of approaches, impact and theoretical underpinnings from 2000 to 2015. *Journal of Moral Education, 46*(2), 129–144.

Martin, M. (2017). SPLC has seen rise in hate crime, domestic terrorism attacks. *National Public Radio*. Retrieved from www.npr.org/2017/05/27/530393081/splc-has-seen-rise-in-hate-crime-domestic-terrorism-attacks

Martin, N., & Montaigne, R. (December 7, 2017). Black mothers keep dying after giving birth. Shalon Irving's story explains why. *NPR All Things Considered*. Retrieved from www.npr.org/2017/12/07/568948782/black-mothers-keep-dying-after-giving-birth-shalon-irvings-story-explains-why

Maxwell, K.E., Fisher, R.A., Thompson, M.C., & Behling, C. (2011). Integrating cognitive and affective learning. In K.E. Maxwell, B.A. Nagda, & M.C. Thompson (Eds.), *Facilitating intergroup dialogues: Bridging differences, catalyzing change*. Sterling, VA: Stylus Publishing

Maxwell, K., Nagda. B. A., & Thompson, M. C. (2011). *Facilitating intergroup dialogues: Bridging differences, catalyzing change*. Sterling, VA: Stylus Press.

Mitchell, D., Hinueber, J., & Edwards, B. (2017). Looking race in the face. *Phi Delta Kappan, 98*(5), 24–29.

Moonesinghe, R., Chang, M., Truman, B. (November 2013). *Health Insurance Coverage—United States, 2008 and 2010*. Centers for Disease Control and Prevention, 62(03), 61–64. Retrieved from www.cdc.gov/mmwr/preview/mmwrhtml/su6203a10.htm?s_cid=su6203a10_w

Morrison, M., Allies for Change Workshop, Lansing Michigan, Fall, 2014.

Morrison, K. Y. (2010). Slave mothers and White fathers: Defining family and status in late colonial Cuba. *Slavery and Abolition, 30*(1), 29–55.

NAACP Legal Defense Fund. (2017). *Locked out of the classroom: How implicit bias contributes to disparities in school discipline*. Retrieved from www.naacpldf.org/files/about-us/Bias_Reportv2017_30_11_FINAL.pdf

Nagda, B. A., & Maxwell, K. E. (2011). Deepening the layers of Understanding and Connection: A critical dialogic approach to facilitating intergroup dialogues. In K. Maxwell (Ed.), *Facilitating intergroup dialogues: Bridging differences, catalyzing change*. Sterling, VA: Stylus Publishing.

National Center for Education Statistics. (2013). *Characteristics of public and private elementary and secondary school teachers in the United States: Results from the 2011–2012 schools and staffing survey*. Retrieved from nces.ed.gov/pubs2013/2013314.pdf

National Center for Education Statistics. (2017). *Characteristics of public elementary and secondary school teachers in the United States: Results from the 2015-2016 national teacher and principal survey*. Retrieved from nces.ed.gov/pubsearch/pubsinfo.asp?pubid=2017072rev

Obear, K. (2013). Navigating triggering events. In L. Landreman (Ed.), *The art of effective facilitation: Reflections from social justice educators* (pp. 151–172), Sterling, VA: Stylus.

Oliver, M., & Shapiro, T. (2006). *Black wealth, White wealth: A new perspective on racial inequality.* (10th Anniversary Ed.) New York, NY: Routledge.

Olsson, J. (2011). Detour-spotting for White anti-racists. *Cultural Bridges to Justice.* Retrieved from www.culturalbridgestojustice.org/resources/written/detour

Oluo, I. (2018). *So you want to talk about race?* New York, NY: Seal Press.

O'Reilly, A. (2017). Hate crimes in U.S. on the rise. *Fox News.* Retrieved from www.foxnews.com/us/2017/08/15/hate-crimes-in-us-on-rise.html

Painter, N. I. (2010). *The history of White people.* New York, NY: W.W. Norton & Company.

Phillips, K. W. (2014). How diversity makes us smarter: Being around people who are different from us makes us more creative, more diligent, and harder-working. *Scientific American, 311*(4), 42–47.

Pierson, E., Simoiu, C., Overgoor, J., Corbett-Davies, S., Ramachandran, V., Phillips, C., Goel, S. (2017). A large-scale analysis of racial disparities in police stops across the United States. Retrieved from openpolicing.stanford.edu/publications/

Plessy v. Ferguson, 163 U.S. 537 (1896).

Pollock, M. (2004). *Colormute: Race talk dilemmas in an American school.* Princeton, NJ: Princeton University Press.

Public Broadcasting Service (2003). The difference between us: Human variation [Episode 1]. *Race—The power of an illusion.* Retrieved from www.pbs.org/race/000_About/002_04-about-01.htm

Quereshi, A. & Okonofua, J. (2017). *Locked out of the classroom: How implicit bias contributes to disparities in school discipline.* NAACP Legal Defense and Educational Fund. Retrieved from www.naacpldf.org/files/about-us/Bias_Reportv2017_30_11_FINAL.pdf

Ramsey, S. (2017). The troubled history of American education after the Brown decision. *The American Historian.* Retrieved from tah.oah.org/february-2017/the-troubled-history-of-american-education-after-the-brown-decision/

Richmond, E. (2012). Schools are more segregated today than during the late 1960s. *The Atlantic.* Retrieved from www.theatlantic.com/national/archive/2012/06/schools-are-more-segregated-today-than-during-the-late-1960s/258348/

Rilke, R. M. (2004). *Letters to a young poet.* (M. D. Herter Norton, Trans.). New York, NY: W. W. Norton.

Rock, D., & Grant, H. (Nov. 4, 2016). Why diverse teams are smarter. *Harvard Business Review.* Retrieved from hbr.org/2016/11/why-diverse-teams-are-smarter

Rosenberg, N. A., Pritchard J. A, Weber, L. A. Cann, H. M., Kidd, K. K., Zhivotovsky, L. A., Feldman, M. W. (Dec. 20, 2002). Genetic structure of human populations. *Science, 298,* 2381–2385. doi: 10.1126/science.1078311

routenberg, r., Thompson, E., & Waterburg, R. (2013). When neutrality is not enough: Wrestling with the challenges of multipartiality. In L. Landreman (Ed.). *The Art of Effective Facilitation,* (pp. 173–197). Sterling, VA: Stylus.

Saunders, H., Sustained Dialogue Institute. Retrieved July 6, 2018 from sustaineddialogue.org/about-us/

Schoem, D. L. & Hurtado, S. (Eds.). (2001). *Intergroup Dialogue: Deliberative democracy in school, college, community, and workplace.* Ann Arbor, MI: University of Michigan Press.

Singleton, G. E. (2015). *Courageous conversations about race: A field guide for achieving equity in schools* (2nd ed.). Thousand Oaks, CA: Sage Publishing.

Smith, T. (April 5, 2017). Fighting hate in schools. *All Things Considered*, National Public Radio. Retrieved from www.npr.org/sections/ed/2017/04/05/522718288/fighting-hate-in-schools

Sorenson, N., Nagda, B. R. A., Gurin, P., & Maxwell, K. (2009). Taking a "hands-on" approach to diversity in higher education: A critical-dialogic model for effective intergroup interaction. *Analyses of Social Issues and Public Policy*, 9(1), 3–35.

Sparks, S. D. & Klein, A. (2018). Discipline disparities grow for students of color, new federal data show. *Education Week*. Retrieved from www.edweek.org/ew/articles/2018/04/24/discipline-disparities-grow-for-students-of-color.html

Spencer, M. S., Brown, M., Griffin, S., & Abdullah, S. (2008). Outcome evaluation of the intergroup project. *Small Group Research*, 39(1), 82–103.

Stanley, C. A. (2007) When counter narratives meet master narratives in the journal editorial-review process. *Educational Researcher*, 36(1), 14–24.

Stevenson, H. C. (2014). *Promoting racial literacy in schools: Differences that make a difference.* New York, NY: Teachers College Press.

Stout, M. (2012). *Native American boarding schools (Landmarks of the American mosaic).* Santa Barbara, CA: Greenwood.

Sue, D. W., (2010) *Microaggressions in everyday life: Race, gender, and sexual orientation.* Hoboken, NJ: John Wiley and Sons.

Sustained Dialogue Institute. (2017–2018). *Sustained Dialogue campus network moderator manual.* Retrieved from sustaineddialogue.org/campus-dialogue-resources/

Tatum, B. D. (2000). The complexity of identity: Who am I? In M. Adams, W. J. Blumenfeld, H. W. Hackman, X. Zúñiga, M. L. Peters (Eds.), *Readings for diversity and social justice: An anthology on racism, antisemitism, sexism, heterosexism, ableism, and classism* (pp. 9–14). New York, NY: Routledge.

Tatum, B. D. (2004). Defining racism: Can we talk? In P. Rothenberg (Ed.), *Race, class, and gender in the United States: An integrated study* (p. 127). New York, NY: Macmillan.

Tatum, B. D. (2017). *Why are all the black kids sitting together in the cafeteria? And other conversations about race.* New York, NY: Basic Books.

Thakral, C., Vasques, P., Bottoms, B., Matthews, A., Hudson, K., & Whitley, S. (2016). Understanding difference through dialogue: A first-year experience for college students. *Journal of Diversity in Higher Education*, 9(2), 130–142.

Tippett, K. (2016). *Becoming wise: An inquiry into the mystery and art of living.* New York, NY: Penguin Books.

Torino, G. (2017). How racism and microaggressions lead to worse health. *Center for Health Journalism*, Retrieved from www.centerforhealthjournalism.org/2017/11/08/how-racism-and-microaggressions-lead-worse-health

Tucker, M. J., Berg, C. J., Callaghan, W. M., Hisa, J. (February 2007). The Black–White disparity in pregnancy-related mortality from five conditions: Differences in prevalence and case-fatality rates. *American Journal of Public Health*, 97(2), 247–251.

Tuckman, B. W. (1965). Developmental sequence in small groups. *Psychological Bulletin, 63*(6), 384–399.

United Nations Ethics Office. (2017). *United Nations Leadership Dialogue 2017.* United Nations. Retrieved from www.un.org/en/ethics/leadership_dialogue.shtml

U.S. Census Bureau. (n.d.) Quick facts. Retrieved from www.census.gov/quickfacts/fact/table/US/PST045217

U.S. Commission on Civil Rights. (2018). *Public education funding inequity in an era of increasing concentration of poverty and resegregation.* Briefing report before the U. S. Commission on Civil Rights held in Washington, DC.

U.S. Department of Education, Office for Civil Rights. (2016). *2013–2014 civil rights data collection: A first look: Key data highlights on equity and opportunity gaps in our nation's public schools.* Retrieved from www2.ed.gov/about/offices/list/ocr/docs/2013-14-first-look.pdf

U.S. Department of Education, Office for Civil Rights. (2018). *Civil rights data collection (CRDC) for the 2015-16 school year.* Retrieved from www2.ed.gov/about/offices/list/ocr/docs/crdc-2015-16.html

U.S. Department of Education, Office of Planning, Evaluation and Policy Development. (2016). *The State of Racial Diversity in the Education Workforce.* Retrieved from www2.ed.gov/rschstat/eval/highered/racial-diversity/state-racial-diversity-workforce.pdf

U.S. Department of Justice, Federal Bureau of Investigation. (2010). *Hate crime statistics.* Retrieved September 26, 2018 from ucr.fbi.gov/hate-crime/2010/narratives/hate-crime-2010-victims

U.S. Department of Justice, Office of Justice Programs, Bureau of Justice Statistics, Snyder, H. (Sept. 2011). *Arrest in the United States, 1980–2009.* NCJ234319. Retrieved from www.bjs.gov/content/pub/pdf/aus8009.pdf

U.S. Senate. *Ethnic Diversity in the Senate.* Retrieved from .senate.gov/senators/EthnicDiversityintheSenate.htm

University of Michigan. (2013). The Program on Intergroup Relations National Intergroup Dialogue Institute.

Warikoo, N. (2017). FBI: Reported hate crimes spike 29% in Michigan, which had 4th highest nationally. *Detroit Free Press.* Retrieved from www.freep.com/story/news/local/michigan/2017/12/10/hate-crimes-michigan/886779001/

Wheatley, M. (2009). *Turning to one another: Simple conversations to restore hope in the future.* San Francisco, CA: Berrett-Koehler Publishers.

White, A. (2009). *From comfort zone to performance management: Understanding development and performance.* Baisy-Thy, Belgium: White & MacLean Publishing.

Wildeman, C., & Wang, E. A. (2017). Mass incarceration, public health, and widening inequality in the USA. *The Lancet, 389*(10077), 1464–1474.

WNYC. (2018, Oct. 26). Knock, knock. *On the Media.* Retrieved from www.wnycstudios.org/story/on-the-media-2018-10-26

Yeakley, A. (2011). In the hands of facilitators: Student experiences in dialogue and implications for facilitator training. In Kelly Maxwell (Ed.), *Facilitating intergroup dialogues: Bridging differences, catalyzing change* (pp. 23–36). Sterling, VA: Stylus Publishing.

Yong, E. (2017). The desirability of storytellers. *The Atlantic*. Retrieved from www. theatlantic.com/science/archive/2017/12/the-origins-of-storytelling/547502/

Yudell, M., Roberts, D., DeSalle, R., Tishkoff., S. (February 2016). Taking race out of human genetics. *Science, 351*(6273), 564–565.

Zak, P. (2014). Why your brain loves a good story. *Harvard Business Review*. Retrieved from hbr.org/2014/10/why-your-brain-loves-good-storytelling

Zinn. H. (1998). *A people's history of the United States*. New York, NY: The New Press.

Zinn, H. (2002). *You can't be neutral on a moving train: A personal history of our times*. Boston, MA: Beacon Press.

Zúñiga, X., Lopez, G., & Ford, K. (2012). Intergroup dialogue: Critical conversations about difference, social identities, and social justice: Guest editors' introduction. *Equity and Excellence in Education, 45*(1), 1–13.

Zúñiga, X., Nagda, B. A., Chesler, M., & Cytron-Walker, A. (2007). Intergroup dialogue in higher education: Meaningful learning about social justice. *ASHE-ERIC Higher Education Report, 32*(4), 1–128. San Francisco, CA: Jossey-Bass.

Index

About the Authors

Shayla Reese Griffin is the Equity, Inclusion, and Social Justice Consultant for the Washtenaw Intermediate School District, a regional service agency, where she provides professional development to P–12 educators in nine school districts in Michigan. Shayla's passion for racial justice stems from her own experience as a Black student in predominantly White, suburban K–12 schools. From an early age, she was aware of how race, class, gender, sexual orientation, and ability were shaping her school experience and found that her teachers lacked the knowledge and skill to help students navigate these realties. Since that time, Shayla has been committed to creating schools in which young people of all backgrounds are valued, successful, and prepared to contribute to a more just world. Shayla earned her bachelor's degree in African American Studies from Spelman College (Atlanta, GA) with a minor in Spanish and her MSW and PhD from the University of Michigan (Ann Arbor). Shayla has developed and facilitated dialogue and professional development series with over a thousand high school students and P–12 educators around issues of race, class, gender, and sexual orientation in more than 15 school districts. In addition, she has taught courses on race, diversity, and social justice at the University of Michigan for the Program on Intergroup Relations, the School of Social Work, the Department of Anthropology, and the School of Education. She is the author of *Those Kids, Our Schools: Race and Reform in an American High School,* which was published in 2015. Shayla resides in Detroit, MI, with her spouse and three children, one of whom is currently a Detroit Public Schools student.

Donna Rich Kaplowitz is the co-director of the Program on Intergroup Relations at the University of Michigan. She holds a Ph.D. in international relations from Johns Hopkins University and has published three books on Cuba. She has studied race in a cross-cultural context and has brought years of work on difficult dialogues in international conflict into a local racial lens. Prior to working at the University of Michigan, Donna taught race dialogues, dialogue facilitation, and civic engagement in public education for twelve years at Michigan State University. She created and designed a near-peer–based race curriculum using preservice teachers as facilitators in public schools. She also developed and served as the first director of Michigan State University's Dialogue program which oversees hundreds of dialogue facilitators and participants (including undergraduate and graduate students, faculty, and staff) each year. Donna's years of experience training college students to lead race dialogues with near peers in high school and college has made her a passionate advocate of intergroup dialogue as a method to deconstruct White supremacy. As a White woman, she is conscious of the fact that race dialogues need to be in collaboration with People of Color. Donna lives in Ann Arbor, MI, with her husband. She is the mother of four grown children.

Sheri Seyka is a public education teacher in East Lansing Public Schools with 22 years of teaching experience. Sheri teaches a variety of English classes at East Lansing High School, including multicultural literature, and serves as the English Department chair. Her work with intercultural dialogue and trained facilitators spans over 5 years, impacting over 900 high school students. During the past 5 years, Sheri, who is White, has recognized an increasing need for race dialogue in the classroom and the need for intercultural dialogue professional development for teachers. Teaming up with professors from Michigan State University's College of Education, she began working on bringing race dialogue curriculum to high school classrooms through preservice English educators. Her years of classroom experience make her an advocate for all students. She believes talking about race is the key to improving intercultural race relations in and beyond the classroom. Sheri lives with her spouse and two children in East Lansing, MI.